Affectionately, **F.D.R.**

Affectionately, **F.D.R.**

A SON'S STORY OF A COURAGEOUS MAN

by

James Roosevelt and Sidney Shalett

WITH SIXTEEN ILLUSTRATIONS IN HALF-TONE

GREENWOOD PRESS, PUBLISHERS
WESTPORT, CONNECTICUT

Library of Congress Cataloging in Publication Data

Roosevelt, James, 1907-
    Affectionately, F. D. R.

    Reprint of the ed. published by George G. Har-
rap, London.
    Includes index.
    1. Roosevelt, Franklin Delano, Pres. U. S.,
1882-1945. 2. Roosevelt, James, 1907-
3. Roosevelt family. I. Shalett, Sidney, joint
author. II. Title.
[E807.R657 1975]   973.917'092'4 [B]
ISBN 0-8371-8329-4   75-22309

To my beloved wife, Irene, who never knew my father, but who believes in his goals and ideals as implicitly as I do.

JAMES ROOSEVELT

The authors wish to thank Harper and Brothers and Messrs Hutchinson and Co., Ltd., for permission to quote from *This Is My Story* (published in Great Britain under the title *The Lady of the White House*) and *This I Remember*, by Eleanor Roosevelt.

Foreword by Sidney Shalett

FIRST there was the great physical drive, the unquenchable ebullience. The world was his footpath ; fortune was the golden dust under his feet ; the end of the rainbow and far beyond was his vista. There were no obstacles ahead that the magnificent legs seemingly could not hurdle. (Yet was there any end, any attainable end, to the road ?)

Then, while the hurdler's legs still carried him forward, there came the time of the searing trial. There was the pain, the awful pain, and the blackness, and when the pain subsided the numbness, the nothingness, were worse, far worse, than the pain. No longer were the legs magnificent ; no longer would the owner—physically—hurdle anything.

But what about the mind, the spirit, the soul—would they stagnate or soar ?

For a time there was no one who knew the answer, not even the owner of the dead limbs and the courageous heart. Then, out of the torment and trial, the handicap and humbling, came a spiritual alchemy, a distillation of human dauntlessness. With it was lifted the opaqueness at the end of the road. And there was the vista, shining as always, but now constant and attainable, ready to be engulfed.

In the process of attaining the objective, with its ultimate by-product of becoming a father-image to millions throughout the world who never saw him, but who knew him, the man found himself enmeshed in another struggle—a struggle to retain his rôle, which he never was willing to relinquish, as a personal father to his own five children. He did not wholly lose this struggle ; he did not wholly win it either, for he was forced into becoming not one but several fathers.

And somewhere along the way a strange and sad and paradoxical thing happened : the engulfer himself was engulfed ; the figure who was the pivot point of millions, the man who rarely was physically alone, became a man alone, a man lonely.

Contents

CONTENTS

chapter

Illustrations

Introduction

NOT ONE BUT THREE FATHERS

SOMETIMES, in looking back, it seems as if there were periods when I had no father at all ; then it seems as if I had not one but three fathers. All of them, of course, were the one man, Franklin Delano Roosevelt—F.D.R.

First, there was the father of the time before polio. That was the period in which my sister, my brothers, and I were prone to call him " Pa-*pa*," in that Harvard-cum-Groton manner that our detractors put on when they want to picture us as a bunch of rarefied, affected snobs. " Pa-*pa* " sort of went with that period. He was the handsomest, strongest, most glamorous, vigorous, physical father in the world.

He also was a busy, ambitious, and, I suspect, somewhat self-centred man. When he was around, which wasn't nearly often enough for us, he inundated us with fun and activity—and with love too—but in his special way, which was both detached and overpowering. Sometimes we felt we didn't have him at all, but when we did have him life was as lively and exciting as any kid could want it to be.

Then there was the father of the post-polio, recovery period. We called him " Pa " then. Struck down by the cruellest blow that could have afflicted such an active man, Pa began the struggle not only for his body, but for his spirit. No part of it was easy ; the proud sprinter experienced the humiliation of learning not just to walk, but first to crawl. He battled also against the psychological pressures exerted by an indomitable, worshipping, but misguided mother, who, in her zeal to protect him, tried to sway him towards the easy way out—a hole in the good Roosevelt earth at Hyde Park into which he could crawl and hide, to look out at the world, but not to be looked at by it. In this period emerged the F.D.R. of greatness of spirit ; he spurned the return to the Hyde Park womb, and chose instead to fight his way back.

These were the lonely years ; for a long while during this time of illness and recovery we had no tangible father, no father-in-being, whom we could touch and talk to at will—only an abstract symbol, a cheery letter-writer, off somewhere on a houseboat or at Warm Springs, fighting by himself to do what had to be done.

Only now do I realize how sorely we missed him during that period. But when we saw him he was so—well, so damned gallant that he made you want to cry and laugh and cling to him and carry him in your arms and lean on him for support all at the same time.

The true greatness of F.D.R., the father, came out almost from the very beginning of his affliction, for even in those first terrible days, when the daggers were cutting deep into agonized muscle and flesh, he was grinning (though he clenched his teeth to do it), jesting and striving to pass it all off as a nothing, a nuisance, to ease the shock on the five scared kids who watched him. And during the period when he was off trying to repair his ruined limbs and to accomplish the harder task of keeping going, of holding his mental resolve firm, he kept seeking in many ways, light-hearted but touching ways, to keep close contact with his often undeserving children.

Finally, there was F.D.R., my third father, the public figure ; first Governor, then President. I, as the eldest son, witnessed the early part of this period more closely than my sister or my brothers, because I was at various times his " legs," his unofficial aide, and eventually one of his White House assistants.

We five Roosevelt children never wholly lost our Pa—our affectionate, witty, loyal, and even over-loyal Pa. He could find time, even while nations shook and the world burned, to write each of us debonair little notes about our personal affairs. He also could and did take infinite pains to bring us into his orbit, to give us front-row seats from which we might witness the shaping of the momentous events in which he was involved. But we did lose a good part of that personal Pa of ours—and not even he was strong enough to prevent it—when we had to begin sharing him with the world.

Before going further with this story of F.D.R. as a parent, rather than as a politician, let me make one basic fact plain— namely, that this book is written as an act of love—a loving son's memories of a loving father. I proudly use that word " love " in connexion with my feeling about Pa. To me he was great—a wonderful father, the most loyal and understanding parent a son or daughter could want.

It has been no easy thing to grow up in the limelight. Ever since I can remember people have been asking questions or reporters have been writing about the doings of those five Roosevelt kids.

One of the most frequently asked questions is : What was it really like to have Franklin and Eleanor Roosevelt as parents ? The simple truth is this : If you strip away the circumstances that Father was President, a maker and moulder of history, and that Mother became a sort of roving one-woman task force for social reform and international goodwill, we Roosevelts were a family with basic human problems not much different from those of any average family. We had the same yearnings, frustrations, and exasperations as anyone. Father and Mother had the same high hopes and ambitions for us, and experienced the same pride—and the same disappointments—as any parents.

Our parents were able to see to it that we were exposed to the best education money could buy, that we had proper religious instruction, adequate dosages of culture, good medical care, healthful exercise, and the correct things to eat. Yet, just as other parents become too busy, there were times when our parents were too engaged or too preoccupied, or, because of factors in their own backgrounds, were loath to give us the kind of face-to-face (or hand-to-backside) guidance that we needed.

Both the background of our family life and the cast of characters were complex. To begin with, not only was Father " That Man " in the White House, but his place in history—and this can be said objectively even by a son—is unique. The people sent him to the White House four times—twice more than any other President has ever been elected. Besides doing more to change the pattern of living in the United States than any President within our time, if not in history, he was Governor of New York State for a couple of terms, and the winner in his tense, personal battle against the disease that crippled him from the waist down. I think even the most rabid Roosevelt-haters—and the pattern seemed to be that you either loved him or hated him—will agree that he was a man not without his intriguing aspects.

Then there is Mother. Wise and naïve, rational and impulsive, determined and uncertain, compassionate and occasionally misguided, Mother has lived a life that in its own way has been as full and fascinating as Father's. She has come a long way from the willowy, luminous-eyed, adolescent girl who deprecated herself as an " ugly duckling " (though Father and later the rest of us always saw and loved her real beauty) and the young bride so painfully unsure of herself that she could panic at the thought of having to face dinner guests. Mother grew to become Father's invaluable and trusted right arm, and, since his death, has continued her evolution into an international figure of acknowledged stature.

Also, ever present in the background, spoiling us outrageously behind our parents' backs and often to their faces, was our strong-willed Granny—and, incidentally, that is what we children called her, not " *Grandmère* " or " Grandma-*ma*." As a matter of fact, my sister, Anna, reminds me that Granny even tolerated our calling her " Ga-Ga," until one day she overheard one of the servants telling another, " Them kids is calling the Old Lady ' Ga-Ga,' and they ain't far wrong ! " That put a stop to that.

Finally, there are the five Roosevelt kids—the restless, tempestuous Roosevelt kids, now—I hope !—grown up. All five of us are highly individualistic persons with independent minds. The opinions which I shall express about Father are my own, and are not necessarily those of Anna, Elliott, Franklin, Jr., or John. In the preparation of this story, however, I have had the assistance of each of them—and of Mother too—and I am grateful for it.

We never have been a tranquil breed. On occasions—usually for minor reasons—we will scrap violently with one another. Yet in times of crisis—and this is a quality which we inherited directly from Father and Mother, who all their lives set us the example of unswerving, unrationed family loyalty—we will close ranks and fight to the death *for* each other.

In the order of our appearances we are :

Anna Eleanor Roosevelt—named after Mother, but known in the family as " Sis." Beautiful and high-spirited as a young girl, she was—and is—imbued with the Roosevelt energy. In fact, when Sis was less than one year old Mother was already writing her mother-in-law :

> My lady Anna is the mischief itself and I will be glad when Nurse returns to manage her, as Nurse Spring and I not being used to her have had some quite hard struggles with little tempers and wildest animal spirits which will break out at inopportune moments !

Sis and I, being closest in age, teamed together in the growing-up years—though I suspect I subconsciously resented the fact that she was my senior ; it seemed intolerable to have an *older* sister.

Anna's life has had its share of glamour ; she rode the campaign trains with Father and was with him during the last seventeen months of his life as an unofficial—and unpaid—member of his personal staff, accompanying him to the Yalta Conference. She also has had her share of heartbreak, two early marriages having ended unhappily. To-day, a handsome, keenly intelligent, hard-working mother and grandmother, Anna is married to a Veterans' Administration doctor, and leads a busy but quiet life. She lives modestly in an old, remodelled farmhouse outside of Syracuse, New York, holds down a full-time public-relations job, and manages to do most of her housework and cooking.

I am the oldest of the four boys. My early years were handicapped by a procession of annoying illnesses ; by growing too fast ; by an overabundance of Roosevelt vitality which often led me to overtax my physique ; and by being outrageously spoiled, as were all of us, by a doting, wealthy Granny, who was in constant competition with Mother over how the five " chicks "—to use that rather saccharine term by which Father, Mother, and Granny habitually referred to us—should be raised. I am a product of Groton and Harvard, as were Father and all my brothers—except Elliott, who, after unwillingly enduring Groton, was enough of a nonconformist to say to hell with

Harvard and make it stick. I have been moderately successful and moderately unsuccessful in various business enterprises, and have been immoderately criticized on both counts. My first marriage ended unhappily, but politely ; my second terminated with some of the most unfortunate publicity it has ever been the lot of a man in public life to receive ; and I am now married quietly and happily for the third time. I have served as a White House secretary under Father, as a United States Marine, and, as I write this, am in my third term as a member of Congress from the Twenty-sixth District of California.

Elliott Roosevelt, next in line, is a born rebel, the hard-luck kid of the tribe, and in many ways the most appealing. From a physical standpoint his childhood made mine resemble a bed of lily-petals. In addition to the usual assortment of ailments, Elliott, though now more than six feet tall, was a runt ; he suffered from weak legs that made braces necessary, and later from a hernia that prevented him from keeping up with us other hellions.

Elliott—nicknamed " Bunny "—was perhaps the only one of us whom Mother babied—possibly, as she herself has speculated, because she saw in him a resemblance to her own much-loved father, after whom Elliott was named. Bunny also was condescended to by Granny, and, being both pugnacious and imaginative, he likes to argue that this was because she never quite forgave him for having been named after a Roosevelt on Mother's side of the family (the Oyster Bay branch), rather than the Hyde Park strain. This argument, however, doesn't hold much water, for Granny was fond of Grandfather Elliott, and she and Grandfather James chose him as godfather to their son, Franklin. It is more likely that Bunny ruffled Granny by his habit of sassing her more than any of the rest of us ever dared.

Like Mother's uncle, President Teddy Roosevelt, whom political enemies called " that damned cowboy," Bunny always had an affinity for the West ; he never really liked the East, and, after spurning Harvard, he put in some hectic years as a rancher and as a Texas radio-network operator. During World War II, although he has poor eyesight, Elliott became an Air Force photo-reconnaissance pilot by signing a physical-disability waiver, flew unarmed planes in combat zones with flak spraying all around him, and rose to the rank of brigadier-general, commanding a wing in North Africa. Along the way in his busy life he has managed to marry four times—including once to the actress Faye Emerson—and has had more than his share of rotten publicity, which is probably what makes him such a human, loyal, sympathetic guy when one of the rest of us is in trouble. At present he seems to have found his niche in life, ranching and mining—out West, of course—and is showing a renewed interest in politics.

Franklin Delano Roosevelt, Jr.—known in the family as " Brud " or " Frankie "—inherited Father's name and a good deal of his looks. Like Father, Franklin, Jr., became a lawyer in New York City, then entered politics. He served in Congress, and for a while it appeared as if he might be headed for higher posts (as, indeed, he still may be), until Tammany Hall (as it once did to Father) cut him down.

In his younger days Frankie was not above taking an occasional punch—and he's big enough to throw a good one—at photographers who invaded what he considered his right to privacy. His wedding to his first wife, the former Ethel du Pont, was probably the most highly publicized amalgamation of two unlikely clans that has ever taken place. During World War II, as a Navy officer, he had a distinguished combat record. As this is written Franklin, Jr., now married for the second time, has put aside politics and the law and is operating an inter-state foreign-car distributorship.

John Aspinwall Roosevelt, youngest of the five children, began life as the real runt of the family, smaller even than Elliott. It must have traumatized him to have been so small among those hulking brothers, though now he is the biggest six feet five inches—of all of us. Though he may dispute this, I suspect Johnny, who was only five when Father was stricken with polio, missed a good deal by never having really known and enjoyed Pa in his physical prime, and for having gone through his formative years during the busy time when Father was Governor, then President.

John is the family enigma. He chose early in life to make a career of business, inflicting great shock on Granny (who otherwise adored him) when she read somewhere that her grandson,

a Hyde Park Roosevelt, was selling ladies' panties in the bargain
basement of a Boston department store. Continuing with his
iconoclasm, he married a Republican, has turned one himself—
and even works in Wall Street.

Johnny, who served in World War II aboard an aircraft-
carrier, has seemed the " quiet one," but he possesses an ex-
plosive temper. His early tantrums sometimes were so violent
that Mother had to lock him in his room. I think that Johnny,
like Samson of old, would pull down a temple on his own head
if he thought that the Philistines were doing him wrong. Like
the rest of us, he has had his share of notoriety, though, unlike
the rest of us, he has never been divorced. He has had his en-
counters with the speed cops, and once—though Johnny always
insisted the incident was greatly magnified—was accused of
dumping a bottle of champagne on a French mayor's head.

Well, there we are, for better or worse. Father must often
have seethed over our orneriness, but rarely, if ever, did he let
us know it. I do not presume to speak for anyone but myself,
but I, for one, freely admit that at one time or other, largely
because I was raised the way I was, I have lived too hard, played
too hard, lived above my means, and perhaps thought more of
James Roosevelt than I have of others. I hope all that is behind
me now ; as my brother Elliott rather sagely and candidly
comments, to some of the Roosevelt children maturity has come
late—and hard.

By the rule-books, Pa certainly had some shortcomings as a
father. These were things forced upon him by a variety of circumstances : his own rather cloistered upbringing and education,
never far from the supervision of a too adoring mother ; the
cruel handicap that crippled him at the peak of his physical
vigour ; and, later, the demanding obligations of the Presidency.
He should have been a lot tougher with all of us. He should
have whaled the daylights out of us many times ; he should have
put us—and kept us—in the doghouse for some of the dreadful
things we did after we got too big to spank ; he should have
counselled us more, instead of leaving us free to steer our own
courses ; and, above all, he should have tried harder to make
us realize that there are a certain number of pennies to every

dollar and that dollars do not grow without limit on family trees—even if you are a Delano and a Roosevelt.

Yet, in lieu of these things we did not get from him, he had other superlative parental qualities. He gave us love : in our own headstrong, often rebellious, thoughtless ways every one of us adored him. We *wanted* his love and respect ; we not only loved him, but we *liked* him—a form of affection harder to come by : we thought he was a pretty wonderful guy.

He—and Mother too—gave us the priceless security of their loyalty. I would be a fool to argue that none of us ever did anything which did not bring Father pain and occasionally shame. Though our exploits were often exaggerated, there were times when a less tolerant and loving father would have shown some of us the door and suggested that we please just go away and not complicate his tremendously important life any further. Elliott, Anna, and I were divorced while he was in the White House. Anna and Elliott, respectively, worked briefly for newspaper and radio chains which fought Father, and Elliott criticized Father's administration on the air. My business activities—though I opened my books and defended every allegation made against me—came under criticism, as did some of Elliott's financial transactions. Elliott had fist fights ; Franklin, Jr. and John, made headlines in various ways.

Yet always, when we were in trouble, Pa stood by us. With him we were never presumed to be guilty until proved innocent. There were times when Father—the President of the United States—publicly came to our defence, though it was to his political detriment to do so. Never to my knowledge did he complain to anyone about what we were doing " to him."

Looking back on it all, I would not swap the tiniest part of the great humanity which Father gave us for all the rule-book upbringing in the world.

Part One

FATHER, THE VIGOROUS COMPANION

1

A Man of Tremendous Strength

MY earliest memory of Father goes back to the time when I was about five years old and he was in the State Senate at Albany, New York. He would walk me to the firehouse to see the horses that drew the fire-wagons. We must have done this fairly often, for I have recollections of having been there more than once when the bells started clanging and the horses raced out of the firehouse, their hooves beating a wonderful, wild tattoo on the cobblestones. I suspect this picture sticks in my mind after the passage of so many years and so many events because it was associated with my earliest physical image of the tall, strong man with the straight back and straight legs who held my hand so firmly and reassuringly when the excitement started.

My most vivid early impression of Father, however, is that he was a man of tremendous strength. I was six years old and we were living in Washington, where Father was Assistant Secretary of the Navy. We had an automobile—a Marmon—and one of my favourite pastimes was to sit at the wheel of the parked car and pretend that I was driving. Thanks to the pneumonia, later followed by a heart murmur, I had contracted as an infant, I was not a strong child. (I had always blamed the pneumonia on the fact that Mother, a fiend for fresh air, used to hang me outside the bedroom of our New York town house in a home-made window-box, but Mother insists it was because I would not—or could not—eat properly.) In any event, I could not push in the clutch-pedal, not even if I cheated and pushed on it with both feet. When I rode next to Father and saw how he dominated the clutch with no effort at all I can recall my exalted, little boy's feeling that my father must be the strongest man in the world.

My sister and my three brothers also have their own significant first images of Father. Anna has told me her earliest recollection also goes back to the Albany period when Father was a rambunctious young State senator. She had been given permission by him to sit—" but quietly ! "—in our living-room while he plotted strategy with his political lieutenants in a hot anti-Tammany battle. All the politicians were puffing cigars, except Father, who smoked a pipe in those days. Suddenly Sis had to run from the parlour to avoid being asphyxiated by the cigar-smoke. From that time on politics really was synonymous in her mind with a " smoke-filled room." Many times have I heard Anna's story supported by our magnificent though often overpowering grandmother, Sara Delano Roosevelt. She would recall with queenly distaste the " horrid, blue tobacco-smoke " that, as Granny told it, was so thick it seeped right through the ceiling, so that the nursery just above had to be moved elsewhere to preserve Baby Elliott—" Bunny "—from nicotinic poisoning.

Elliott's earliest memory is of seeing Father give me the first and only spanking I ever remember receiving from him, and thinking how " dreadfully cruel " it was (Bunny really is notoriously tender-hearted) for Father " to use the bristle side of the hairbrush on Jimmy's backside." On the other hand, Johnny, the youngest, remembers Father's unfailing compassion whenever one of the children was in trouble : " we would go and cry on his shoulder, and Pa would melt."

The memory that stays with Franklin, Jr.—" Brud "—is of a scene that I too shall never forget—that of standing on the porch at Campobello, watching Father being carried out on a stretcher, and recalling how he tried to wipe away the scare of it by smiling wonderfully at us and cheerily singing out, " I'll be seeing you chicks soon ! "

Strength and excitement, politics and a smoke-filled room, paternal authority (although there wasn't much of that), fun, tragedy, courage, and warmly human sympathy—all in all, a rather revealing album of first memories that the five of us have retained of the protean parent of ours.

He has been gone now since April 12, 1945. There hardly has been a day when I have not missed his incomparable companionship and that delightful, devastating faculty of his for letting the air out of windbags.

The Irreverent Traditionalist

The first American-born Roosevelt, from whom both Father's and Mother's branches of the family stemmed, was Nicholas, son of Claes Martenszen van Rosenvelt. Claes came to Nieuw Amsterdam—later New York—from Holland around 1649. From Nicholas' line two Presidents—Theodore Roosevelt, who was Mother's uncle, and Father—were produced. Mother, blithely ignoring the fundamental conflict in the political affiliations of the two branches, sometimes quips that " the only difference between my side of the family and Franklin's is that the Oyster Bay Roosevelts are ' REW-sevelts ' and the Hyde Park Roosevelts are ' ROSE-evelts.' "

On Grandmother's side Father was a Delano, a clan of Flemish descent which numbered in its company some swashbuckling sea-captains, China traders, and other colourful characters. The first Delano—then de la Noye—in America was one Philippe, who arrived in the Massachusetts Bay Colony in 1621, much earlier, as Granny was fond of remarking, than the Johnny-come-lately Roosevelts. Our redoubtable grandmother considered her side of the family infinitely the superior of the two lines, and often commented, with the finality of a Supreme Court justice handing down an opinion, that " Franklin is a *Delano*, not a Roosevelt at all."

At heart Father was as tradition-loving as any Daughter of the American Revolution—even though, as President, he once jolted that august society by reminding it that " you and I . . . are descended from immigrants and revolutionists." (That speech was delivered in 1938, when I was a White House Secretary, and I've always regretted that I did not go along to hear him startle the good ladies.) The difference was that Father mixed his reverence with irreverence, and refused to be stuffy about his ancestors.

In fact, when he was around anyone who took the ancestor business too seriously—Granny, for instance—he loved to whack away with devastating slashes that let some of the sap run out of the family tree.   Sometimes when " important people " were dining at Hyde Park I've heard him exasperate Granny beyond all endurance by. dropping sly hints that old Claes left Holland because he was a horse-thief or worse, or suggesting the existence of other skeletons in the family closet.   Pointing to one of the family portraits on the wall, he would allude to that particular ancestor as " that old drunk," or would take off, to his mother's unspeakable anguish, on the subject of the Delanos who went into the China trade, implying that they smuggled everything from opium to immigrants. 'Sometimes he sounded as if he were taking his text, chapter and verse, straight from the columnist Westbrook Pegler, who seems to advocate the sterilization and/or extermination (retroactive) of all Roosevelts from old Claes on. Father played this trick so often that Granny could not have failed to have realized his game, but she never learned to take it, and always rewarded him with the reaction he was striving for— an explosively reproachful exclamation of " Oh, Franklin ! "

Yet Father himself was a walking encyclopedia of knowledge about the family tree.   When I was one of his White House secretaries, if some one were to write a letter requesting information on some ancient or obscure Roosevelt or Delano, I always knew the one who would have the answer on the top of his head—Pa.

I never saw my grandfather, James Roosevelt, who died when Father was a freshman at Harvard.   He wore mutton-chop whiskers straight out of Dickens, and, from what Father told me of him, he looked, thought, and acted the part of a benevolent country squire.   Grandfather was a businessman with a sub- stantial—though not ostentatious—fortune, derived largely from coal and transportation interests.   In commenting on his father's ingrained personal conservatism Father often told me how Grandfather always kept at least five hundred dollars in gold on hand (something he would not have been able to do after Father became President and took the country off the gold standard) as a precaution against any emergency.

A widower, Grandfather was fifty-two years old in 1880 when, at the home of the Theodore Roosevelts, he met his distant cousin, Sara Delano, for the first time. The beautiful, spirited " Sally " Delano was twenty-six—exactly half his age.

Grandfather James and Sara were married in October 1880 ; on January 30, 1882, Franklin Delano Roosevelt was born. The birth took place at home, and both Grandmother and the future President almost died from an overdose of chloroform. Granny, nevertheless, often commented on " how nice " it was for a baby to be born " in his own home."

Some biographers have written off Grandfather James as a thoroughgoing stuffed shirt. Certainly Father did not regard him as such. William D. Hassett, former Presidential secretary, whom Father affectionately called his " Bartlett, Roget, and Buckle," relates in his *Off the Record with F.D.R.* how Father once told him that Grandfather would not let Grandmother accept a dinner invitation from Mrs Cornelius Vanderbilt because he did not want to receive the Vanderbilts in his own home. " Yet he was no snob," Hassett quotes Father as saying. " He was the most generous and kindly of men and always liberal in his outlook."

All the evidence I have gathered from conversations with Father, Granny, and others—now gone—indicates that, despite his father's advanced years, there was a happy, companionable relationship between the two. From stories Father told me of his father's tolerance towards some of his youthful escapades, I doubt that Grandfather James could have been entirely humourless. For instance, Father once told me how he filched from his father's medicine cabinet a couple of effervescent powders and secreted them in the old-fashioned china object that stood under the bed of his dignified German governess. Nature and the effervescent powders combined to produce the desired effect, and the hysterical *Fräulein* ran to Grandmother with news of the terrifying symptom that had beset her. The incident duly came to Grandfather's attention ; he put two and two together, summoned young Franklin, and gravely told him, " Consider yourself spanked ! " But Granny was never told.

Granny's volume provides an interesting, if rose-tinted, picture of Father's early life. I say " rose-tinted " advisedly ; among other things, it contains the rather remarkable assertion : " We never tried . . . his father and I, to influence him against his own tastes and inclinations or to shape his life." She pictured

him as a manly, precocious little fellow, and indignantly denied
that he was " lonely " because he grew up as an only child. She
admitted he was " spoiled "—not by her, of course, but by his
adoring nurses.

But Granny revealed perhaps more than she realized about
her possessive feelings towards her only son. She described
how she and Grandfather came tearing home from Europe when
Father came down with a bad case of scarlet fever which went
into a period of prolonged complications. As visits were pro-
hibited, Granny told how she circumvented the quarantine.
" Several times each day," she related, " I would climb a tall,
rickety ladder, and, by seating myself on the top, managed to
see into the room and talk with our small, convalescent scapegrace. He loved to see me appear over the window ledge."
Whenever I envision the commanding figure of my grandmother,
clambering in rustling skirts up a shaky ladder to converse through
a window with her little boy, I involuntarily steal one of Father's
favourite phrases—" *I love it !* " I'm certain that's exactly what
Father must have said when he read this passage of Granny's
recollections.

As part of the pattern of Father's early life, he went to Europe
eight times during his first fourteen years, shepherded by various
governesses and tutors, and his parents. On his last trip he
bicycled through Germany with a tutor. He liked to boast to
my brothers and me—presumably to prove to us that he had
been a regular guy—that he had been arrested four times in one
day for stealing cherries, wheeling his bike into the waiting-room
of a railroad station, pedalling into a town after sunset (*verboten*),
and running over and killing a goose. As the years went by he
improved bit by bit on this story, finally insisting that the goose
really had " committed suicide " by sticking its neck through
the spokes. Our little brother, Johnny, must have remembered
Pa's escapade, for, on his own memorable trip through Europe
in 1937, in which a fast motor-car substituted for a bicycle, John
wrote me : " We've had three casualties thus far on the road, all
of them yesterday coming back from Budapest. The score now
stands at two ducks, one chicken and thousands of furious peasants
whom we made scatter to the fields by means of cut-out and
siren."

In September 1896—a bit behind schedule, for his mother was reluctant to let him leave the nest—Father entered Groton. "It is hard to leave our darling boy," Granny noted in her diary. "James and I feel this parting very much." There, under the guidance of the Rev. Dr Endicott Peabody, who was to become a major influence in the spiritual and traditional side of Father's life, Father's personality was moulded by the rigid pattern of discipline and respectability that dominated the Groton way of life. Conformity, a sense of obligation, and acceptance of that peculiar Grotonian tenet best described as "playing the game" seemingly came naturally to him.

After Groton the natural progression was to Harvard. Even at Harvard Father had the maternal influence with which to cope, for, after his father's death, his doting Mama—though she insists in her book that she abstained from interfering in his life—came to Cambridge to be near her cherished son.

To me the miracle is that Father was strong enough in later life to rise above his Hyde Park-parental-Groton-Harvard background and to become such a human, sympathetic, understanding individual.

The Women in Father's Life

Father was a man who enjoyed feminine companionship. He was at his sparkling best as a conversationalist when his audience included a few admiring and attractive ladies ; this was an entirely natural circumstance, for Father was a great showman, who enjoyed being the centre of attention.

Certainly Mother understood this side of Father. She has written teasingly of the "lovely ladies who worshipped at this shrine," and how difficult it was sometimes to get him to break up a gathering when he had an admiring feminine gallery.

In this respect Mother knew him better—or at least was more honest about it—than Granny, who contended it was a surprise to her when her boy Franklin came out with the news of his engagement to Cousin Eleanor, "because he had never been in any sense a ladies' man." I'm afraid Granny either wasn't very observant in the days when Father was a typical, normal young college man, or she was a little forgetful. She should have remembered the letter he wrote her from England in August

1903 apropos of his attendance at a very social British garden party. " As I knew the uncivilized English custom of never introducing people," Father related,

> . . . I walked up to the best looking dame in the bunch & said " howdy ? " Things at once went like oil & I was soon having flirtations with three of the nobility at the same time. I had a walk with the hostesses' niece over the entire house which was really perfect in every way—I mean the house. . . . Then I inspected the gardens with another " chawmer " & ended up by jollying the hostess herself all by her lonesome for ten minutes while a uniformed Lord stood by & never got in anything except an occasional " aw " or an " I sy."

The two women who exerted the strongest influence on Father's life were, of course, his wife and his mother. I would place them in that order.

Mother's rôle was vital both in our scheme of family living and in the evolution of Father's career. While her importance naturally increased after he was stricken with polio, she was a major factor even earlier in his humanitarian development. Always, even when she was the anxious, uncertain housewife, by her own admission fearful of practically everything and everybody—most of all of her formidable mother-in-law—there was the latent spark of social crusader in Mother. She taught and did settlement work ; let a good cause rear its head and Mother came running.

It is not an easy thing to-day to catch my fabulous mother in a state of repose, for Eleanor Roosevelt in her seventies is as active as I can remember her in her fifties, if not more so. Occasionally, however, we find time for a visit around the fireside or on the rolling lawn of her Val-Kill Cottage on the land near Hyde Park that Father gave her as the site for the now defunct furniture factory which she once started with two friends. Then, if the conversation swings that way, Mother will be quite frank about the upbringing of her five children. If there were short-comings in our raising—and she thinks there were—Mother, even though she points out that Father wasn't much help as a disciplinarian, admits that she must take a good deal of the blame because of things she *didn't* do.

Mother's own upbringing did little to prepare her for becoming a wife and mother. Her mother, Anna Eleanor Hall, whom Mother remembers as "one of the most beautiful women I have ever seen," died before Mother was eight. Two years later she lost her adored and adoring father, Elliott Roosevelt ; his life dogged by misfortunes, he had taken to drink, which accounts for Mother's lifelong antagonism to alcohol. Mother was raised by her Grandmother Hall, a strict disciplinarian.

In almost everything I can remember her doing, Mother seemed torn between the desire to raise her own children with reasoned discipline and, on the other hand, not to interfere in our lives. In certain of her letters to Father she complains severely—sometimes even bitterly—about our conduct and our failings. Yet almost never were these criticisms conveyed directly to us—and we rarely heard anything of them from Father.

For example, during Father's White House days Mother learned, while on a trip, that a member of the family was delinquent in meeting certain obligations. "Something has to be done to make —— realize it is dishonest not to pay bills," she wrote Father. "I suggest you ask him to list *all* he owes. Pay it yourself & then take out of his allowance $100 a quarter. Tell him he *has* to live on his income . . . until he earns his own money. . . . Forbid Granny to give him anything. . . . I think it is serious & must stop now."

In May 1941, when I was temporarily out of the country on a Marine Corps mission, Mother, misinformed and consequently alarmed about the details of a business transaction which she thought might cause me trouble, wrote Father : "He always trusts everybody and never has learned . . . that some people are not worthy of trust. . . . He himself has no experience or knowledge of what it means to count pennies." Mother's characterization of me was quite true : I was brought up in a way that gave me little understanding of any need for counting pennies, and I did trust people too much—perhaps I still do. Where I feel Mother made her mistake, however, was in writing about it to Father on the basis of information which came to her from a second party, rather than waiting and taking it up directly with me.

As for the matriarchal Sara Delano Roosevelt, I cannot fully agree with frequently advanced theories that her influence on

Father was wholly adverse. Certainly she would have dominated him could she have done so, but Father, the inheritor of Grandmother's own stubbornness, was tough enough to resist her; indeed, I feel she strengthened his character by increasing his capacity for resistance.

I do not dispute, however, that his mother's influence had much to do with the kind of parent that Father became. I firmly believe that one of the reasons he shied away from excessive managing of his children was his memory of how much of that sort of thing he had to put up with from his own mama.

There was a definite, rather marvellous regality about Granny. She was a blueblood through and through, and not even kings and queens fazed her. In June 1934 she wrote Father from England of having taken tea " quite alone " with King George V and Queen Mary at Buckingham Palace. She reported that she had given the King a message from Father, relating to their common interest in collecting stamps, and that the King was " very pleased." " The Queen is quieter & a little shy which is a good thing," Granny went on approvingly. " She was *very* nice & asked about you as he did & how you could get about. I even got up & stood behind a chair & put one hand lightly on the back as you do."

The following year, when Father cruised to the Bahamas and met the Duke of Kent he dashed off a note to Granny that he had told the Duke " to be sure to tell his father and mother how much I appreciated their kindness to you last summer ! " The picture of his unabashed " Ma-*ma* " giving the King and Queen of England a demonstration of how her son, the President of the United States, coped with his physical disability must have stayed with Pa for a long time !

In the early years Granny's ace in the hole—though she would not have approved of such a vulgar metaphor—was the fact that she held the purse-strings in the family. For years she squeezed all of us Father included—in this golden loop. What many persons do not realize is that Father was not a rich man ; in fact, for a long period he was extremely strapped. Under the terms of Grandfather's will the bulk of the estate was controlled by Granny—and how well she knew it ! Father himself, conditioned since childhood to an expensive standard of living, grew up largely dependent on his mother—a circumstance which I am convinced drove him into some of the wilder business ventures he undertook during his middle years in his efforts to make himself financially independent.

Granny adored Father beyond all reason; also she never stopped trying to manage him, even after he became President. I have been able to reconstruct this picture with fidelity, not only from my own memories of incidents, but from personal letters that have been preserved. Fortunately for history, the Roosevelts—especially Pa—had what amounted almost to a mania for saving correspondence and other scraps of paper that might be of interest or value to posterity. Incidentally, the finest way I know to ruin one's eyesight—mine isn't very good, anyway—is to try to decipher early letters of the Roosevelt clan. (I have come across passages in some of Mother's letters which not even she can read!) Not only are the various handwritings generally atrocious, but Granny and Mother particularly had a habit of finishing up a letter by writing criss-cross across the first page—an old-fashioned custom called " lacework letters." I asked Mother recently why she and Granny did this, and she replied, " I suppose we were trying to economize on writing-paper." I herewith reproduce a sample—one of Mother's undated letters to Father, written shortly after I was born—to illustrate what I mean.

In perusing Granny's letters to Father I never cease to marvel at how relentlessly she smothered him with gratuitous advice on personal matters, ranging from how she thought his married children should conduct their lives to the advisability of keeping his digestive tract regular. I have seen one letter, written by Grandmother to " Darling Son " in 1934, just before he was about to go off on a Presidential cruise to tropical waters. As if he still were her little boy, she counselled him : " Keep yourself in order & your blood cool in going through strange climates."

There are innumerable other letters in this vein. " Do be careful of your throat and don't ' speak ' until you have to ! " says one note, which starts off by asking if he would like to give Eleanor a $16.70 umbrella for her birthday. A spell of hot weather found her writing Father anxiously : " Do be careful about food and avoid fish and bad water, get some french Vichy

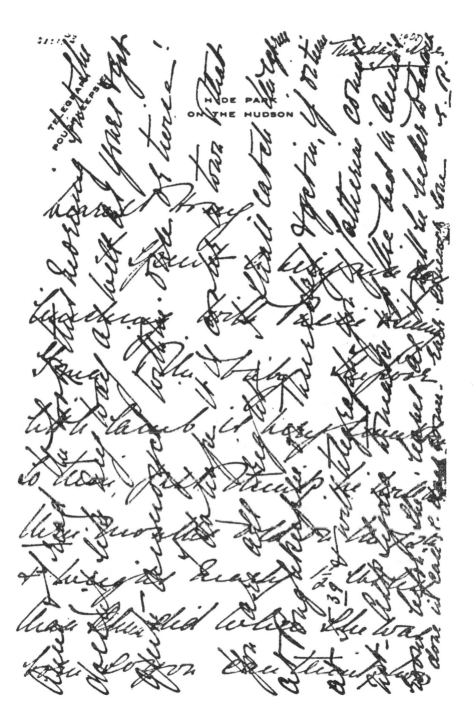

HYDE PARK
ON THE HUDSON

and have in your house, not to drink with meals, but between meals, and on going to bed. . . . I hope you wear the thinnest of clothes."

Then there was the time when, after a running battle on her part to curb our little brother, Johnny, from using such words as " damn " and " hell," Granny became indignant at the dinner-table when Father let a " damn " slip into his conversation. " Our little Johnny," she announced in tones that oozed distaste, " learns his language from the stable, and Franklin, apparently, learns it from Johnny." Father just let the criticism roll over him.

Though Father rarely exploded, I know for a fact that he seethed under this drip-drip of maternal advice ; how he escaped the ulcers that have afflicted me since early life I shall never know ! I also know that, despite the exasperations, he loved his mother deeply, though he never stopped resisting her attempts to tell him what to do and what not to do.

Probably the thing that subconsciously irritated Mother most was the tone of Granny's constant but oblique needlings. When Mother had anything on her mind, usually—except in the instances when she went to Father with complaints about us—she came right out and said it to the parties involved. Granny, however, leaned towards an arch and infuriating subtleness. For example, it was perfectly obvious in a letter she wrote Father from Hyde Park in October 1914, a couple of months after Franklin, Jr., was born, that she didn't think Mother was taking care of " Baby " very well. What she wrote, however, was : " I think in consequence of Eleanor's having had two hard days & being up rather late, Baby is a little fussy & hungry."

During World War I, when Father was in Paris and Mother was working herself to a frazzle in various home-front activities, Granny took pains to let him know that " Eleanor is well & I hope will add a *little* layer of fat to her frame before you get back."

The basic trouble was that Granny, though she would have denied it indignantly had anyone accused her of it, never quite forgave Mother for marrying her boy, Franklin, right out of college at a time when Granny was looking forward to enjoying a few years with Franklin all to herself. In family conversations Mother has told the story—and frankly—to all of us. She was the ugly duckling, or so she thought, and Franklin, her fifth cousin, whom she knew not too well, was the handsome, glamorous Prince Charming. They saw each other at " proper " parties, and Mother was overwhelmed when he began to show her attentions.

As they began seeing one another Mother gave the self-sure young Hyde Park gentleman, with his narrow window on life, one of his first lessons in the realities of human existence. She was doing settlement work in New York City's slums, even though, as she has written, " the streets filled with foreign looking people, crowded and dirty, filled me with a certain amount of terror."

On one of Father's week-end visits to New York City during his Harvard senior year he ventured down to the Rivington Street Settlement House, where Mother was working. He made the trip in stages by trolley and " el " (the old elevated transit line). This was the beginning of his education. Mother's little girls at the settlement house clustered around him, later asking her if he was her " feller "—" an expression," Mother says, " which meant nothing to me at that time ! "

She took him with her on a visit to one of her sick charges. " He was absolutely shaken when he saw the cold-water tenement where the child lived, and kept saying he simply could not believe human beings lived that way," Mother recalls.

Father proposed during the autumn of 1903 ; he was twenty-one and she was not quite nineteen. Mother and Grandmother differ as to exactly what happened, but the established facts indicate that Mother's memory is more accurate. Mother, though she treats the incident gently in her autobiography, has made it plain in reminiscing within the family circle that Granny's reaction was one of regal affront.

Father finished Harvard in the spring of 1904. Actually he had earned his bachelor's degree in July 1903, after three years of study, but stayed on in the graduate school for his fourth year. In February of 1904 Granny took him and his lifelong friend and college room-mate, Lathrop Brown, on a West Indies cruise. As Mother observed in *This Is My Story*, Granny's idea was " to make her son think this matter over—which at the time, of course, I resented." But despite the diversions of the cruise " Franklin's feelings did not change." The engagement was recognized, and, on March 17, 1905, Franklin and Eleanor Roosevelt were married.

One of the diversions which Granny had not anticipated and about which she became mightily upset was a meeting aboard ship between Father and an attractive French woman. Father never talked much about the " French lady," as he called her, but the family legend—undoubtedly magnified over the years— was that she became quite interested in the handsome young Harvard graduate. (It did not sway Father in his devotion to his fiancée, however.) The mystery, which has intrigued all of us over the years, has been somewhat clarified for me by Lathrop Brown, who recalls : " The ' Famous French Lady ' is a character which has grown in the telling. Many ladies of thirty can flatter youngsters of twenty-one and annoy the mothers of same. I think that here is a clear case of F.D.R. being pleased by the lady's attention, and equally pleased to find how annoyed his mother was about it."

In any event, it is interesting to note that Father, a man who rarely forgot anything, remembered over all the years that the enchantress had settled down in Trinidad. In 1936, when he was President and I accompanied him on his South American goodwill tour, he wrote his mother that he might stop in Trinidad on the way back, and added teasingly, " And perhaps I may meet the famous French lady ! "

Granny's version in *My Boy Franklin* is that " Franklin, unknown to any of us, had become engaged to his distant cousin, Anna Eleanor Roosevelt, a delightful child of nineteen, whom I had known and loved since babyhood," and that he told her about it *after* the West Indies cruise. Contemporary letters, however, show that Father and Mother broke the news to Granny on December 1, 1903, which was not too long after Father had popped the question. On December 2, 1903, we find Mother writing her future mother-in-law—addressing her as " Dearest Cousin Sally "—to thank her " for being so good to me yesterday." " I know just how you feel and how hard it must be," wrote Mother, " but I do so want you to learn to love me a little. You must know that I will always try to do what you wish for I have grown to love you very dearly during the past summer." She went on to say : " It is impossible for me to tell you how I feel toward Franklin, I can only say that my one great wish is always to prove worthy of him."

And two days later Father, apologizing for having been "absolutely rushed to death" with class elections and such, wrote his "Dearest Mama" as follows:

> I know what pain I must have caused you and you know I wouldn't do it if I really could have helped it—*mais tu sais, me voila!* Thats all that could be said—I know my mind, have known it for a long time, and know that I could never think otherwise: Result: I am the happiest man just now in the world; likewise the luckiest—And for you, dear Mummy, you know that nothing can ever change what we have always been & always will be to each other—only now you have two children to love & to love you—and Eleanor as you know will always be a daughter to you in every true way.

Mother in those days basically wanted one thing above all else—to be loved by every one. Having had no mother of her own from the time she was eight, she desperately wanted Grandmother to accept her as a real daughter. This is shown—rather poignantly—in letters written by Mother to Granny while on her honeymoon. "You are always just the sweetest, dearest Mama . . . and I shall look forward to our next long evening together, when I shall want to be kissed all the time!" she wrote in one frank avowal of daughterly love. Said another: "Goodbye dearest and a thousand thanks and kisses. I feel as though we would have such long arrears of kisses and cuddly times to make up when we get home!"

No one who has read Mother's letters to "Dearest Mama" could deny that she exerted herself far above and beyond the call of duty to be a good daughter-in-law in every way, even standing by almost supinely while Granny managed everything for her. In her own way Granny, who was as well-meaning as the Scriptures, also was devoted to Mother—but she never ceased trying to dominate her. Eventually Granny lost out when Mother began to grow in other directions—and to build for herself a life larger than the one bounded by "Ma-ma," the "chicks," the sewing circle, and social obligations. Mother became a personage in her own right, not to be dominated by anyone, not even by Father. Thus, in the end, it was Mother who triumphed and became the stronger and the bigger of the two.

2

Early Days: Of Names, Nurses, and Other Tribulations

WE resided—and visited—in a lot of places before Father and Mother moved into the White House. When I was growing up I seemed constantly on the move between New York, Albany, Washington, Hyde Park, Campobello, Warm Springs, the Florida keys—also Groton and Harvard. Sometimes I felt as if I were a white-collar gipsy.

I was born two days before Christmas, 1907, in New York, a gentler, more leisurely paced city than the metropolis of to-day. My first residence was the town house at 125 East Thirty-sixth Street—then a silk-stocking neighbourhood—in which I was born. The house was conveniently located within three blocks of my grandmother's residence, which was no surprise, for Granny herself had selected it. In writing of the " relief and joy " with which she welcomed me into the world Mother noted : " I had been worried for fear I would never have a son, knowing that both my mother-in-law and my husband wanted a boy to name after my husband's father."

Actually there was a bit of tradition-flouting, going back to Father's birth, in the fact that I was christened James—after my grandfather—rather than Isaac. There had been a long-standing custom in the Roosevelt family—adhered to with reasonable fidelity—of alternately bestowing the names Isaac and James on the first-born son of each generation. Grandfather James was the son of my Great-grandfather Isaac. When his first son by his first marriage came along he broke the chain by calling him—rather excessively, I always thought—James Roosevelt Roosevelt, known in the family as " Uncle Rosy." When

Father entered the world Grandfather, as I heard the story, was all set to appease tradition by calling him Isaac. He reckoned, however, without Granny. She detested " Isaac," and was determined that her son would bear a really *distinguished* name, so the child was christened Franklin Delano Roosevelt, after one of her favourite uncles, Franklin Hughes Delano. Originally, Grandmother planned to name him Warren Delano Roosevelt, after her father, but her brother, Warren Delano, had just lost an infant son who bore the same name ; he told his sister it would grieve him if she chose that name, so the future President became Franklin instead of Warren.

In due course, when I was born, the family blithely reverted to James on the convenient theory that it was Father, not I, who should have been tagged Isaac. My only regret is that, had tradition been respected, there would have been an " Ike "—Ike Roosevelt !—in the White House long before the advent of a certain military man.

I must confess there were times when I would rather have been called Ike, Adam, Ebenezer, Mohammed, or anything in preference to my given name. I am thinking of the occasions when Granny would come to visit me at Groton. She would sweep me up along with two or three of my favourite chums whom I was trying to impress with my manliness, take us to Parents' House for luncheon, and address me loudly and distinctly as " Jamesie-boy." Those were the times when I was deeply grateful for the true-blue spirit implanted within the Grotonian breast. Not one of the fellows ever peached on me.

Even after I entered Harvard Granny occasionally lapsed into usage of this dreadful appellation. In January 1928, when I was visiting Father at Warm Springs, she wrote him : " It is a happiness to me to know that Jamesie-boy is with you, a dear companion." I considered desperate appeals to get Granny to cut it out, but they would have done no good ; she merely would have felt I was spurning her affection and would have gone into one of her famous " hurts." My familiarity with Granny's capacity for magnificent martyrdom went back to the time when I was five years old, and she wrote Father :

James refused to believe that I am your Mother, & says " no, he has a mother somewhere else "—I said " but why don't you think

I am father's mother," & he said in a decided tone " Why, he never sees you & you don't kiss him." He is certainly a funny little boy, but I daresay Anna w^d say the same so I think a little *home* education might do them good ! Ever, Mama.

All I know about the house in which I was born is what Mother has told me of her " curious arrangement " for airing my sister and me in the city. Mother had come under the sway of the three health principles to which Granny was passionately dedicated —fresh air, castor-oil, and wholesome, home-grown food, all to be absorbed in enormous quantities. To read some of the Roosevelt family correspondence, it would seem that we were always being stuffed with food, flushed with castor-oil, and exposed to the elements. In any event, when Anna and I were infants Mother dreamed up some sort of chicken-wire, boxlike contraption to hang out of a window, and in it she periodically deposited us—separately—for airings. Anna, awakening one morning in the chicken-wire box and liking it not at all, screamed so violently that an irate neighbour threatened to report Mother to the Society for the Prevention of Cruelty to Children. That put an end to the chicken-cage airings.

Lest I be suspected of exaggerating about Granny and the fresh air, I quote from a letter she wrote my parents in March 1915. We were living in Washington, and Granny had come to watch over " the chicks " while Father and Mother were in San Francisco. Reporting on the welfare of Franklin, Jr., then an infant, Granny wrote : " Babs is splendid, has his one big movement in the morning as before & I do nothing but preach fresh air to Nurse who takes it in a chastened spirit." (Little Franklin then was being referred to as " Babs," apparently a diminutive for " Baby," which was the pet name Father invented for Mother on their honeymoon.) Granny went on at some length to describe a sort of reconnaissance patrol she set up outside our house to make certain we were getting enough air. " I noticed . . . that sometimes when he [Franklin] was supposed to be sleeping in the open . . . they [the windows] were closed again in an hour," she related. " Yesterday they were open from ten to two . . . so I hope by watching that he may have more air."

Even when Sis was grown, married, and expecting her first baby Granny was writing Father : " I consider Anna's athletic exercises . . . *too much* for her. . . . A nice little walk daily in the fresh air is all Anna needs."

In the late summer of 1908, in order to build me up after my bout with pneumonia, Father and Mother rented a house on the ocean at Sea Bright, New Jersey. I was to be exposed to all that healthful, fresh sea air, and it was close enough for Father, then clerking with a Wall Street law firm, to commute. Granny, who had never even known anybody who had spent a summer in Sea Bright, took this unprecedented development with fortitude. To Mother, who had written of some of the difficulties involved, she replied : " I think the cottage on the ocean sounds perfect, as the *air* is what you go for, and really if it is healthy the furniture makes absolutely no difference." Granny did mention in the same letter that *she* was sitting on the " South Verandah " at Hyde Park " in a delicious breeze."

As it turned out, it wasn't a very healthful or serene holiday. The house was on stilts, and once Anna pushed me in my carriage off the edge of the high, unrailed porch. I retaliated at some point by stabbing her in the hand with a pencil. Another time a storm blew the ocean right into our parlour. My parents never tried that experiment again.

As for me, for the next several winters I kept coming down with colds and flu, and finally developed a heart murmur and some sort of nervous affliction. The first meant that Mother or Father had to lug me up and down the steps. The second meant I had to lie flat on the floor for a certain period each day. This was supposed to accomplish something called " relaxing the muscles." The only way poor Mother could keep me quiet during this exercise—or non-exercise—was to get down on the floor, too, and read to me.

An Aggressively Bountiful Provider

As Mother has written, during the first ten years of her married life she " was always just getting over a baby or about to have one," so her activities were rather restricted. The third child born to my parents in 1909 was the first Franklin Delano Roosevelt, Jr., who lived less than eight months. Mother, who had a chronic guilt complex and a tendency to blame herself illogically

for anything, reproached herself " for having done so little about
the care of this baby." When Elliott was born the following
year Mother blamed herself because he " suffered for a great
many years with a rather unhappy disposition." She has written :

" In all probability I was partly
to blame, for certainly no one
could have behaved more fool-
ishly than I did practically up to
the time of Elliott's arrival."

After Elliott's birth almost
four years elapsed before the
arrival of the second Franklin
Delano, Jr., who entered the
world without giving Mother
any causes for self-reproach.
The last child, John, was born
on March 13, 1916.

As the family began to expand,
Granny, always the aggressively
bountiful provider, set to work
to build us a new town house at
49 East Sixty-fifth Street. In her
personal correspondence files
at the Franklin D. Roosevelt Library at Hyde Park there is a
little sketch she drew of the projected house, with the legend
in her handwriting : " A Christmas present to Franklin &
Eleanor from Mama—Number & Street not yet quite decided."
What emerged was a narrow, four-storey house of brick and
stone. While Granny was at it she constructed herself an adjoining, identical residence with connecting doors, so that the dining-
and drawing-rooms could be combined and we really could be
all together. Father, who always enjoyed building anything,
joined enthusiastically in the planning. Mother, who liked
neither the house nor the idea of all that propinquity, unhappily
withdrew from the whole affair.

The adjoining houses on East Sixty-fifth Street remained in
the family through the growing-up periods of all the children,
through Father's convalescence from polio, and through most
of his years as President ; the property was not sold until after

Grandmother's death in 1941.   Our half was the scene of some lively escapades.   Anna and I would lurk on the roof and drop water-bombs—paper bags filled with water—on the heads of approaching callers or innocent pedestrians.   All of us were skilled in concocting stink-bombs to set off when the house was full of important guests.   Elliott and Johnny once tested a new air-rifle—quite accurately—against the horribly expensive stained-glass windows of our neighbour, a *Social Register* Mrs Laidlaw.   For a high-strung person with a potentially volatile temper, Father was remarkably patient and controlled.   However, those early boisterous years provoked him to occasional explosions, which, in turn, kept poor Mother—in those days almost obsessively shy, timid, and anxious to please every one—fluttering about nervously in her efforts to keep us reasonably subdued.

Mother's stratagem for keeping us quiet was to read to us ; she read us stories until she must have hated the sight of a nursery-book.   When I was less than two years old she took Anna and me on a sailing expedition at Campobello, concerning which she wrote Father that we " quarreled a lot " because Sis " wanted to have and do everything that James had or did."   Observing that " James goes round and round the cockpit . . . and Anna kicks him whenever she can ! "   Mother closed with an appeal that had the ring of desperation :   " Will you bring them up one or two picture books ? "

We carried our exuberance with us wherever we went.   In May 1914, when Mother was visiting one of her favourite uncles, Henry Parish, at Llewellyn Park, Orange, New Jersey, with Anna and me in tow, she wrote to Father ·   " The children have been the wildest things you ever saw & about ready to jump out of their skins but I think it is the sudden cessation of all regular work & a new person who's [*sic*] authority they still question over them."

" *Old Battleaxe* "

One of the hazards of life during this period for Anna, Elliott, Franklin, Jr., and me—Johnny escaped it by virtue of his tender years—was the procession of " proper " English " nannies " foisted on our household by well-meaning Granny.   Mother, though she disliked some of the early martinets as much as we did, had not yet developed gumption to stand up to Granny on such things. Father's attitude on nurses and other household affairs was strictly hands off.

One English nurse in particular, whom I shall refer to merely as " Old Battleaxe," did dreadful things to us. Once this non-admirable creature pushed Sis to the floor, knelt on her chest, and cuffed her around a bit in order to drive home the importance of conducting oneself as a lady at all times. Elliott caught it when he managed to upset Franklin in his high chair ; Bunny laughed uproariously as baby brother hit the floor, but his innocent merriment was hushed when Nursie flung him in a closet and turned the key with such force that it broke off in the lock. For some idiotic reason no one did anything about it until Father came home about three hours later and rescued him. It was one of the few times we ever saw Father show livid anger around the house. This frightened Elliott more than being locked in the closet ; yet Old Battleaxe stayed on.

On another occasion the same nurse later locked little Franklin in a closet and broke the key again. " I've had claustrophobia ever since ! " Franklin says.

Of all the children, I took the most drastic punishment from Old Battleaxe. We would eat with her occasionally, and I, un-fortunately, was fascinated with her habit of slathering her meat with a thick layer of English mustard—the " hot " variety. I could not keep myself from staring, and this enraged her. " Keep on gawking," she threatened me one day, " and I'll make you eat the whole of this mustard-pot ! " I tried to look elsewhere, but her performance with the mustard drew my eyes like a magnet. One day the harridan *did* make me eat the entire contents of the mustard-pot, spoonful by spoonful. I was miserably ill, and to this day I cannot abide even mild mustard—not even on a hot dog at the ball game. I am certain that the experience led to the chronic stomach ailment from which I have suffered most of my life.

Another time she became enraged when she thought I had fibbed to her about brushing my teeth. She made me dress in my sister's clothing, hung a sign on my back reading I AM A LIAR, and forced me to walk up and down the sidewalk outside our East Sixty-fifth Street home, enduring the hoots and jeers of my playmates and the stares of adult passers-by. Even to-day I have seen Mother's eyes mist up as she recalls : " It was the cruellest thing that ever happened to a child. Heaven knows what it must have done to James." And in telling of the incident Mother invariably adds, " I *still* feel guilty when I think of it."

Old Battleaxe's downfall finally came when Mother one day had a legitimate occasion to put something away in the nurse's dresser and found a whole drawer full of empty whisky- and gin-bottles ! Unbeknownst to any of us, Old Battleaxe was a secret drinker. As boozing was the cardinal sin not only to Mother, but to Granny, Old Battleaxe was immediately discharged. This was the first step in Mother's personal Declaration of Independence in her relations with her mother-in-law, as from that day on Mother not only selected her own nurses, but began to make more decisions on her own. " From the time I got rid of that person and took over the selection of the type of nurse I wanted," Mother reminisced recently, " I began to have more confidence in my ability to handle the children."

When Old Battleaxe finally went Father, though he never had been kneed, closeted, mustarded, or placarded, was as happy as any of us kids.

After the forced abdication of our English torturess we had some lovely nurses selected by Mother. One who redeemed our faith in the British Empire was Elspeth Connochie, a Scots-woman, beloved by all of us. " Connie," who is still alive as this is written, helped bring Elliott through his difficult physical period, and became a confidante to Anna. She remembers Franklin, Jr., as " a perfect little darling " and well she might, for in the family correspondence is a letter telling of how Frankie once told her how nice it would be if Ada, another nurse, who had disciplined him by forbidding him to ride his tricycle on the sidewalk, should die, so he and Connie could start having fun again.

I apparently lacked Brother's winning ways, for a letter of June 1918 finds Mother reporting to Father that " Connochie had a fearful scene with James last night & then talked to me 20 minutes about him. . . . I hope things will go better."

Connie was pretty much responsible for enforcing rules of conduct, as Father and Mother were " no disciplinarians." She remembers how she would appeal to Father to put a halt to the rough-housing between Elliott and me, but that Father merely laughed and told her, " Oh, let them scrap—it's good exercise for them ! "

Granny had a fetish against permitting us to spend the night out at the homes of other children, and vice versa. When Father and Mother went to the Versailles Peace Conference in 1919 Granny wrote them aggrievedly that Connie had. permitted me to spend two nights away from home. " If I had been asked *before* permission was given of course I never sh^d allow a small boy to visit a friend overnight especially in the same town," she wrote. " It is always a mistake. . . . Of course Connochie wants to have the children look back with pleasure on her time in charge." In a later epistle Granny reported further : " Connochie & I had a talk last evening. . . . I asked her not to invite any boy to *stay* here as I felt it was always a mistake for children to *visit* & she C^d ask any of them for tea & lunch."

Apparently Mother was influenced by Granny's prejudice against promiscuous socializing, for a letter from Campobello in the summer of 1916 finds her reporting to Father that we had made friends with some summer people named Duckworth, whose children had a pony which they let us ride. " Do you think it dreadful of me to let the children pick up acquaintances ? " wrote Mother, who to-day is the friendliest of persons, prone to " pick up " an acquaintance with anyone she suspects may be interesting.

Another of the delightful nurses with whom Mother replaced the early tyrants was Seline Thiel, a young Swiss girl, known to us as Mademoiselle, or sometimes " Mammie." It was a huge joke in our nautical family that Mademoiselle always seemed to be falling off one of our boats at Campobello. In July 1921— the month before Father was stricken with polio—Mother wrote him : " Mlle. fell in again this a.m. while cleaning the ' Vireo.' " Father thought this was hilarious, and wrote back : " Tell Mlle. to postpone her next bath till she can fall off the rocks on our next cliff walk." Mother, however, regarded it as no laughing matter, for she noted : " [I] had to give her a little of your gin in hot lemonade as she has never warmed up since." When Mother voluntarily gave anyone gin in any form it was a real emergency.

3

Hyde Park was Really " Home "

OF all the places in which I ever lived Grandmother's place at
Hyde Park—Father's birthplace—was the spot that was really
" home." Even to-day I feel the same way—though the old
family home has become a national historic site.

My happiest memories of Father, my most carefree experiences
of childhood, all seem centred there around the last-century
mansion on the green brow overlooking that most beautiful of
rivers, the Hudson, which Father loved so well and taught all
of us to love.

Hyde Park was the place to which all of us flocked for summer
vacations and holidays, particularly at Christmas-time. It was
at the hearthside there that Father was at his best in readings of
Dickens's *A Christmas Carol*—a performance which he stretched
out over three evenings. As I write this I can almost hear his
clear, confident voice once again, soaring into the higher registers
for the part of Tiny Tim, then shifting to a snarly imitation of
mean old Scrooge. How we would thrill as Father rolled out
that final, soaring line, " *And so, as Tiny Tim observed, God
Bless Us, Every One* " !

Father's love for Hyde Park was deep and abiding ; he
cherished it with a nostalgic affection hard to describe. Father
himself came as close as I ever heard to expressing this feeling
when, in November 1939, in laying the corner-stone for the
library that bears his name on the Hyde Park grounds, he
reminisced :

> Half a century ago a small boy took special delight in climbing
> an old tree, now unhappily gone, to pick and eat ripe Seckel pears.

That was about one hundred feet to the west of where I am standing now. And just to the north he used to lie flat between the strawberry rows and eat sun-warmed strawberries—the best in the world. In the spring of the year, in rubber hip boots, he sailed his first toy boats in the surface water formed by the melting snow. In the summer with his dog he dug into woodchuck holes in this same field.

My own feeling for Hyde Park is much the same as Father's. Never did I feel any particularly strong ties to our New York, Washington, and Albany residences, and, though I lived briefly in the White House, I certainly never regarded that place as home. Whenever I was staying at the White House, in fact, I kept having the absurd but almost nightmarish feeling that some day—perhaps while I was in the shower—the line of tourists might somehow stray from the public rooms to the private living-quarters, and the White House usher would announce, " And there on your right is Jimmy Roosevelt. Go ahead and pinch him, if you please, to make sure he's real ! " (This nightmare is not so absurd as it sounds. Once Mother, who was always flouting tradition, was showing a group of lobstermen through the ordinarily off-limits family living-quarters. After taking them through Father's bedroom and her own suite she escorted them into another bedchamber, relating, " And here is where my daughter, Anna——" At this point she broke off, and everybody beat it out of there as fast as they could, for there, sound asleep on the bed, was Anna.)

The rambling, old-fashioned, and, to me, thoroughly gracious residence at Hyde Park originally was a clap-board frame house, built in 1826 and purchased by Grandfather James in 1867. Over the years it underwent so many structural changes that the mansion which stands to-day is hardly recognizable as the house in which Father was born. Its clap-boards were removed and the frame covered with grey stucco ; a porch with curving balusters, a white colonnaded portico, with outside trim and a widow's walk to match, were added. The last major changes—conceived by Father—were the two-storey wings of native field-stone at each end. When these were completed in 1916 Father and Granny agreed that the house was " right."

It was Father's idea that the Hyde Park estate become a place where his papers might be housed and people might visit. Each year now some two hundred thousand persons from every state in the Union and many far-off lands go there to see how Father and his family lived. Father himself made the first gift of land to the Government, and the Franklin D. Roosevelt Library was established by a joint resolution of Congress in 1939. In 1944 the home became a national historic site. Since Father's death Mother, Anna, my brothers, and I have waived our life interest in the house and grounds. The Government acquired additional land as a gift from the Franklin D. Roosevelt Foundation, and now holds full title to approximately 110 acres and all the buildings in the area.

The library, built and equipped by funds donated by thousands of private citizens, was started and completed in Father's lifetime. It was there that he spent many of his working hours during the months when the Hyde Park home became the summer White House. It is both an archive and a museum, containing thousands of manuscripts, books, and historic papers, in addition to an incredible variety of memorabilia, such as childhood mementoes, personal objects, and gifts presented him as President.

Often I have an overwhelming yearning to return to our beloved Hyde Park home. My room there was the little bed-room that once had been Father's. I slept in the same brass bed he had used as a boy. In the closet and in the drawers of an antique maple chest I would leave year-round what I considered my most precious possessions—a favourite sweater, a woollen stocking cap, my baseball-glove, my ice-skates, a book that once was Father's so that these things would be there for me to use when I came to stay for all-too-brief periods. In truth, the place must have bewitched and bemused me, for an early letter finds Mother writing to Father impatiently that " James . . . does fool things. . . . For instance, after a whole day of rain he placed his sandals on the roof for the night." I haven't the faintest recol-lection of placing my sandals on the roof or why I did it, unless it was connected with some roof-climbing expedition, but I'm sure that, to a small boy, enjoying life to the fullest at his grand-mother's place, the finest place in the world, there must have been a good reason for it. What I do remember was asking myself time and time again why Father ever had to leave this Paradise, and why we had to troop after him to such places as

New York and Albany, where he persisted in dabbling in such grubby occupations as law and politics.

In the winter-time at Hyde Park there was ice-skating and hockey on the pond, and coasting behind the South Porch down the long hill leading to the river. Father was like a kid himself on these sledding expeditions. He would chase us back up the steep road at a pace so fast our lungs would ache with the hurt of the cold air and hard breathing. Spills were frequent, but it was our code to treat them with great hilarity. Once Sis almost had her insides squashed when the overloaded sled flipped over and Cousin Theodore Douglas Robinson, no featherweight, landed on her midriff. But no one, Father included, gave her the slightest sympathy.

In the summers Father taught us to swim in a natural pond on the adjoining estate of our wealthy neighbour, Colonel Archibald Rogers, an original associate of John D. Rockefeller. Pa's teaching method was pretty basic : he tied one end of a rope to a strong pole, hitched the other end around our waists, and threw us in. After swallowing a certain amount of water and flailing about, while Pa dangled us like minnows from his pole, shouting encouragement at us all the while, we discovered it really was possible to stay afloat. Of course, if we remained under for any length of time which Father regarded as excessive he would yank us up for air. It really was a wretched way to teach anyone to swim, but it was the way Father had learned, and—traditionalist that he was—it was the way he was going to teach us. Furthermore, it worked ; we all became fairly strong swimmers, even though to this day my stroke is nothing to cause Johnny Weissmuller any envy-pangs.

We also rode at Hyde Park. In this department Anna took the honours. Thanks to Granny and affluent Delano relatives, Sis had a succession of ponies and horses, and she rode them skilfully and daringly—side-saddle, astride, and even bareback—with her long blonde hair streaming behind her like a pennant.

Even when Sis was a tiny little girl Father would place her in front of him on his favourite horse, Bobby, and they would canter over the Hyde Park countryside. Eventually Sis learned to ride Bobby by herself, but she was one of the few persons who did, as Father, an incorrigible practical joker, had taught Bobby some disconcerting tricks. He trained him so that on certain stretches of terrain no amount of whipping or spurring could induce him to execute anything more than a slow walk. Coming to another spot, however, Bobby, with no urging, would break suddenly into a wild gallop. Ever so innocently, Father would invite unsuspecting guests to ride " my favourite mount." Inevitably they would return—usually on foot—with their confidence badly shaken.

Even poor Mother was duped one day when Bobby ran away with her at Father's secret spot. All of us tell her she was traumatized by Father's horse, and I believe Mother still blames Bobby for the fact that she has never been at home in the saddle.

I rode, but with nothing like the enthusiasm for sailing which I inherited from Father. Apropos of my riding, a letter which Mother wrote Father from Hyde Park the summer before my seventh birthday is another illustration of the casualness with which physical mishaps were treated in our family. " Anna and James got their ride," Mother reported, " but unfortunately James fell off & Daisy got away. . . . He slid off over her tail & her hoof must have touched his chest & chin as both are scratched." Hinting at the increasingly stronger conflict between Granny and herself over how we were to be raised, Mother continued : " He did not seem really hurt at all but he cried hard & Mama brought him in & had him lying down before I knew anything was wrong. . . . I would have made him get on again if only for assurance." In this regard Father sided with Mother, for I can remember a later incident in Washington when he made me mount my pony and try again after I had taken a bad fall in attempting a high jump.

All of us were incorrigible dog-lovers. There was usually a Scottie in the family, starting with the first Duffy, bought in Scotland by Father and Mother on their honeymoon. A later Duffy was the family pet when Father was stricken with polio in 1921, and Mother to-day has acquired a Mr Duffy. Fala, most famous of all of Father's Scotties, is buried at Hyde Park near the foot of Father's grave. Another favourite pet—Chief, a police dog won by Anna in a raffle—is also buried in the rose-garden.

Ours Was No Ordinary Family

At Hyde Park I became aware that, in so far as lines of authority were concerned, ours was no ordinary family. This was Granny's home, and we all knew it. She laid down the rules, and all of us —even Father and Mother—accepted them. We "chicks" quickly learned that the best way to circumvent "Pa and Mummy" when we wanted something they wouldn't give us was to appeal to Granny.

I do not want to give the impression that Father was just a guest at Hyde Park, or that he accepted Granny's orders supinely. She paid the bills, but he planned and directed the operation of the place, and, even after he became President, took close interest in the smallest details. Right up to the end of her life Granny wrote letters to him at the White House about such matters as new plumbing.

Occasionally, however, Father came up against Granny on some point on which she would not yield. For instance, for years he tried to persuade her to curtail our ridiculously large dairy herd, arguing that one could import champagne and caviare for what it cost to produce the Roosevelt milk and butter. Granny told him with a finality that brooked no argument that Grandpapa James had started the dairy, that Roosevelts had always produced their own *safe* milk and butter, and that Uncle Rosy and all our relatives in the county counted on us to supply their needs. Inevitably, she closed the discussion with the dictum : " And so long as I am alive, Franklin, it is a matter of no consequence to me whether the cows make money or not." And that's the way it was.

One thing about it—we did eat well. I remember the cream was so thick you could eat it with a spoon. As a matter of fact, during the first years of my married life in Cambridge, Granny eased my always strained budget by shipping us dairy products three times a week from Hyde Park—probably the most expensive milk route on the Eastern seaboard. We even got eggs from the Hyde Park chickens. There was precedent for Granny's largess : during World War I she had supplied Father and Mother with apples and vegetables. In 1919 Mother was writing her from Washington : " Could we have a barrel of potatoes as ours is nearly empty ? "

Father also lost an early debate with Granny over one of my first ventures at earning money by raising vegetables at Hyde Park. Granny's idea of teaching me self-sufficiency was to provide the land, the seeds (free), and lots of advice, then purchase my crop at prices 50 per cent. above the market. Father contended with some asperity that it was " unrealistic " to pay me 150 per cent. of parity. All he got was a hurt response that surely " dear James " should be encouraged in his commendable display of initiative.

I was also permitted to work a couple of hours a day on the farm at Hyde Park, and, in advance of my 1918 summer visit, I wrote Granny rather anxiously that Father had agreed that I might " get paid for it." It is surprising that Granny sanctioned such labour on my part. Perhaps it was in harmony with some theory of hers that it was all right for " gentry " to work on their own land : Granny herself made a fetish of personally tending her rose-garden. Once when I told her I had to wash my hands because they were " dirty " she reproved me : " A gentleman's hands may be *soiled*, James, but they are never *dirty*."

This attitude was anathema to Mother, who always believed that young people should make themselves useful. However, she did not stand up to Granny about it, feeling that the responsibility was Father's—and Father, undoubtedly discouraged by constantly losing such arguments with his mother, shunned the subject.

To this day Anna recalls that she was raised " more by my grandmother than by my parents." Over and over again Granny would tell her such things as : " No *lady* ever crosses her limbs when seated. A lady sits with her limbs straight in front of her and her knees together."

Imperious, lovable, well meaning, over-generous Granny gave Father and Mother a bad time in so far as we were concerned. Even after we entered college she continued to spoil us with her extravagant dispensations, frequently overriding Father and Mother in the process. For example, when I was at Harvard Father finally agreed that I might have a car, if I saved the money for it. I did accumulate the cash and bought an ancient Ford roadster, which I called Ebenezer. One winter night, when I left it parked outside with the top down, a snowstorm of blizzard proportions descended, and Ebenezer was ruined beyond all redemption. I went to Pa with my tale of woe. He told me it was too bad, but that it was my fault, and I would have to wait until I could afford to buy another car before Ebenezer could be replaced. I promptly approached Granny with my hard-luck story, telling her that I would be unable to keep up my social obligations without a car. Christmas was at hand, so my present from her that year was a brand-new Chrysler runabout, grander than anything I could have afforded had I saved for the rest of my college career.

Father was horrified, and this was one of the few times he had words with Granny over how she was spoiling us. Yet he did not step in and say I could not have the car ; he did not say to me or to any of the rest of us, " Now, look, you're *my* children, and *I* am going to say what you may or may not have ! " As a result, all of us later went through a difficult readjustment period because we had become accustomed to getting pretty much what we wanted and when we wanted it, without having to earn it, or without learning that perhaps we could live without it. When we no longer had Granny to provide it for us it was a jolt.

The car incident was repeated by Granny with Franklin, Jr., when he wrecked the little roadster which Father and Mother had given him as his graduation present from Groton. They decided it would be a good lesson for him to be without a car ; Frankie merely went to Granny, and almost immediately had a larger, more expensive auto than the one he had wrecked. In her book *This I Remember* Mother writes :

> When we objected, she looked at us quite blandly and said she hadn't realized that we disapproved. She never heard anything she did not want to hear, and this was one of the occasions when she was all ears to her grandson and deaf to the remarks of his parents.

Mother went on to say :

> She often got angry with me because I seldom told them what was right or what was wrong. The reason I didn't was that I was never sure I knew myself. However . . . she had no doubts and never hesitated to tell the children what she thought. As a result, they often fooled her. The two youngest members of the family, particularly, always treated her with an affectionate *camaraderie* which won from her almost anything they desired.

How right Mother was—only it was by no means only the two

youngest children. Every one of us got lavish gifts from Granny.
It was Granny—not our parents—who took Anna and me on
our first trip to Europe. She gave us horses, watches, knick-
knacks, allowances—and all those cars. Sis, in fact, got two cars
from Granny, the second being a gift to replace a vintage jalopy
that Anna, by this time a married woman with her own children,
was driving when Father went to the White House. Granny
simply did not think it was dignified for the President's daughter
to be seen in such a vehicle.

Father was a man who rarely confided to anyone about family
matters, but when he was Governor he exploded one day to
Frances Perkins, his Industrial Commissioner (later his Secretary
of Labor when he went to the White House), that Granny's
continued interference was making it impossible for him to
" discipline those boys ! " Relating how he and Mother had
decided to punish Franklin, Jr., and Johnny for some atrocious
conduct by taking away their pony, Father told Miss Perkins :
" We thought we had made some impression. Well . . . last
week my mother buys . . . two horses for them ! . . . Now what am
I going to do ? "

Granny's generosity manifested itself in many ways. When
Anna was expecting her first baby—Eleanor (Sistie) Dall—in
1927 Granny, who wanted to help Anna with her doctor's bill,
but did not want her to know it, conspired with Father to have
it appear that the cheque came from him. In a letter which,
with her great sense of melodrama, she marked " Private &
Confidential " she wrote ·

> Dearest Son :
> Will you please send to Anna a cheque for $1,000, with a personal
> letter telling her that you want to pay her doctor's bill ? *I* w^d give
> it but I want it to come from *you*. Eleanor has already given her a
> cheque for her nurse. . . . Your loving, Mummy.

This generosity continued up to her last days and was extended
to her numerous great-grandchildren.

In all candour, Father also was the recipient of many large
gifts from his mother. She gave him the house in which we lived
in New York ; a summer house, separate from hers, on Campobello ; the boats which Father sailed ; and innumerable other
major items. She also frequently bailed out Father when he

was hard-pressed, as witnessed by the following letter which he wrote her in February 1920 :

> Dearest Mama—
>
> You are not only an angel which I always knew, but the kind which comes at the critical moment in life ! For the question was not one of paying Dr. Mitchell for removing James' insides, the Dr. can wait, I know he is or must be rich, but of paying the gas man and the butcher lest the infants starve to death, and your cheque which is much too much of a Birthday present will do that. It is so dear of you.

In matters involving public issues and personalities Father permitted no interference by his mother. When she undertook to " advise " him on affairs of state—and it was as natural as breathing for her to attempt to do so—he either ignored her or, if she persisted, shut her up sharply. When he said, " Ma-*ma*, I don't want to hear any more about that ! " the discussion was closed. I once heard him turn off some critical remarks Granny was starting to make about James A. Farley, who managed Father's first two Presidential campaigns, in just such manner.

Granny had a peculiar sort of attitude towards some of Father's political associates who were not Hyde Park-born : she might dislike them and would run them down to Father, but let outsiders criticize, and Granny loyally would rise to their defence.

For example, she never cared for Governor Alfred E. Smith, and she sniped at him constantly to Father until he made it plain that he wanted to hear no more on the subject. One evening, however, when Granny was dining at the home of the younger J. P. Morgan, that august capitalist remarked that he could not understand how Franklin, who after all was " one of us," could associate with this Smith person. " I understand," said Morgan, " that the fellow even uses brass spittoons in the Executive Mansion at Albany." Granny could not have agreed with Morgan more, but she could not let the implied criticism of her boy Franklin go unchallenged. In a commanding voice she announced to the company at large that Governor Smith had certain commendable qualities—though she was not prepared to enunciate just what they were. " It is true, I understand, that he does have—er— *spittoons* in the Executive Mansion," she admitted. " However, I am reliably informed that, when he uses them, he *never* misses."

Once Father secretly enjoyed one of Granny's political block-busters, though, for practical reasons, he had to conceal his amusement. During the 1932 campaign he brought the late Senator Huey Long of Louisiana, then a potent political figure, to Hyde Park for luncheon. As usual, the "Kingfish" held forth loudly on his favourite subject—Huey Long. Granny endured it as long as she could, then, in a stage whisper that could have been heard down at the stables, inquired, "*Who* is that *dreadful* person?"

A Place of Wonderful Memories

But Hyde Park was more than psychological conflicts with Grandmother. As I said at the outset of this chapter, Hyde Park was "home"—a place of wonderful memories.

Hyde Park was the place where a tall, skinny boy of ten or eleven watched his fearless father—the very model of a country squire—sit up all night with a shotgun to trap a burglar. That was the summer when a wave of burglaries struck Dutchess County and the estate-owners were indignant over the sheriff's failure to stop it immediately. Granny thought it was scandalous that such things were tolerated and that decent citizens were preyed on in their homes by law-breakers.

One night a rumour came to Father that burglars might visit the Roosevelt place. Squire Roosevelt got his shotgun and, about one o'clock in the morning, came into my room and took a seat by my window, which commanded a strategic view of the front lawn.

I was awakened by some movement of his, and sat bolt upright in bed. For a moment I was scared stiff when I saw him sitting there grimly with his gun.

"What is it, Pa?" I asked shakily.

"There may be a burglar in the vicinity," he informed me in a voice that was strangely formal. "I intend to remain here all night, if necessary, to apprehend him. You are to pay no attention to me. Go back to sleep!"

Go back to sleep! Pa said that as if he were telling me to blow my nose or go to the bathroom, but I could no more sleep than I could fly!

Finally, almost as the dawn was breaking, we heard the sound of steps outside—*crunch, crunch, crunch !*—on the gravel drive-way. Father stood up—suddenly he was at least eight feet tall—and pointed his gun through the top half of the open window. In tones that seemed to me capable of frightening even Jack the Ripper he thundered, " Halt ! Who's there ? "

" Don't shoot, Mr Roosevelt ! " answered a scared voice, which we recognized as that of our groom. " It's me ! "

The fellow had some lame excuse as to why he was prowling at that hour. Father ordered him back to his quarters, telling him he would speak with him in the morning. Then he turned to me and said impatiently, " Now, for heaven's sake, get back to sleep ! I can't understand why you haven't been asleep all along ! "

We never saw that groom again, incidentally. In the morning he was gone. For years Father wondered if he might not have been working with a burglary gang.

Christmases were especially wonderful times at Hyde Park. The celebration took on a Currier and Ives flavour, and even after Granny died and Father was busy with the affairs of the Presidency he managed to get to Hyde Park for Christmas for the traditional feast and the distribution of presents to the large tribe of children and grandchildren, and all the employees.

Father's yuletide reading of the saga of Tiny Tim and Scrooge was inspired by Groton days : he remembered nostalgically how the Rev. Dr Peabody, the headmaster, read it to the boys every Christmas. Another holiday touch that stemmed at least in part from the old school was the carving of the turkey. Both of us had been taught at Groton, as part of the proper education of a gentleman, the fine art of carving a fowl. Father took in-ordinate pride in his carving skill, and as I, the eldest son, entered upon manhood he naturally expected me to carry on the tradition.

This presented Father with a dilemma. As head of the family, he could not surrender the carving-knife to me. Yet he wanted to put me to the test to determine my capabilities.

One Christmas at Hyde Park, when I was a Harvard under-graduate, Granny arranged what even for us was an inordinately large family dinner, requiring two enormous turkeys to feed every one. Father hit upon the idea of staging a contest. He would carve one bird, and I would carve the other.

Now, as President Pa may have been a liberal, but as a carver and a dispenser of food in general he was an arch-conservative. Over the years he had added a sort of Rooseveltian-Dutch-economy twist to his technique, and he sliced his white meat so thin that, as he boasted, " you can almost *read* through it ! "

Under the " contest " rules I was to serve one end of the table, Father the other, and the competition was to determine who could carve and serve in the quickest time and still have some meat left on the carcass. After making his usual fuss about the carving-knife not being sharp enough Pa started off in fine form and beat me hands down on the speed element. However, he was so stingy with the turkey that the guests at his end had consumed their portions and were sending their plates back for more while I was still serving adequate portions on the first go-round. By the time he dished out seconds—grumbling and, of course, hugely enjoying it all—Pa's turkey carcass was practically stripped. In the end my plodding liberality balanced off his speedy conservatism, and we argued for years over who had won the contest. (Now, however, I must confess that I have fallen into his ways, and I can carve a turkey just as thinly and stingily as Pa ever did.)

Another Christmas custom at Hyde Park which I never shall forget was the tree-trimming ceremony. Again, Father always took charge—and he was a perfectionist. Though fear of fire was his only physical phobia, Father adhered to tradition, just as it was in Grandfather James's time, and insisted on decorating the tree with candles rather than electric bulbs.

He had his own fire-protection ritual. A bucket of water was kept near the tree, and Father tied the biggest sponge he could find to the end of a cane, so he could instantly douse any vagrant sparks

Before polio Father placed and balanced each candle himself, and there would be much loud-mouthed, joyous bickering among all of us as to the artistic merits, or demerits of his production.

After polio he was still the impresario, but, of course, he could no longer do the whole job himself. He would place as many candles as he could on the lower limbs of the tree, and we would help with the rest. Even when I became a grown man with children of my own it sometimes hit me like a blow in the stomach to see Pa sitting there in his wheel-chair, unable to reach the higher branches.

4

World War I Days in Washington

HAD I not been such a callow youth during the World War I era when Father was in Washington as Assistant Secretary of the Navy, I might have been able to contribute some valuable historic footnotes on his reactions to great events and personalities. Alas ! my most persistent memory is of how Father reacted when the " Bolshevikis," as we used to call them, tried to blow up our across-the-street neighbour, United States Attorney-General A. Mitchell Palmer, with a home-made bomb.

It was June 1919. We were living at 2131 R Street, in the north-west section of Washington. My sister and three brothers were visiting Grandmother in Hyde Park. I—eleven years old at the time—had been left behind because I was supposed to be boning up for entrance examinations for Groton. Father and Mother were out to dinner, and I had gone to bed. Suddenly there was a loud bang, a crash of window-panes, and I heard our superstitious cook start screaming, " The world has come to an end ! " Barefooted, I ran over the broken glass to the front bedroom window to see what had happened. I distinctly remember being awakened by the blast, even though Mother next day wrote Granny that " James did not hear the explosion but heard the ensuing confusion."

Just at this time Father and Mother were returning home ; had they been a few minutes earlier they might have been blown to bits. Father had parked his prized Stutz, successor to our Marmon, in the garage he rented several blocks away, when he heard the blast. He told me later how he joked : " That souvenir shell I brought home from France must have fallen off the mantel ! " Then, hearing sirens and realizing something really had happened, he started running. Mother, hobbled by her long skirt, trailed after him.

I'll never forget how uncommonly unnerved Father was when he dashed upstairs and found me standing at the window in my pyjamas. He grabbed me in an embrace that almost cracked my ribs. What I did not know was that the bomb-thrower, while failing to kill Attorney-General Palmer, had blown himself to pieces. Parts of him were on our front steps, and Father had no way of knowing that it was not I who had been blown up.

About this time Mother, her skirt hoisted above her ankles, arrived, and cold water was cast on my emotional scene with Father. " What are you doing out of bed at this hour, James ? " she inquired, as if bombings and dismembered anarchists on the porch were everyday occurrences. " Get yourself straight to bed ! " Then she proceeded to soothe the hysterical cook.

Father went over to see if Mr Palmer was hurt and if he could be of help in any way. He was back before Mother was able to pack me off to bed. " Say," said Father, seemingly more intrigued by his discovery than by the bombing, " I never knew before that Mitchell Palmer was a Quaker. He was ' theeing ' and ' thouing ' me all over the place—' thank thee, Franklin ! ' and all that." That was typical of Father : set him down in any unusual situation, and he always seemed to come up with some unexpected piece of information.

Next morning Father was still feeling unusually tender and solicitous towards me. I curdled that situation quickly, however, by going outside to investigate while Pa was having his breakfast. I poked around in the debris, found an interesting-looking object, and brought it in to him, asking, " What's this ? " I've never seen such a reaction from Father ! He paled, grabbed it from me with his napkin—it was a piece of the anarchist's collar-bone—and took it out to the police. He never did finish his breakfast.

In her letter to Granny Mother delicately glossed over this phase of the morning's events, merely reporting : " James glories in every new bone found."

In any event, while the excitement lasted I was quite popular with my friends, for I could get them past the police lines one at a time. Had I been mercenary I could have turned a profit on the concession.

When President Woodrow Wilson—always one of Father's political idols—invited him to come to Washington as Assistant Secretary of the Navy under the late Josephus Daniels of North Carolina, Father, then in his second term as a State senator at Albany, accepted with delight. Not only did he love the Navy, but he was getting fed up with his disillusioning battles with the heavy-handed Tammany politicians.

Father in those days was cocky, impatient, and ambitious, and it is a miracle that Josephus, the sage Tar Heel editor, liked and tolerated him as much as he did. Early in their association Father referred to his chief as " the funniest-looking hillbilly " he had ever seen—a remark I know he later regretted—and he also passed a number of youthfully bumptious remarks about Secretary Daniels's good friend and fellow cabinet member, William Jennings Bryan, then Secretary of State. At one point, before the United States became involved in World War I, Father wrote Mother : " These dear good people like W.J.B. and J.D. have as much conception of what a general European war means as Elliott [then four years old] has of higher mathematics," and that " Mr. Daniels [was] feeling . . . very sad that his faith in human nature and civilization and similar idealistic nonsense was receiving such a rude shock." At another point he wrote : " I am *running* the real work, although Josephus is here ! He is bewildered by it all, very sweet but very sad ! " [1]

It was no secret to Secretary Daniels that his youthful assistant was impatient with him, but he maintained an almost saintly forbearance towards Father's brashness. As the War progressed a mutually reciprocated respect and affection developed between

[1] Josephus Daniels had more understanding of America's preparedness problem than Father realized at that time. In 1937, when I was a White House assistant, Daniels wrote me, commenting favourably on a Navy Day speech in which I had deplored the steps taken at the 1921 Naval Disarmament conference. His letter related how he had witnessed the scene at the conference when President Harding's Secretary of State, Charles Evans Hughes, proposed the scrapping of several nearly completed U.S. warships, and Mark Sullivan, the newspaper columnist, and William Jennings Bryan, " arose with all the others and applauded the proposition." Daniels wrote : " Mr Sullivan said it was the greatest event in decades. I kept my seat, and Mr Bryan said ' get up Daniels, this a great thing for peace.' I said ' no, I see nothing very great in this ; moreover, I am not disposed to applaud at my own funeral.' "—J.R.

the two men. After he became President Father appointed Daniels Ambassador to Mexico and continued to address him in their correspondence as " Dear Chief."

When we first came to Washington we lived in a little house at 1733 N Street, N.W., owned by my mother's Aunt Anna (" Auntie Bye "). " When we moved down to Washington," Mother has written drily, " my mother-in-law, as usual, helped us to get settled." Anna and I were installed in private schools ; Elliott was still too young for schooling, and the two younger boys had not been born. As the family grew we had to move to the larger house on R Street.

Father's physical appearance and vitality excited attention after his arrival on the Washington scene. He was in one of his sporadic economy periods. He was spending so much money on his various collections—stamps, ship models, early American naval prints, and so forth—that he felt he had to stint himself on clothing and transportation. Accordingly, to save car fare, he would walk to his office in the old State, War, and Navy Building next to the White House. I have been told by intimates who remembered him from those days that the " Government girls " on their way to work would cast appraising glances at the tall young man in the high collar and bowler hat, hurrying along as if the Germans were on his coat-tails.

Indeed, the Washington gossip mill being as maliciously active then as it is now, there was the usual amount of talk, seeking to cast the handsome young Assistant Secretary in the rôle of " ladies' man," particularly since he was a summer bachelor for the periods when Mother would take " the chicks " to Hyde Park or Campobello. I think the record of their long and successful marital partnership is the best and most dignified answer to such rumours.

Spendthrift and Shoe-saver

Father was earning five thousand dollars a year as Assistant Secretary, and our chronic condition of genteel non-affluence continued. Mother's budget troubles became worse as time went on. Father and Mother had worked out a system whereby certain expenses, such as rent, food, school, and medical care,

were his responsibilities, while Mother used part of her independent income towards clothing for herself and the children.
On family presents and charities they went fifty-fifty. One of
Mother's letters to Granny from that period woefully catalogues
all of our numerous and expensive ailments, and notes : " I
know F. won't be happy as there is a bill here now for all the
babies' ear troubles for $223 ! Children are an expensive luxury
aren't they ? " Granny must have taken a hint, for shortly after
Mother's letter Father was writing her : " You have saved my
life, or, rather, the various Doctors' lives, by making it possible
for me to pay them promptly ! "

Father had a terrible time making his salary stretch. He even
relied on Granny for help in meeting some of his insurance
premiums. " I enclose an insurance card on my life but your
pocket ! " said one letter of this period. Years later Father, in
reminiscent mood, recalled to his World War II Press secretary,
Jonathan Daniels, son of Josephus, how his World War I salary
" just went," he didn't know where. " I couldn't keep an
account with myself," he said. " After about six months of
this, certain complaints came from back home about paying the
grocery bill. . . . So I began taking my salary by check and putting
it in the bank, and taking perhaps five dollars cash for the week."

Mother, of course, could tell Father where his money went,
for she discovered early in her married life that she was wed to
an incurable collector. Father would wear a jacket until it was
threadbare—and even then he could not bear to discard it, but
would pass it on to one of the boys. He would erupt with all
his Dutch stubbornness if anyone suggested it was necessary to
pay more than two dollars for a shirt. Mother had to prod him
to order new clothes. Yet let some firm come up with a stamp
or book or autograph which he coveted, and he would go
after it.

It wasn't that Father didn't like fine clothing and accessories.
He adored them. In fact, in his early Groton and Harvard
letters he chattered like a schoolgirl debutante about his apparel—
for instance, " My dress suit looked like a dream and was much
admired." It was simply that, in later life, he much preferred
to spend his money on other things. Consequently, Granny
sent him fancy pyjamas, dressing-gowns, and smoking-jackets,

1908. I haven't changed much in appearance, only in size

Father and Mother with their children in Washington, 1916

Franklin D. Roosevelt Library

Here I am in a wrinkled outfit, about 1917, at Campobello

The Family at Campobello, 1920
Franklin D. Roosevelt Library

and Mother gave him the practical gifts, such as shirts, ties, and handkerchiefs.

One thing Father definitely could not see " wasting money on " was dining out. In my growing-up years I cannot recall a single instance—except when we were travelling—when Father splurged by taking us out to dinner.

Father was paradoxical about some of his economies : for instance, he had a weakness for expensive English shoes. He compensated for this extravagance by becoming a shoe-saver and keeping all his old shoes. Since his shoes took little wear after his illness a tremendous quantity of them built up. For a while he could parcel some of these out to Elliott, who has small feet, as had Father, but the rest of us had much bigger underpinnings and could not wear them.

We used to kid Pa about his clothes closet being a regular second-hand junk-shop in which we could find anything we needed, but I must admit that his hand-me-downs often came in handy. Until recently, when it fell apart, I wore a tweed jacket which he had passed on to me. Conversely, Pa would latch on to any of our old clothes that he liked—if we would give them up.

This habit of clothes-swapping caused a notable mix-up at the marriage of Franklin, Jr., to Ethel du Pont. I had no silk hat to wear, and I announced to the family that I was hanged if I was going to buy a plug hat just because my brother was marrying a du Pont. Pa told me to calm down, that he would look in his closet at the White House and was certain he had an old one somewhere. Sure enough, he had one—slightly vintage in style and a bit too big for me, but, by stuffing a little paper in the sweatband, I managed to keep it from falling over my ears, and it did fine.

It was a good wedding-party, and I managed to mislay the hat, which had Father's initials in it. Even in that Republican stronghold the initials " F.D.R." had a certain collector's value, and some character, thinking he had the President's top-hat, walked off with it. Another eager-beaver acquaintance found out about it, tracked down and reclaimed the hat, and returned it to Father with a note that made it apparent he felt he was performing a deed similar to rescuing the Magna Carta from a ragpicker's bag. Father, who always enjoyed such gestures, wrote the Good Samaritan a personal letter, explaining : " The hat was not mine at all. It was Jimmy's, handed down to him by a benevolent parent."

" I did think," he added, " that Jimmy had shown complete sobriety at the wedding but I am beginning to wonder in view of the fact that he apparently had not even discovered the fact that he had lost his hat ! "

Mother's Social Ordeals

On the social front back in World War I days there were two schools of thought as to how Father took to the livelier side of Washington life. Father himself sometimes insisted that the socializing was a " great nuisance " ; others who remember this period tell me he had a whale of a good time at parties.

As for Mother, with the painful shyness that weighed so heavily on her in those days, the social calls she was obliged to make as wife of the Assistant Secretary were an ordeal. How well I remember the ritual, for, as I grew older, Mother would make me dress in my blue suit and long black stockings and go along to deposit her calling-cards at the homes where she did not have to pay a formal visit. I was as reluctant as Mother about knocking on those strange doors, but I could not talk her out of pressing me into service as her footman. I felt greatly imposed upon !

One of my favourite stories about our Washington social life concerns the Sunday when Father was preparing to enjoy a rare, quiet evening at home with the family.

The cook was off, so Mother fixed an early supper of scrambled eggs—the only dish she cooks, as she herself will tell you. Mother was in a dressing-gown and Father was in his smoking-jacket, when the front-door bell rang. There stood some guests in full-dress Navy uniforms and evening gowns. They had been invited for dinner, but Mother had written it down on her calendar for the following Sunday.

Father took it in his stride, for it was the sort of situation that appealed to the outlandish strain in his sense of humour. He did something about producing cocktails, while Mother disappeared into the kitchen and whipped up more scrambled eggs. " Franklin and I thought it was rather funny," Mother recalled recently, " but I do not think our guests felt the same way. They left quite early."

Mother's shyness stayed with her for many years, even after she became active in public life. Sometimes it manifested itself even with us. Around 1930 or 1931, when Father was Governor, Anna, my brothers, and I hired an artist to do a portrait of Mother secretly—he worked from photographs and sketches he made of her at public gatherings—to present to Father on his birthday, which we were celebrating at Hyde Park. We hid the painting behind some drapes. When we unveiled it Father was genuinely delighted and kept exclaiming over it, but Mother was so upset that she fled from the room.

Another part of official life which Mother hated were the visits to battleships and cruisers to witness target practice and such. Secretary Daniels frequently invited her—and occasionally Anna, me, and even little Elliott—on such junkets. While she loathed going, because she was never a particularly keen sailor and was always afraid she was going to embarrass Father by becoming actively ill, she felt she could not say no to her husband's chief.

Mother and all of us—even little Elliott, when he joined the expeditions—were carefully coached by Father on the fine points of Navy protocol, such as who walked ahead of whom, how to salute the quarterdeck, what parts of the ship the ladies shouldn't visit, and so forth.

Father frequently took us for outings on the *Sylph*, a sleek 124-foot converted yacht, painted a gleaming white, which formerly had been used by Presidents McKinley, Uncle Teddy, and Taft, and now was assigned to the Secretary of the Navy's office. In April 1918, after an overnight voyage on this elegant vessel, Sis gleefully tattled in a letter to Granny that it had been quite rough, but " no one was sick except the Captain. . . . I am not supposed to know it but one of the officers told me and James."

The following month Father took us again on the *Sylph* to see George Washington's home at Mount Vernon. If there were any spit-and-polish naval officers aboard they must have suffered, for there were fifteen children in the party, and, as I wrote

Granny, " We ran aroud [*sic*] the decks and ran relay races and played ' Hide and go seek.' " Next year Father got pretty sore when the *Sylph*'s crew, taking us ashore in a motor-launch, disregarded his advice on how to approach the landing and got stuck in the mud. The Navy sent another motor-launch to the rescue, and, as Anna somewhat uncharitably reported to Granny : " All the fat ladies including Mother got into the motor boat. . . . Then we managed to get out of the mud."

My particular disgrace occurred when Father took me with him to a grand review of the fleet at Yorktown. The review was followed by a sumptuous, thirteen-course official banquet. Coming back across Chesapeake Bay dirty weather set in, and I promptly lost all thirteen courses, much to Father's disgust.

I would be less than candid if I did not report that Father both enjoyed and made use of his perquisites of office. I remember his being brought to Campobello for week-end visits several times aboard Navy destroyers ; on one occasion he even brought in the *Vireo*, our sailing-boat, aboard a destroyer's deck. In 1916, when a polio epidemic of frightening proportions hit Campobello, Father finally persuaded Secretary Daniels, who was rightfully fearful of possible public criticism, to let him send the U.S.S. *Dolphin*, an unarmoured former naval cruiser, then being used by the Secretary's office, to evacuate all of us from the island.

Busy as Father was in those Washington days, he found time to do things for and with his children. To me he was not only a father, but, when he had the time, a grand playmate—and he was always a good friend whom I did not hesitate to ask for any reasonable favour. He would cart my tool-box or other forgotten gear from Washington to Campobello, and his letters to Mother when she was on the island or at Hyde Park never failed to contain some special message for one or all of us children. When a pet bunny died, for instance, he took time to write : " I'm *too* sad about the bunny's demise—and only hope the funeral & making of the tombstone will console the chicks. I wonder if it was the lop-sided one ? "

When he was home he always came up for a romp at bedtime, and he had a ritual of asking the younger boys, " Are you snug as a bug in a rug ? " Even after we became strapping six-footers my brothers and I always kissed Pa on the cheek when we greeted him, and he was genuinely surprised if anyone commented on the custom. " I always kissed my father," he would say.

It was a family custom for Mother to read to us in the evenings. We also gathered frequently around the piano, with Granny at the keyboard, for family " sings." Although piano lessons were inflicted briefly and futilely on Anna and me, there was not, in my opinion, a decent musical talent in the family, though all of us—especially Father—were convinced we had magnificent voices. None of us was bashful about opening our mouths and singing, particularly in church, though Father, whose robust voice ranged between baritone and tenor, sometimes sang so loudly that we children were just a little embarrassed.

Though Episcopalian, Father particularly enjoyed hearing and singing the rousing Methodist and Baptist hymns, and occasionally attended churches of those denominations for that reason. " I *love* to sing with the Methodys ! " he would reply if anyone took him to task for deserting his own church. Once, during World War II, he took Winston Churchill with him to a Methodist Christmas service, and Frances Perkins relates how he told her, " It is good for Winston to sing hymns with the Methodys." He was particularly enchanted that year with the spirited rendition of one of his favourite hymns, " Oh, Little Town of Bethlehem," to which he, no doubt, and possibly the doughty Prime Minister contributed.

Any pastime involving physical exertion found favour with Father He was the leading spirit in organized games of field hockey with players mostly recruited from the British Embassy, and baseball with mixed groups of Father's friends and ours. Pa got terribly angry with Anna and me on the baseball field one afternoon. He had drafted a new recruit—a powerfully built young Britisher who later became his country's Ambassador to Washington, Sir Ronald Lindsay. The future Ambassador had never played baseball—only cricket—so Anna and I thoughtfully offered to " instruct " him. One of the points we carefully drilled into him was that the proper way to slide for base was to dive head first for the bag. The first time he did it his patrician nose cut a furrow in the dust, and he came up bleeding and minus a good deal of skin. Father caught on to what we had done and was giving us an awful bawling out when Lindsay, a good fellow, saved us by starting to laugh uproariously.

Father's passion for the strenuous life occasionally did him in. When World War I broke out he was one of the leading disciples of the " fitness " programme launched by the Navy in Washington under the guidance of Walter Camp, the one-time famous Yale football coach and father of the " daily dozen " setting-up exercises. Camp himself wrote admiringly of Father : " Mr Roosevelt is a beautifully built man, with the long muscles of the athlete . . . his heart and lungs cry for more exercise . . . his effect upon others is . . . salutary in that he imparts some of his own vitality."

The programme was not easy to sell, but, under proddings by Father and other athletic young officials, various Cabinet and sub-Cabinet members, including Father's close friend, Secretary of the Interior Franklin K. Lane, and President Wilson's son-in-law, Secretary of the Treasury William G. McAdoo, were seduced into turning out for callisthenics and a brisk trot in Potomac Park. Secretary Daniels, a man who believed that exercise was a fine thing for athletes, gave his slightly cynical blessing to the fitness crusade, but wouldn't have a thing to do with it himself. He stayed perfectly healthy throughout the War, but the programme, as Jonathan Daniels notes in his book on that era, *End of Innocence*, " almost disrupted the war effort before it was begun," for, among other casualties, Secretary Lane suffered a heart attack, and Father came down with colds and sore throats, one after the other.

Father also loved to tell the story of another " physical hazard " to which he was exposed—" above and beyond the call of duty "— during World War I. (His friend Charles F. Palmer, a war-time special assistant to the President in the housing field, and now chairman of the Franklin D. Roosevelt Warm Springs Memorial Commission, advises me that Father related the story so vividly at a private White House dinner one evening that Governor Herbert Lehman of New York, an avid listener, dropped his raspberry sherbet in the finger-bowl.) As Father told it, Marie Dressler, the actress, later famous for her portrayal of Tugboat Annie, had come to Washington to plug Liberty Bond sales.

Father was detailed by Secretary Daniels to escort her to the outdoor platform where she was speaking and introduce her to the crowd. Miss Dressler suddenly decided she wanted to be seen better, hopped up on the wooden rail of the platform, and yelled at Father, " Hold my legs ! "

" I did so—gingerly ! " Father related. " Suddenly, in her fervour, Miss Dressler—no lightweight—jumped. The rail collapsed, and she fell backward with me under her. It almost killed me."

Father was also an enthusiastic golfer. According to Mother, he was often on the golf-course on Sunday mornings, " leaving me to take the children to church." He usually went around in the high eighties. One summer at Campobello Mother tried to learn the game, so that she could play it with him, but, after watching her hack out divots for a while, Father pointedly observed that it might be just as well if she developed some other interest. Mother thereupon took up walking.

The time came in Washington when Father decided I should earn my allowance—twenty-five cents a week—by caddying for him, so I too got to skip church occasionally in favour of the golf-course. I loved it, and would have forgone my allowance for the privilege. He played with various men in public life. Several times I caddied for Father when his partner was Senator Warren G. Harding, who in 1920 was to head the Republican ticket that defeated the Democratic slate on which Father was the Vice-Presidential nominee. All I remember about Harding was that he seemed amiable and that Father enjoyed golfing with him.

The diversions which Mother organized for us were on the gentler side. For example, she was ingenious at arranging Easter surprises. She would conceal gifts in papier-mâché Easter eggs— toy tanks for Johnny and Franklin, skates for Elliott and me, and gloves and other such feminine frippery for Sis. She also got us into a dancing class sponsored by Lady Spring-Rice, wife of Father's good friend the delightfully witty and notoriously absent-minded British Ambassador, Sir Cecil Spring-Rice. We called her ladyship " Springy," and I, together with the other small fry of Washington officialdom who were sent to the Embassy classes, professed to loathe the weekly dancing lessons.

At that, I fared better than Franklin and Johnny, who some years later were sent to a fashionable New York City dancing school ; one of Mother's letters to Father, which I'm sure my brothers would like to have burned, recounts : " The little boys have their last dancing class to-morrow afternoon and are doing a minuet in costume with wigs, they are so sweet ! "

Father frequently had us visit him at the Navy Department, where we were enthralled by the fighting-ship models on display ; this caused him trouble on at least one occasion, when Baby Elliott wouldn't go home. " There is only one thing that interferes with their perfect enjoyment . . .," he once said, " and that is my inability to take the boats out of the ' windows,' as they call the glass cases, and sail them in the bath tub or the river or any other wet places."

We were also taken to see historical events. An early letter of mine to Granny tells how Anna and I accompanied our parents " as near to the Capitol as we could get " when President Wilson was inaugurated in 1917. While Father and Mother walked to the ceremony, Anna and I " sat in the car [and] ate are lunch " ; then, " after the President at finished is speech," we all went to see the inaugural parade.

I saw President Wilson several times and was introduced to him, but Father, rather surprisingly, never took us to the White House. As a matter of fact, I never set foot in the White House until I went there with Father in 1933. An early letter from Anna to Granny reminds me that once, when Father was away from Washington, we tried to go sightseeing there, but, as Anna wrote, " we could not get in because . . . they were afraid of German spys."

With his sense of history, Father was always seeking opportunities for the children to meet world figures. I think I almost cured him of this the day he and Mother took Anna and me to Mount Vernon to meet the visiting King Albert I, Queen Elizabeth, and Crown Prince Leopold of Belgium. Father had met the heroic King Albert on the Belgian battle-front in 1918, and was determined that we should see him. Mother coached us assiduously on how I was to bow and how Anna was to curtsy and kiss the Queen's hand.

We got that over with, and I was standing around gawking

at Leopold, who was about six years my senior. The future king, an early prototype of the present-day hot-rodder, spotted a motor-cycle in the entourage of guards and wangled permission to ride it. Then he turned to me and told me to hop on behind him. Before Father or Mother had a chance to say no I was straddling the motor-cycle with my arms around the Crown Prince's middle and we were tearing through the Virginia countryside. We stayed out well over an hour, and I never had such a wild ride in my life—including even several I have taken with my brother Franklin. Father and Mother—not to mention the King and Queen—were awfully mad.

Years later, when Father was President, I visited Brussels as the guest of the late Ambassador Joseph Davies, and had a reunion with Leopold, who by this time had become king. I asked him if he remembered giving me the motor-cycle ride at Mount Vernon, but he just looked at me blankly.

Father Goes to See the War

The events of World War I, naturally, were very much on the minds of all of us—all the more so since Anna, Elliott, and I were convinced that it was our dashing Pa who was practically winning the War singlehanded, at least so far as the naval end of things was concerned. Historians have speculated a good deal on Father's supposed frustration over not having been in uniform during the First World War. From what I recall hearing him say on this subject, I think that some of the historians are way off base. It is true that Father wanted to get into uniform, and that he was told, first by Secretary Daniels, later by President Wilson, that it was his duty to stay on the job in Washington. Father was not a man given to brooding over a decision once it had been made, so, after his first turn-down, he accepted the situation and plunged wholeheartedly into doing his job at the Navy Department, which, of course, he loved.

When he returned from his 1918 inspection of the battlefronts he was all fired up to renew his efforts to get into uniform. However, on the trip home he contracted double pneumonia. By the time he recovered President Wilson advised him that an armistice was imminent. Years later, when Father was President, he, like Wilson, was importuned by various young congressmen and Government officials who wanted to get into uniform ; in persuading them not to leave their posts he made effective use of the story of how President Wilson had kept him on the home front.

Father's trip to the war zones was an exciting experience for him—and, vicariously, for me. I was ten years old at the time, and avidly followed newspaper accounts of his trip. " I wish I could have been there to see King George of England when you did. . . .," I wrote Father. " An article on the front page of the times . . . said you had made the best impression of any man over there."

Father's exuberant, energetic nature was illustrated by some sidelights of his 1918 trip. He chose, characteristically, to go over on a destroyer, the U.S.S. *Dyer*, commanded by a Captain Poteet, and he thoroughly enjoyed the rough crossing. His destroyer costume—" my own invention," he wrote in his shipboard diary—consisted of " khaki riding trousers, golf stockings, flannel shirt and leather coat." Whenever a submarine alert was sounded Father, regardless of what he was doing, was one of the first to reach the bridge. Twice he arrived there " in pajamas and bare feet." " I . . . apologized to Poteet . . .," Father wrote, " but he said it made an excellent and distinctive uniform for a flag officer as long as the Secretary of the Navy does not try to change it to the old fashioned night-gown and carpet slippers."

Father almost got his head blown off during the crossing, because of his insistence on being in the thick of things. During a gun drill, he recorded in his diary,

> a green youngster pulled the lanyard of the port gun when it was trained as far forward as it would go. McCauley [Captain Edward McCauley, Jr., U.S.N., Father's aide for the trip] and I happened to be standing in the port wing of the bridge, and when the blooming thing went by only a few feet outboard, we thought the end had come. Captain Poteet seemed annoyed !

Years later, when Father was President, he was reminded of his experience on the *Dyer*. He was travelling to the Teheran and Cairo conferences aboard the then new battleship U.S.S. *Iowa*, along with practically all the top brass of the United States high command—including Generals Marshall, Arnold, and Somervell and Admirals Leahy and King. A torpedo was inadvertently fired from an escorting destroyer and exploded perilously close to the *Iowa*, which had to manœuvre sharply to get out of the way. Father witnessed the whole performance.

Despite the excitement and pressure of his trip Pa was like any typical husband and father in his concern over what to bring home for Mother and the kids. Even before the *Dyer* docked in England he had written Mother a letter, ready to go back on the next boat, urging : " I do wish you would write me if you can think of any small thing which Mama or the children would like me to get. I would ask you to do the same in regard to yourself, but I fear you would suggest tablecloths or feather dusters." It was—and still is—a standing joke in the family that Mother's gift notions always run to the practical side. Dutifully and typically, she lived up to her reputation by writing back that Mama could use a black bag from Paris ; Anna needed " 6 new nightgowns & 6 prs. drawers," and Elliott and I could use " those knot stockings with turnover tops . . . you can get them cheaper in London than here." For herself she specified " nothing unless you see some wash cotton white gloves size 6½ short & short white kid same size the kind you pull on, no buttons."

Whether I knew of Mother's uninspired suggestion at the time I cannot say, but I have come across a letter I wrote Pa which indicates that I would certainly have taken a dim view of knit stockings with turn-over tops as a gift from the war front. " Please get me the ' Kaiser's Helmet ' and if you can the Kaiser himself," I asked. There must be at least half a million surviving former small boys from this period who penned identical requests to their daddies overseas.

Father was diligent about keeping Anna and me posted on progress of the conflict through war maps, which he kept in his study at home. He also brought us in to listen when British and French officers would come to our house to brief him on developments at the front. All of this made a vivid impression on us, and, in January 1917, Sis was writing Granny : " Last night we played that I was a train nurse and James was the doctor and Elliott was the wound. I was dressed in a white skirt and white apron, and James in his boy scout suit and Elliott in his cow boy suit and we had lots of fun."

The War was one of the milestones in Mother's growing awareness of world events. In August 1915, exiled, as usual, with " the chicks " at Campobello, she was urging Father in Washington to wire her " if any very exciting events take place. . . . The Germans are certainly not treating us with great consideration."

Mother's naïveté in those days landed her in an embarrassing predicament with the Press—perhaps her first major experience in how one's words may sometimes be twisted. It came about through a Washington dispatch printed in the *New York Times* under a dateline of July 16, 1917. Mother was bubbling with enthusiasm to help win the War through such efforts as canteen work, knitting, and food conservation. (Indeed, there is a wartime letter from me to Granny in which I report somewhat apprehensively that Mother was " up at five this morning to go to the canteen—do not you think that Mother should not go so early ? ")

In due course Mother's efforts came to the attention of the Press, and the *Times* carried a story stating that " the food-saving program " at the home of Assistant Secretary and Mrs Roosevelt had been singled out by the Food Administration's conservation section as a " model " for large households. It went on to quote Mother as saying that there were seven in the family (correct), that ten servants were employed (incorrect), and that all the servants had signed pledge-cards and took part in daily conferences on ways and means of saving food. " Making the ten servants help me do my saving has not only been possible but highly profitable," Mother was quoted further. " Since I have started following the home-card instructions prices have risen, but my bills are no larger." To this day Mother does not know where the woman reporter who wrote the story came up with those " ten servants "—unless she added up every one employed by us and Granny combined in Washington, Hyde Park, New York, and Campobello.

No one—not even Mother—knows how Father really felt about this publicity, portraying her as the brave little housewife struggling along with only ten servants. However, he reacted typically—by teasing her unmercifully. The day after the article

appeared a letter from Father was on its way to Mother at Campobello, stating :

> All I can say is that your latest newspaper campaign is a corker
> and I am proud to be the husband of the Originator, Discoverer
> and Inventor of the New Household Economy for Millionaires !
> Please have a photo taken showing the family, the ten cooperating
> servants, the scraps saved from the table and the hand book. I will
> have it published in the Sunday Times.

Father added : " Uncle Fred [Delano] says, ' It's fine, but
Gee how mad Eleanor will be ! ' " How right he was, for two
days later Mother responded : " I do think it was horrid of that
woman to use my name in that way and I feel dreadfully about
it." To her credit, however, Mother did not claim she was
entirely misquoted, but admitted : " So much is not true and
yet some of it I did say. I never will be caught again that's sure
and I'd like to crawl away for shame."

During the latter part of the War period we kept a symbolical
empty chair at our table for " Mr Hoover." This was supposed
to signify our willingness to cut down on food, as Herbert Hoover
was President Wilson's war-time Food Administrator, and
" hooverizing " then was an accepted synonym for going without
food voluntarily, instead of involuntarily, as came about during
the depression of the late twenties. As a matter of fact, the
Herbert Hoovers and the young Franklin D. Roosevelts were on
friendly social terms and dined with each other occasionally.
Mr Hoover had not come out yet as a Republican, and Father
even considered him good *Democratic* Presidential material. In
a letter to their mutual friend Hugh Gibson, the career diplomat,
Father remarked : " I had some nice talks with Herbert Hoover.
. . . He is certainly a wonder, and I wish we could make him
President of the United States. There could not be a better one."
I think I am safe in saying that Father changed his mind about
this with the passage of years. And, just to show how history
repeats itself, I too, in 1948, had some things to say in public
about what a fine candidate a certain general named Eisenhower
would make—on the Democratic ticket ! Mr Truman has never
forgiven me.

Mother accompanied Father when he went to Europe again

in 1919 to transact certain business for the Navy. He spent a good deal of time as an observer at the Versailles Peace Conference, and became a convert to President Wilson's tragically unrealized ideals for a League of Nations. This politically significant conversion was strengthened on the return trip, when Father and Mother travelled on the transport s.s. *George Washington*, which brought the tired President back to the United States.[1] Father saw a good deal of Mr Wilson, and the contact generated in him the enthusiasm for the League which Father, as the Democratic Vice-Presidential nominee, later carried into the 1920 campaign.

Granny also took full cognizance of the War, and no account of her war-time activities would be complete without mention of how she exposed the French war hero Marshal Joffre to whooping cough in order that he might have the pleasure of meeting the Roosevelt children.

Anna, Elliott, and I had all come down with whooping cough in May 1917, and we were bundled off to Granny's place for protection of Frankie and John. That was the month the hero of the Marne visited New York, and Granny was determined that, germs or not, we were going to meet him.

Anna and I had reached the stage where we were reasonably non-infectious, but Elliott was slow in getting rid of his symptoms. May 10—the day of Joffre's arrival—came, and Elliott was still puny. How Granny must have wrestled with her conscience! Her sense of history triumphed over her sense of hygiene, however, and all of us, including the pale and barking Elliott, were bundled up and taken to the imposing Frick mansion on Fifth Avenue in response to a special invitation which Granny had arranged through the Marshal's aide, Colonel Fabry, who knew Father.

Granny's subsequent letter to Father and Mother described how " the perfectly charming brave Joffre spoke to me of *my*

---

[1] As Assistant Secretary, Father was responsible for selecting the transport on which President Wilson was to travel, and he chose the s.s. *Washington*. He also arranged for the purchase of a replica of George Washington's desk, on which President Wilson wrote his drafts of the Covenant of the League of Nations and various other historic documents. Later Father bought this desk from the Government and used it at Hyde Park. I inherited it from Father, and now use it in my home.—J.R.

son in a most *lovely* . . . [here, Granny dropped a word in her rapture]. I felt . . . rather like shedding a tear but managed to behave decently."

The gallant Marshal then " kissed all three children " on the cheeks, and Granny, quite overcome, noted that we " were all *so* sweet and appreciative." All I can remember of the incident, however, is how peculiar it seemed for this old bird with the white walrus moustache to be bussing me, a perfect stranger. In retrospect, I like to think of what a delicious international incident it would have created had the hero of the Marne come down with an infantile disease from kissing the Roosevelt children.

5

Father spared the Rod

As a disciplinarian in the old-fashioned mould Father was the world's worst. Generally speaking, he was too tender-hearted to spank us, and when it came to advising us on major decisions it was almost a fetish with him just to tell us what he thought and not try to impose his will upon us. Never did he insist that " you must do as I say."

We kids, naturally, loved him for these traits, though Mother did not always appreciate the fact that if there were any unpleasant punishment to be dished out the responsibility was shunted over to her.

Sometimes in retrospect, however, I think that Father really gave us a subtle, psychological form of discipline. He sought to guide us by personal example, with a minimum of preachment. That there were failures along the line was more our fault than his. Certainly he was a very human father—I remember many examples of his wisdom and deep consideration for our problems—even at times when his own troubles were almost unendurable.

The only spanking I ever remember getting from Father occurred one Sunday morning when we were living in Washington and I was a lad of ten or so. That Sunday Mother's will had prevailed, and Father was going with the family to church, instead of to the golf-links. We attended St Thomas's Episcopal Church at that time. Father was a vestryman, and, as such, attired himself with impeccable formality in cutaway coat, striped pants, and high silk hat.

That morning I decided to rebel : I would not accompany my

parents. Father and Mother had a very big bed, and I got under-
neath it, taking a position exactly in the centre, where I thought
no one could reach me.

Father said come out. I said *no*. Father took off his silk hat,
got down on his hands and knees, crawled under the bed—striped
pants, cutaway, and all—dragged me out, and proceeded to give
me a thorough treatment with the hairbrush. I went to church.

The occasion is so memorable because it was so rare. Mother
tells me there was one earlier incident in Albany involving me,
when she literally put the hairbrush in his hand and said,
" Franklin, you *must* spank this child," but I was too young to
remember it. So far as I have been able to establish, I was the
only one of the five children who was ever actually spanked by
Father.

Though it was foreign to her gentle and reasonable nature,
Mother was gradually forced into becoming the administrator
of whatever punishment was meted out in our family. I remember
one occasion when she yanked violent-tempered young Johnny
from the dinner-table, lugged him upstairs, and literally heaved
him into his room. Despite her soft spot for Elliott, she also
punished him when necessary. " Elliott bit James hard the
other day," one of her early Campobello letters to Father relates.

> . . . I spanked him & explained that no matter whose fault it was
> boys didn't bite. His feelings were much hurt & he made such a
> long upper lip he looked like a rabbit but at the end of the spanking
> (with my slipper) he said " It didn't hurt so very much, Mother."

Father's reply—a typical one—was : " I love the description of
Elliott's spanking ! "

Usually when Mother tried to pass responsibility to Father
the punishment simply was not administered. A typical example
was the time when Elliott, a born rebel, outrageously insulted
one of Mother's school-teacher friends, Miss Marion Dickerman,
who was trying to tutor him. Mother took him in to Father
with a demand that he deal firmly with the situation. Elliott
tells me :

" Father sat me on his knee, put his arm around me affectionately, and we began talking about everything except what I had
said to Mother's friend.

" In half an hour Mother came back and said, ' Is everything settled ? '

" Father replied, ' Everything is settled.'

" There had been no discipline, of course, but, out of loyalty to Father, I went back to being tutored."

Even on matters of discipline where physical punishment was not involved Pa was a softie. Once, after Franklin, Jr., was involved in a speeding scrape, Father " revoked " Franklin's driver's licence for an indefinite period, but then Brud talked him into limiting the suspension to a couple of weeks. Before Brud left Pa told him that it was Mother who had insisted on the punishment.

In those early days Mother seemed driven by some inner compulsion to write detailed letters—usually to Granny—about her problems with the children. Back in our early Washington period, when I was going on eleven and Anna was twelve, Mother related to Granny how Anna and I had each been allowed to invite a friend over for the day, and how violent hostilities— ending in fisticuffs and, as I remember it, hair-pulling—began when the two girls decided to snoot my chum and me. " When the guests left," wrote Mother, " I told them there would be no more [guests] for a time. . . . Then there were united tears and assurances that they enjoyed the fights."

Despite these outbursts, Anna and I, by reason of age, were close. For the same reason Franklin, Jr., and Johnny, though vastly different in personalities, were a team. Elliott was in the middle in more ways than one : every one ganged up on him, particularly Sis and I, who felt that Mother " coddled " him.

Frankie was always the sunshine boy, the budding politician of the family. I have found a letter which I wrote to Granny in March 1918 relating : " I went out for a walk with little Franklin this morning and every time he saw a child he would say hallow as if he new them." Another letter, written by Granny to Father from Hyde Park during this period, contains this passage :

My garden club meeting was pleasant, & Franklin, Jr. & Johnnie handed cakes & sandwiches & behaved like perfect gentlemen. The evening before, F. Jr. said " Granny, I intend to run for the Presidency, & am beginning my campaign at your tea." I said : " how will you do that ? "

" Oh, I shall get to know people, & when my name comes up, they will vote for me "—So I answered, " That's a good idea & if you wait on people quietly & do not drop the sandwiches & cakes, & are helpful, people *may* say : " Oh that must be one of those nice little boys who helped us. I think I will give my vote to him." He took it quite seriously & went to sleep.

Being undersized in his early days and a moody child by nature, Johnny was rather jealous of the more robust, happy-go-lucky Franklin. I remember that the two of them once went to a place where there was an alleged X-ray gadget that was supposed to reveal the size of one's bones. Frankie shoved his arm under the contraption, and his bones showed up big and strong. Then Johnny extended his arm for the test, and by comparison the bones appeared puny. Poor Johnny was terribly upset and sulked for days.

Mother recalls how Father sometimes let her down badly in her attempts to control Johnny. Once, after one of Johnny's eruptions, she ordered him to his room, then followed him there, intending to have a heart-to-heart talk. Johnny wasn't there, so she went to Father's study and found him crying on Pa's shoulder. Father had his arm around him and was attempting to console him. Knowing that he was undermining her efforts to enforce discipline, he looked " quite guilty," Mother remembers.

Elliott had a temper too. He himself has reminded me of the time he threw a hunting knife at Miss Jean Sherwood, another of Mother's friends who had rashly consented to tutor him. Fortunately his aim was bad. Even earlier, when Bunny was three years old, Mother told Father in a letter how " Elliott went for me with both fists " because she had to discipline a dog. " He throws stones at him," she wrote, " but no one else may touch him ! "

Though it was Mother who was always hovering over Bunny, Elliott had a strong attachment to Father. In 1913, when Father was so involved with his Navy post that he was separated from the family for most of the summer, we find Mother writing : " Elliott feels a calamity approaching." The following year Mother wrote Father from Campobello : " Elliott sends love and wants you to return at once as he has ' no one to take care of him.' "

Elliott's spells of yearning for Father seemed to hit him hardest when Father had to leave us after a holiday. In August 1915, after Father had returned to Washington from Campobello, Mother, addressing him as " Dearest Honey," an endearment she used frequently in her letters of that period, wrote :

> It seems very lonely and strange without you. . . . Elliott after he got home last night gave way completely & I found him alone in the day nursery waiting for his supper and crying hard. When pressed for a reason he said " I don't want *my* father to go away." I consoled him by suggesting that he make you lots of boats & horses before you got back & he told me this a.m. he was " working hard ! "

Father was quite capable of venting scathing sarcasm and cold wrath on an offender, but it was a fleeting sort of thing with him. Basically he could not bear to stay angry with anyone he loved for more than a short while. Anna recalls an incident which occurred at Hyde Park during Father's most difficult period of convalescence from polio. It was at the time when Father's nerves were raw from his first experiences with the terrible imprisonment of the wheel-chair and the physical pain of his struggles to learn to walk again, plus the pressures of his own inner conflicts. One day Father asked Anna to help him put away some books. She dropped them, and Father, in a sudden, unreasonable fury, upbraided her severely.

Sis ran crying from the room. Yet the storm was over as quickly as it flared. Mother went to Anna and quietly tried to explain to her something of the terrible tension that was weighing on Father. Sis listened, dried her eyes, and returned to the library, ready to make up. She found Father already in control of himself ; he greeted her with affection and made her feel as if the incident never happened.

My own memories of Father as the symbol of authority go back to the time when I was the scared, youthful miscreant, caught in an act for which I still feel shame, and he was the judge— calm, deliberate, wise, and fair.

Christmas was coming, and Anna had requested a wrist-watch. Somehow I learned she was not going to get it. Mentally conditioned to the premise that if you want something you get it, I stole ten dollars from Father's wallet, and bought Sis the watch.

Father summoned me to his study and quietly asked me where I had got the money. Before he let me answer he went on to say that it was a fine and generous thing I had done for Sis. But, he said, something obviously was wrong, for I could not have saved up that much money on my twenty-five-cent-a-week allowance, and he knew I had received no recent funds from Granny.

Then he waited for me to talk.

I was so unnerved by his calm, detached, judicial approach that I knew only one thing : I could not lie to him. So I confessed I had taken the money from his wallet.

" Yes," he said sadly, " I thought you had."

Father sat back and reflected for perhaps a full minute. Each second of silence hurt. Then he began to speak, and, again, his quietness was worse than any fury or threats. He told me, in plain, simple language, that I had done a grievous thing—the sort of thing for which persons went to jail. He went on to say that I was his son and that he had no intention this time of reporting the incident to the police.

But he told me forcefully that I had been wrong—morally as well as legally. He pointed out that, if you want to bring happiness to loved ones by giving them something they want, you work and sacrifice—not steal—to earn the wherewithal, otherwise the act of giving is an empty, ugly thing.

Then he told me that what I had done could be forgiven only once. I can reconstruct his words almost exactly : " If it does happen again I shall have no choice—and I shall not hesitate, though I would regret it—but to call the police, and let them handle the matter as they see fit."

The lesson was not lost on me. I made arrangements to repay Father the money I had taken. From that day on I never took anything that did not belong to me.

The sequel to the story illustrates Father's really wonderful qualities of loyalty, consideration, and dependability. He told me voluntarily that our discussion was a private matter between us, and that unless the offence was repeated he would never reveal it.

Only recently, as I prepared to disclose in this volume the story of my youthful indiscretion, I finally asked Mother and

Anna if Father had ever talked. He had never said a word to either of them. That was Father. Your problems were your own, not matters to be gossiped about with others ; if you had a confidence with him he respected it.

Pa Goes to Bat for Elliott

There were times—not often—when Father did feel it necessary to discuss a private problem of some member of the family with another in order to get information on which he might take some constructive action. As the eldest boy, he talked with me occasionally about my younger brothers' school problems and, less frequently, about other family matters. If Father became convinced that any of us was being maligned or treated unfairly he would stand up for us against anyone—even against the formidable Headmaster Peabody of Groton.

There was one such instance just before Christmas in 1927. Father received a letter from Dr Peabody criticizing Elliott rather severely for his conduct in a football game. He wrote :

My dear Franklin :
   I am a bit disturbed in regard to Elliott's lack of self-control. In the Milton match he was turned off the field. He assured us that his " kneeing " of a man was accidental, and I of course believe him. At the same time, it is a fact that he gets over-excited and allows himself to go blindly, so that in a way he was responsible for the offence. I could see this in Elliott last year when I coached him in rowing. If he was criticized he would seem to become angry, with himself, he would explain, but it made him an unpleasant person to coach and one felt that there was something wrong within. . . .
   I have not talked this over with Elliott as I shall do next term, but I think it would be an excellent plan for you to make a beginning if you agree with me in counting the fault a rather serious one.

Father asked me—I was at Harvard at the time—to look into the matter and give him an objective report on what had happened. I was able to tell Father with perfect honesty that I was convinced the kneeing had been unintentional.

Father was disturbed by the incident—particularly in view of his high regard for Dr Peabody. On becoming convinced, however, that Elliott had been unfairly accused he wrote back on

January 9, 1928, a long, handwritten letter that was remarkable
for the vigour with which he defended Elliott against the headmaster's charges. The letter is perhaps the most forthright and
revealing statement on record of Father's feelings towards the
problems of his adolescent children. He wrote :

My dear Mr. Peabody :
I have of course been greatly concerned by your letter about
Elliott, and he and Eleanor and I have had many talks during the
holiday.
. . . I do not quite understand—Elliott tells me that not only
was the " kneeing " episode in the Milton game entirely accidental,
but was so recognized by the coach & after the game, by the referee
& umpire—I don't see why, if this was the fact, it can in any way be
charged to lack of self-control. . . .
Now I am not making any excuses for a quick temper, which at
times he shows & which we have recognized for many years, but I
am a little surprised that it is being discovered at School in his 5th
Form year.
He is extremely sensitive to praise or blame. The first four years
he struggled at or near the bottom of his Form. This year he has
done really better in his scholastic work—but apparently no one has
given him an encouraging word.
It is the feeling of never being patted on the back that has brought
him today to a personal feeling of complete discouragement.
For instance for three years he has been taken out of the play
because of his studies. This year he is freer to be in the play & his
studies are better, but he expects to be removed again.
What I am trying to get at is the thought that he is unhappy,
sensitive and discouraged ; that a continuation of this attitude on
his part is unthinkable, but will continue at Groton if the attitude
or supposed attitude towards him remains the same.
Further, I think that if you could all try the experiment of encouraging him when he does well in studies or sport, patting him
on the back occasionally, and if anything goes badly to talk it over
with him—give him a chance to explain, instead of assuming that
it is an " angry spirit ", it might work out vastly better. At least it
is in my opinion worth the trial, and at least, it may change Elliott's
attitude of utter discouragement at the present time.
An inferiority complex at Elliott's age is an unfortunate thing
and dangerous for after life—Even at a cost of an occasional bit of
over praise it is worth it if it shall bring back a degree of self-
confidence with which to face life.
In my judgment any lack of self control cannot be corrected while

there is such a lack of self confidence. If the School can treat this lack of self confidence as a special case, calling for special individual treatment, Elliott will come out of it benefited by the experience he has been through.

I know it is hard to treat exceptional problems in an exceptional way, but I know too that you have done so with success many times before ! . . .

Eleanor joins me in love to you all, & I hope we shall all meet next month.

Affectionately yours,
Franklin D. Roosevelt

Dr Peabody replied by thanking Father for the suggestions " whereby we may deal with . . . [Elliott] more wisely in the future." He went on to say that he did not doubt Elliott's statement that the kneeing was accidental. " There still remains the fact," the headmaster wrote,

that Elliott has been in the habit of opening a football contest with great excitement and in a temper that seemed almost ferocious. . . . I cannot help thinking that his conduct has generally been such as to justify the report among the boys that Elliott said that he wished that he had hit his apponent harder and that the opposing player had called him a name. . . . My point is that his conduct has been such as to give him the reputation of being a fierce player who does not care particularly whether he hurts people or not.

The incident rested there ; there is no doubt that it was one of the factors that soured Elliott on Groton.

Though Father spared the rod, and occasionally consoled us when we were emotionally upset, neither he nor Mother believed in coddling us over physical hurts. There was the time when Father was Governor and I came down at Harvard with double pneumonia. I ran a 103-degree fever, and, in my delirium, boarded a train for Albany. I was so sick that the conductor kept coming over to ask anxiously if I thought I was going to make it. I staggered into the Executive Mansion, interrupting Father and Mother in the middle of a dinner-party, and told Mother dramatically I had come home to die !

" Well," she said, " the best place for sick people is in bed. Go upstairs and get a good night's sleep—and what time do you want breakfast in the morning ? "

I went to bed all right, but I didn't eat breakfast for quite a number of mornings, for I was sick for nearly six weeks.

Mother has since admitted she was often in a state of turmoil over bottling up her feelings. With her wonderful honesty, she will now tell any of us that she thinks it was a mistake for her and, to a lesser extent, for Father to have been so seemingly hard-boiled about our aches and pains.

To me the classic illustration of Mother's inner conflict—with Father in the middle !—is contained in correspondence from a 1913 Campobello vacation, when Elliott, then not quite three years old and hampered with braces to correct his bowed legs, suffered a serious accident.

Mother broke the news to Father in Washington in a letter which began with a blithe description of a " splendid " cruise to St Andrews and some other chitchat. Then she wrote : " When I got home I found that poor baby Elliott had fallen into the ashes of a fire the children had on the beach."

At this point she digressed to advise Father that Anna and I had been burning rubbish and that the beach " looks quite nice." Then, getting back to Elliott's problem, she related that " Nurse left the chicks with Germaine " while she went to chat with another nurse, and Baby Elliott fell into the fire. " In getting up [he] must have put one hand in the ashes," Mother related. " The ashes got under the straps of his braces & burned . . . but he only cried a little. . . . Nurse says they are only skin burns. . . . He ate more supper than usual & has gone placidly to sleep so it can't hurt much."

In her next bulletin Mother, while noting that " baby has been quite cheerful all day & he walks about quite regardless of his bandaged legs," admitted : " His hand . . . [is] one large blister. . . . I . . . [am] very thankful that it is no worse . . . it makes me shudder."

Meanwhile Father, who certainly had no cause to be over-alarmed by her first report, had responded calmly. In her next letter Mother turned on him for not being more sympathetic about the incident which she herself had under-played ! " You are casual about Elliott's burn," she chided, " but he had a very bad hand & it won't be healed for some time . . . he is a very brave young man."

Father and the " Birds and Bees "

Father was by no means a prurient man. In after-hours conversations among male companions with whom he felt at home he could be earthy and even ribald. He did not hesitate to jest broadly on racy topics ; yet he couched his language in rather classical terms, for gutter talk offended him.

I was with him during his first " hundred days " in the White House, when he paid an unheralded courtesy call on retired Supreme Court Associate Justice Oliver Wendell Holmes. I never shall forget Father's monumental glee when we found that wonderful old Yankee browsing through his noted collection of French novels which he kept hidden behind his law books.

In one respect, however, Father was extremely old-fashioned. When it came to instructing his sons about sex matters he simply couldn't do it.

When the time arrived to tell us boys about the " birds and bees " Pa—typically—relegated responsibility to Mother. Mother —typically—read us a book. It was a very learned book. In my case she might as well have been reading me Homer's *Iliad* in the original Greek.

This reticence of Father's manifested itself in the fact that he never told in my presence a story with which he loved to regale certain friends about one of our scapegrace Delano—*né* de la Noye—ancestors. In fact, until I read a book, *Franklin Roosevelt and the Delano Influence*, written by my cousin, Daniel W. Delano, Jr., I never even knew that on October 20, 1667, one Thomas Delano, son of Philippe, the first de la Noye to settle in America, had been fined in Plymouth Colony " ' for having carnall [*sic*] copulation with his *now* wife before marriage,' the evidence being a lusty son born that day . . . named Benoni Delano." Cousin Daniel refers to the incident as " the first shot-gun wedding in American history." Father would improve on the story, according to Bill Hassett, his former secretary and biographer, by blaming it on the original Philippe himself.

There was one occasion, however, as I was about to set off for college, when Father did have a conversation with me that might be broadly interpreted as a " facts of life " lecture. The story sheds considerable light on Father's own reactions to violations of the mores of polite society. He told me—and it was the first

time in our relationship that the name had passed his lips—of the
" misspent life " of his own half-nephew, James Roosevelt
Roosevelt, Jr., known in the family as " Taddy " and regarded
by Father as the real black sheep of the Roosevelts.[1]

Taddy was the son of " Uncle Rosy," Father's considerably
older, widowed half-brother. From the very beginning of his
school career Father, a very proper young Hyde Park product,
was embarrassed by the eccentric Taddy. At Groton Taddy was
a favourite target for hazing and ridicule. In his brief stay at
Harvard he was an outright scandal. In 1900 a shocked young
F.D.R. was writing his parents : " Taddy . . . may be off on a
bat now for ought I know." And later, reporting that Taddy was
about to be expelled, he moralized : " I have never heard of such
assininity [sic] and every one up here . . . thinks him a fool."

As Father told me the story, the reasons for Taddy's vagaries
soon broke in the Press. He had been slipping down to New
York, had taken up with " a woman known as ' Sadie of the
Tenderloin,' " and, Father related with great distaste, had
" even married her ! " Meanwhile he had come into a considerable fortune, left him by his late wealthy mother.

Uncle Rosy moved in quickly and broke up the marriage. As
Father recalled it, Taddy thereupon returned to Sadie and
married her a second time. (I have not been able to verify this
detail, and I suspect it may have been one of Father's bits of
dramatic embellishment.) Later, however, Taddy definitely broke
with Tenderloin Sadie, and there was, of course, a cash settlement.

At Harvard Father was deeply mortified. Even though Taddy
disappeared from the university, there is reason to believe that
Father felt in later years that the scandal had hurt him socially
and had kept him out of Porcellian, most exclusive of the student
clubs. In any event, five days after the newspapers had their
field-day with the Taddy-and-Sadie affair Father, in a letter to
" My darling Mama and Papa," wrote :

> The disgusting business about Taddy did not come as a very
> great surprise to me or anyone in Cambridge. I have heard the

---

[1] The story of Taddy has been recounted by several of Father's biographers
and is related in the collection of Father's personal letters, edited by my brother,
Elliott.—J.R.

rumor ever since I have been here, but in the absence of facts the best course has been silence. I do not wonder that it has upset Papa [Grandfather James had suffered another of the series of heart-attacks that brought on his death shortly after], but although the disgrace to the name has been the worst part of the affair one can never again consider him [Taddy] a true Roosevelt. It will be well for him not only to go to parts unknown, but to stay there and begin life anew.

That was exactly what Taddy did. The family broke off relations with him, and Taddy became a recluse, an eccentric, and a miser. All that was known of him for sure was that he spent little of his inherited wealth. Until his death in 1958 he would come occasionally into the office of his New York bank, dressed like a tramp, carrying thousands of dollars' worth of securities or cash bundled up in an old newspaper.

This was the story which Father told me with genuine repugnance, intending it as a horrible example of what happens to young men who are careless in their ways. Alas for Father's good intentions ! He was such a masterful storyteller that, instead of being righteously horrified, I was intrigued by the saga of this romantic kinsman I had never seen, who disappeared from hallowed Harvard into the wicked Tenderloin, married the alluring woman of his choice (possibly twice), and wound up with all those millions. As a morality lecture Father's story of the black-sheep Taddy was completely wasted.

" *A Gentleman Learns His Capacity* "

Drinking was always a topic of much discussion in the Roosevelt family. Granny frowned on it : a small, aristocratic sip of champagne or light wine was as far as she would go. Mother—due to tragic experiences in her family with alcohol—was almost fanatically against it, though to-day she accepts the fact that people will drink. Father, though actually a mild, purely social drinker, whose limit was two drinks before dinner and little or nothing afterwards, constituted the dissenting minority. Constantly bombarded with none too subtle hints from Granny and Mother, he got his " Dutch " up on the subject. Even at Hyde Park, where Granny's will usually was supreme, he refused to be browbeaten. When Granny kept making disparaging comments

Father finally decreed that cocktails henceforth would be served in his own little study, to which Granny was not invited.

Granny then tried a new form of attack—martyrdom. She would drift in, assuming a wholly spurious meekness, take a brave sip from Father's glass—Socrates tasting the hemlock !— and say, " Now, Franklin, haven't you had enough of your . . . *cocktails* ? "

As we gradually came of age we joined forces with Father to constitute at least a numerical majority in favour of the pre-dinner cocktail. He rather welcomed our support. Many times after he became President I heard him spin one of his favourite stories to visitors, for whom he was mixing one of his radical concoctions, of how he " learned to make a *really* dry Martini."

" I used to mix my Martinis nice and gentle—one and one-half parts of gin to one part of vermouth," Father would relate. " Then Anna became old enough for a cocktail and said, ' Pa, this is awful—you've got to make them drier—two-to-one.' So I made them two-to-one.

" Then Jimmy came along and said, ' These aren't fit to drink —you should make them three-to-one,' and I did. Along came Elliott, who made me change it to four-to-one ; then Franklin, who called for five-to-one, and now Johnny, who insists that a really dry Martini should be six-to-one. So if you don't like what I'm serving you, don't blame me ! "

I was not always so tolerant. From somewhere in her volumin-ous heaps of memorabilia Mother has unearthed for me a letter which I wrote my parents in 1924 on the subject of Father's foibles. I was a pretty stuffy character in those days, but this letter was the stuffiest I ever wrote. I told of an inspiring temperance lecture I had just heard at Groton, and said :

I think if you could have heard it you would have agreed . . . that while it is perfectly legal to drink bootleg liquor it is only encouring [*sic*] a man when you buy from him to break the law and that certainly isn't living up to the standards of good Citizenship is it ? You know it's always been rather of a shock to me when I come home from School to find the closet next to my room so full of liquor and I know Elliott thinks also that if it must be around, it might be in smaller quantities. I suppose you think I'm an old ass but I really mean it.

I have no recollection of Father ever replying. Mother says he didn't.

There has been a great deal of foolishness written about Father's drinking habits and his alleged propensity for mixing up weird and utterly unpalatable concoctions which the hapless guest could not refuse because it was made for him by the President of the United States. Many of these stories have been puffed up out of all perspective, often by Father himself. Where lighter matters were concerned, Pa was never one to let a little fact stand in the way of a good yarn.

Actually Father was a conservative drinker. Having been with him on some informal occasions—cruises and such, when all affairs of state and business were far out of mind—there have been times when I have seen Father become a little relaxed, but never out of control. He had no use for what he called " a falling-down drunk." He was more interested in the good conversation that went with conviviality than he was in the drinks.

Being a bold and imaginative sort of person in all fields, and a showman to boot, Pa occasionally liked to convert the cocktail hour into a sort of dramatic exercise in experimentation. When he was in the mood and had a new guest whom he wanted to impress he would make a real alchemist's ritual out of the simple act of concocting a Martini. He would surround himself with a variety of impressive measuring devices and carefully, painstakingly, almost with bated breath, would ration out the precise amounts of gin and vermouth—sometimes even two kinds of vermouth—and maybe an unorthodox dash of Pernod. Then, just about the time the awed guest was convinced he had just seen the President prepare the most carefully constructed Martini in the history of Martini-making, Pa would look up innocently, start chatting about some irrelevant subject, and, without even glancing at the pitcher, would slosh in an extra wallop of gin.

Father sometimes mixed an outrageous cocktail which he learned to make when he visited Haiti as Assistant Secretary of the Navy. I never could abide it, and I have had to consult my brother Elliott, who insists he likes the stuff, for the recipe. Elliott informs me he makes it often for his friends, telling them that it was Father's own cocktail, and I tell him that if he continues serving this abomination he won't have any friends.

It has no particular name—Father just called it " my Haitian libation." As I have no intention of corrupting the nation's drinking habits by revealing the exact formula for this deplorable invention, I will disclose only that the drink involves a mixture of Haitian rum, which is dark and strong, flavoured with extra-dark brown sugar and orange-juice. It looks vile and tastes the same.

Even after they must have—or should have—given up on Father, Mother and Granny sent him periodic alarms about the children. In April 1928 Mother, the perennial voice of conscience in the family, was writing Father at Warm Springs complaining of the late hours I kept on an Easter visit, coincidental with the annual New York performance of the Harvard Hasty Pudding show. " The . . . show was good," she told Father, " but I was so sleepy I didn't find it easy to keep awake ! " She went on to explain that I had been out until four o'clock one morning and six o'clock the next, and that " this sleeping in hour periods while you wait for the boys to come in is a bit wearing." She acknowledged, however, that " even my suspicious nature could not imagine that he'd had too much to drink ! " (*Thank you, Mother !*)

In August 1929, when she took Franklin, Jr., and John on an exhaustive and exhausting trip to Europe, in a letter from Luxemburg, addressed to Father in the Executive Mansion at Albany, Mother good-naturedly poked fun at her own prejudices. She told of visiting a fair with the boys, and related : " The others had some champagne that is made here for dinner & drank your health & wished you were present. I joined in—in Evian water ! F., Jr., has had a taste of everything & likes it but I won't let him have it as a rule ! "

On September 2, 1933, writing from New York, Mother penned a less good-natured note to Father, care of the White House. " Will you," she wrote bluntly, " speak seriously & firmly to F., Jr. & John about drinking & fast driving ? I really think it's important." None of us remembers exactly what particular incident prompted this communiqué, but all of us agree the odds are 999 to 1 that Father didn't do it.

Granny, on her last visit to Paris two years before her death, also took up the cause. She wrote Father at the White House :

I have worried about young Franklin & Johnny ever since I left, that horrid fashion of cocktails has done both of them harm. One thing leads to another & several things have made me sense danger, but *I* can say & do nothing. Please don't allude to this to *anyone* & please don't laugh at me, or say, " Mama is so silly to be worried " —I *know* I am right.

Father paid no attention to these letters, but, as I and my brothers approached the drinking age, he gave each of us the same advice : " A *gentleman* learns his capacity and tries not to exceed it. If he must drink excessively he does it at a time when he does not have to be in touch with anyone. I assume you are a gentleman."

On one memorable occasion Father felt his code of gentlemanly conduct had been violated, and he landed on one of the boys with both feet. It was one of the few times any of us ever was dressed down so strongly by Father—and it illustrates that the same sort of embarrassing incident that can happen to any parent also happened to Father.

The incident occurred when Father was Governor and a group of young Roosevelts, Delanos, and their friends were having a house-party at Hyde Park. The festivities moved to the home of a relative. Father and Mother went along as chaperons.

One of my brothers had brought along a friend, who was paying court to an attractive young lady. The friend plied her with just one cocktail too many. Mother, observing the young lady's condition, told Father. Father immediately broke up the party, and he and Mother started back to Hyde Park with the girl between them.

Unfortunately my brother's friend, in a misguided remedial attempt, had induced the girl to drink a quart of milk. On the ride home, huddled between Father and Mother in the back seat of the Governor's car, she became actively ill—and I shall leave it to the reader to surmise in whose direction she leaned !

Father summoned both my brother and his erring friend to his study and gave them a lecture such as neither of them had ever heard. When he finished the other young man, actually with tears in his eyes, looked at Father, thanked him, and said, " I wish my own father would talk to me as you have." The irony of it is that, as we have grown older, we sometimes wish Pa had talked more often to *us* in the same vein.

Father and Mother with Anna, myself, and Elliott at Hyde Park, 1918

Franklin D. Roosevelt Library

The Family in Washington, June 1919

At my desk
in the White
House, 1933

At Hyde Park in June 1932, when Father was still Governor

6

Religion and Father

FATHER never preached much to us—or to anyone—about piety and virtue, but to him religion was a real and personal thing from which he drew much strength and comfort. Piety was not something he put on like a cloak at election-time; his feelings were deep and unshakeable, stemming from the two strongest influences in his early life—home and Groton.

In Hyde Park Father worshipped at St James's Episcopal Church. His father—my Grandfather James—became a vestry-man there in 1858, then junior warden, and finally senior warden, the highest lay post in the church, serving until his death in 1900. Father became a vestryman in 1906, and followed in his father's footsteps, also serving as senior warden until the time of his death.

All my life I had known how much the church meant to him, but not until recently did I learn of an incident which makes me realize that Father may have been somewhat of a frustrated clergyman at heart. The story came to me from the Rev. Frank R. Wilson, who was rector of St James's when Father was senior warden, and who is now associate rector of St John's Church, Lafayette Square, the "Church of the Presidents" across from the White House, where Father, as President, often worshipped.

The story goes back to the period when Father was Governor. The Rev. Mr Wilson, then a young rector, came down with a sudden appendicitis attack one Saturday afternoon. Granny, who was a "pillar of the church" in the fullest sense of the phrase, took it upon herself to telephone the Executive Mansion to tell Father what had happened. Soon after Granny hung up

Father was on the telephone personally, talking with Mrs Wilson. " Please tell the rector," Father said, " that if he needs me I will come from Albany to Hyde Park in time to take over the 11 o'clock services as a lay reader to-morrow morning."

The young rector was overwhelmed, but, in his own words, " would not dream of imposing on the Governor." He told his wife to thank Father and to advise him that he had already made arrangements for a retired clergyman to officiate.

" Well," said Father on receiving this information, " tell him that if he ever needs me I stand ready."

As the Rev. Mr Wilson reached this point in recalling this incident of nearly thirty years ago it was suggested to him that Father must have been disappointed, as he probably would have liked very much to have read the services. The rector reflected a moment ; then, in most unclergyman-like language which I hope he will forgive me for repeating, he exclaimed, " I never thought of that ! Dammit, I should have let him do it ! "

To the best of Mr Wilson's recollection Father never did lead the services at St James's. The desire to conduct a religious service stayed with him, however, and I was with him on Easter Sunday in 1934, when he finally satisfied this ambition under most unusual circumstances.

Father was President then, and was taking one of his cruises aboard the *Nourmahal*, the private yacht of his distant kinsman and Dutchess County neighbour Vincent Astor. Two United States Navy destroyers were escorting us, and when we entered the waters of the Bahamas a British light cruiser joined the convoy.

Without telling him why, Father advised Vincent he would like a calm, quiet anchorage on Easter morning. They studied the charts together, and at Father's suggestion, possibly with an eye towards the historic background of the location, anchor was dropped off San Salvador, or Watling's Island, where, most historians agree, Christopher Columbus first landed in the New World on October 12, 1492.

There, on Easter Sunday morning, Father had signals run up inviting all the officers and men of the two U.S. destroyers and the British cruiser to come aboard for divine services. The *Nourmahal* was a big ship, but the aggregation almost swamped us. Father produced a large number of printed programmes—

neither Vincent nor I even knew the programmes had been prepared—and had them passed around. The programmes bore
the legend " DIVINE SERVICE, EASTER," and were dated April 1,
1934. (Just before Vincent Astor died he showed me one on
which Father had written, " For Vincent to put in The Log of
the *Nourmahal*. Franklin D. Roosevelt.")

With his " congregation " of British and American sailors
assembled, Father proceeded to conduct the entire service.
(Years later Father was to sit with Winston Churchill on the
deck of a mightier vessel, the British battleship *Prince of Wales*,
in the presence of another congregation of British and American
sailors, and launch the momentous Atlantic Charter meetings
with a divine service.) On the *Nourmahal* that day Father
delivered a simple, short sermon, stressing the religious significance of the spot where we were anchored. He said that Columbus
had arrived there and discovered America only through his
belief in divine guidance, and that this belief in a Supreme Being
gave Columbus courage and confidence to sail on when threatened
by disaster and mutiny.

Later Father told us with some elation that " this is the first
time I have ever conducted a service and preached a sermon all
by myself."

All throughout his years in the White House Father saw to
it that there were special services on his inauguration anniversaries,
at which divine guidance was sought. Whenever possible he
had the Rev. Mr Wilson and Dr Peabody come to Washington
to assist in conducting these special services. The old headmaster
was present for the last time on March 4, 1944—he died later
that year.

If Father attended church less regularly than he might have
during his Presidential years it was because he was irked by the
fact that he could have no privacy in his worship. All of us in
the family have heard him express himself forcefully along the
lines which Frances Perkins recorded so well in her book : " I
can do almost everything in the ' Goldfish Bowl ' of the President's
life, but I'll be hanged if I can say my prayers in it ! " He went
on to say : " It bothers me to feel like something in the zoo being
looked at by all the tourists in Washington when I go to Church."

After Father came to Washington as President I heard him

express his resentment over a sort of undercover tug-of-war on the part of certain churches to " land " him as a parishioner. He went most frequently to St John's, Lafayette Square, because he did not feel this sort of pressure there.

Soon after his inauguration Father had a rather startling personal experience, indirectly connected with the church, that drove home to him the fact that nothing about the private life— or even the after-life—of a President could be considered sacred. At the time he first told me about it he did not think it amusing, though later he came to regard it in a wry way as rather funny.

As I heard the story from both Father and his appointments secretary, Marvin McIntyre, a meeting with the President had been requested by the Right Rev. James E. Freeman, the distinguished Episcopal Bishop of Washington. It was during the hectic first " hundred days," and Father was terribly pressed for time. However, as a good churchman, he did not want to refuse the bishop.

The bishop had been with Father only a short time when Marvin McIntyre got the buzzer which signified that Father wanted the appointment interrupted. As soon as the distinguished churchman had been shown out Father summoned Mac again and, almost spluttering with indignation, told him that the bishop had wanted Father to agree to help the " prestige " of the National Cathedral, still in process of construction and in need of donations, by agreeing, if he died in office, to be buried there.

" If that man ever asks to see me again, don't let him in ! " Father, the staunch Episcopalian, the faithful senior warden, exclaimed. " He's nothing but a body-snatcher ! " [1]

One of the reasons Father had such a deep love for St James's at Hyde Park was that he felt less " on exhibit " there. Also

[1] In *The Roosevelt I Knew* Frances Perkins relates a slightly different version of the " body-snatcher " story, placing the encounter with the bishop outside the National Cathedral after Father had attended services there one Sunday morning. Miss Perkins advises : " F.D.R. told it to me either that night . . . or the next day. . . . It was immediate, and he was hot and mad. . . . A year or so later, when he was driving me around Hyde Park, he pointed out the Rose Garden where he was to be buried and said . . . ' That's where I am going to be buried and don't you let any Bishop or anyone else bury me in any cathedral ! ' " I am certain that the bishop did approach Father on this occasion ; however, I also believe that the bishop called on Father at the White House to make the same request.—J.R.

he was thoroughly at home within the walls of the simple old Gothic structure, where, since Grandfather James's time, the Roosevelts had occupied the third pew from the front on the north side of the church. His father's memorial plaque is on the wall, and both of his beloved parents rest in the tranquil churchyard.

Father was eager for all of us to be active in church affairs. He encouraged us to do so, but, as usual, he did it through suggestions rather than by saying, " You *must* do so-and-so." If we were going to participate he wanted it to come not as the result of his coercion, but from the heart.

In my case perhaps he went a little further than with the others in indicating his desires for me to be active in the church ; this was because, to Father, the tradition of the eldest son continuing in the footsteps of the father was as natural a thing as the rise and fall of the tides. Through his encouragement I became a vestryman at St James's.

Not even the pressures of the Presidency ever made Father forget his responsibilities as senior warden of the Hyde Park church. In my files I find a White House memo, dated May 19, 1937, reading :

> Last Autumn St. James' Church had an anniversary drive and raised $1,600 towards repairs, etc. I think you ought to give something. If you do not make an annual subscription, I think you should, as a member of the Vestry, send a check, for say $25.00.

I sent the twenty-five dollars, and, at the bottom of the memo which I returned to him, is my pencilled notation, " Yes, you chisler ! " [*sic*]

In December 1943, about the time Pa was returning from Teheran, where he met Stalin and Churchill, I, then a lieutenant-colonel in the Marine Corps, was writing the " Senior Warden," care of St James's, Hyde Park, to enclose another small contribution for the church. In February 1944 he took time to reply : " At last I have come down in my basket to your note . . . with its grand contribution. . . . I am sure all the Vestry will be made very happy and I will speak to them about it when we have a Vestry meeting the end of this month." The senior warden, who was spending unprecedented billions of dollars in fighting the

Axis, also took time to advise me that it had been necessary to increase the fire insurance on the church. However, the expenditure was being balanced by the lower salary paid the retired clergyman who was filling in for the Rev. Mr Wilson, by now a Navy chaplain. " For the second year in a row," Father proudly wrote, " we came out without any deficit or any big drives to make both ends meet."

Though his sense of personal identification with St James's was strong, Pa never behaved in a proprietary fashion towards the church. The Rev. Mr Wilson tells how, when he was considering the call to become the rector of St James's, Father personally invited him to come with Mrs Wilson for a visit at the Hyde Park house. " I went with my heart in my throat, expecting to hear all sort of conditions, provisions and so forth," Mr Wilson relates. " He greeted me warmly, and said, ' I want you to understand that if you take the post you will be the rector, and whatever you say, whatever you decide to do, we will be with you.' My heart went right back in place and stayed there all the time I was rector. That's the way it was."

As I functioned as a sort of aide-de-camp to Father on the occasion of the visit of King George VI and Queen Elizabeth to the United States in 1939, I had a small part in arranging one of the most memorable days in the long history of St James's Church—the special services which Father had set up for the King and Queen. This was a function which he regarded with the utmost seriousness, supervising practically every detail himself.

Long before the visit was officially announced Father called in the rector and told him in confidence that the King and Queen were coming and that he wanted them to worship with him at his church. It was Father's idea that the rector should handle the service by himself, but this was one of the times when Mr Wilson took a firm stand against the wishes of his senior warden, insisting that the presiding bishop of the Episcopal Church, Bishop Henry St George Tucker, be invited to deliver the sermon. Mr Wilson also had the inspiration of inviting the young Canadian rector from the Campobello church, where Father had worshipped, to assist, and this symbolical extending of hands across the border for the occasion pleased Father greatly.

Father, Mother, and Grandmother entertained the rector and

Mrs Wilson frequently at Hyde Park and Campobello, and Father also invited them numerous times to the White House. Mr Wilson modestly insists this was a courtesy which Father would have extended to any rector of St James's. I know, however, that Father thought highly of his minister as an individual.

As an old Navy man, Father was gratified when, with the outbreak of World War II, his minister chose to become a chaplain in that branch of the armed forces. In March 1943, when time came for the anniversary services at the " Church of the Presidents," Mr Wilson was in training at the Navy chaplains' school at Norfolk, Virginia. Father personally directed the Navy Chief of Chaplains to cut special orders, instructing Mr Wilson to report to Washington, without telling him why. When he arrived he was told to go to the White House, where he would be a guest, and that he was invited to attend the services next day.

As an extra touch planned by Father, the chaplain was also " ordered " to report to the railroad station to meet an un-identified " very important person," who turned out to be Mrs Wilson. I can just visualize Father's pleasure, in the midst of a war in which he was commander-in-chief, arranging this very personal surprise for his rector !

At the time of the 1944 inauguration Chaplain Wilson was overseas. Father did not forget Mrs Wilson, who was invited to the White House as usual.

The classic illustration of Father's basic, simple, rather un-questioning religious faith was told me many years ago by Mother. Once, when we were growing up, Mother went to Father after much deliberation and asked him if perhaps they should not give some thought as to what they wanted the children taught in regard to religion. She pointed out to him that neither of them held fundamentalist views towards everything in the Bible, although her Grandmother Hall had raised her " to believe every word : if the Bible said that Jonah was swallowed by a whale, he was, regardless of the fact that a whale does not have a large enough throat opening to swallow a man."

" Your Father looked at me rather quizzically," Mother related, " and said, ' What you were taught never hurt you, did it ? '

" ' No,' I answered, ' I suppose not—even though it never gave me any chance to think these things out for myself.'

" ' Well,' he said, ' since it didn't hurt you, why not let the children have the same kind of teaching and then think things out for themselves when they grow up, just as you did ? '

" That was the end of that discussion. We never spoke of it again."

Tradition and Family

Tradition and family also meant much to Father. Though he joked about his " horse-thief " ancestors, he was extremely proud of his Dutch descent. In February 1935 he sent me a note from the White House, calling attention to the fact that both he and his father before him had been members of the Holland Society, and that I, as the eldest son, should carry on the tradition. He was so anxious for me to join, in fact, that he offered to pay for a life membership for me—an offer which I accepted. Franklin, Jr., also joined the Holland Society, but did not get the free life membership from Father.

Father was a Mason, and Franklin, Elliott, and I all followed him into that order. Father thought it would be a good idea for us to broaden our circle of acquaintances, so Gus Gennerich, of the White House Secret Service detail, became our sponsor, and we joined Gus's lodge in Yorkville, a German-American neighbourhood in New York City.

Later, when Franklin, Jr., and I were elevated to the Third Degree of the Masonic Order, Father came up from Washington to preside at the ceremony, which took place at the Grand Lodge in down-town New York. The White House was swamped with letters from Masons all over the Eastern seaboard, requesting invitations to witness the ceremony.

Pa inherited his love for tradition from Granny, who opposed *any* break with the past. Even the thought of a much-needed new schoolhouse in Hyde Park upset Granny. In February 1928, when such a move was under foot, she wrote an indignant letter to Father at Warm Springs, stating :

> I *hate* the idea of a new schoolhouse, the old one is all right & has had a lot of money spent on it. I should prefer to pay a man to see the children *across* to the playground if they can't look out for themselves. This constant pulling down & building anew is much overdone, & I am fond of the schoolhouse. Also a new one will

not educate the children any better. You will say " my Mummy is a back number & knows nothing about it."

In his own way Pa was as much of a sentimentalist as Granny about anything connected with tradition and family, and his memory for names, dates, and details was fantastic. His long-time secretary, Grace Tully, relates in her book *F.D.R., My Boss* how, in signing a document at the White House one day, he looked at the date and remarked that it was the anniversary of his father's birth. She asked how old Grandfather James would have been, and, without hesitation, Father replied, " He would have been 112 to-day."

When I was in the White House as Father's administrative assistant we occasionally received letters from distant relatives who had fallen on hard times during the depression and needed employment. Father would pass along these queries to the proper agencies. However, he requested no preferential treatment, and a number of our needy kinsmen were turned down. I remember one Massachusetts Delano—I am glad to say I never knew him—who, when he could not get the job he was seeking, sent me an irate final blast : " Since I am a typical American and one of the Delano family, it is hard to reconcile the fact that foreigners in our Country are given pick and shovel jobs, while I, a typical American, destitute, yet not looking for charity, cannot even get a pick & shovel job." To the best of my recollection I never showed that letter to Father ; he would not have liked it !

One bit of tradition that always moved me, no matter how many times I heard it and participated in it, was the toast Father gave at midnight just as the New Year was coming in. He began this custom before he went to the White House, and kept it up for the rest of his life. The family would be together, including as many of the grandchildren as were old enough to stay up. About one minute before midnight Pa would rap for silence—a hard thing to achieve when a crowd of Roosevelts was assembled— and, looking at his watch, would count off the last few seconds. When the hour of midnight struck and the New Year was at hand he would raise his glass high and say, " To the United States of America ! " Then all of us, standing, would repeat the toast.

7

Those Roosevelt Kids at School

On the subject of schooling, in so far as my brothers and I were concerned, Father knew his mind perfectly. Schooling to him meant Groton and Harvard, and, with the exception of Elliott, who managed to escape Harvard, that's where we all went.

The story of our collective schooling is indeed a harrowing tale. The harrowing part of it began for Father and Mother when we entered kindergarten, and, in my case, ceased only when I left Harvard—minus a diploma because I had failed German. Pa may have been the glamorous young Assistant Secretary of the Navy, the squire of Hyde Park, the Governor of New York, and the President of the United States, but, in the process of seeing to our education, he was spared none of the trials and tribulations of the average parent.

One of my earliest communications on the subject of schooling was a letter I wrote Granny in 1918, when I was attending St Albans, the National (Episcopal) Cathedral School in Washington. I wrote : " I am getting pretty well at school." (In September 1896 Father, in the first letter he wrote his parents from Groton, wrote : " I am getting on finely." His salutation, an example of his schoolboy humour, was : " Dear Mommerr & Popperr.")

I was not getting on " well " enough, however, to know how to spell " colonel," for in the same letter I referred to a " Conel " Lodge showing us around Mount Vernon. My spelling was always interesting : I find letters in which I wrote " twelf " (for twelve), " telicot " (delicate), " perple " (purple), " golloshis " (galoshes), " sieze " (size), and even " Pokipsie " for " Pough-keepsie "—though I suspect the last was merely a bit of laziness.

Again, I must go back to precedents set by Father, whose early letters disclose such original spellings as " pictuer," " gardan," " brige " (bridge), " camfer " (camphor), and " joice " (joists).

Later that year Mother was writing Granny :

> James stands 13th in a class of 19 with a dreadful mark in arithmetic. Elliott is 4th in a class of 12. I think James is much ashamed but it is all his careless way of working & liking to have a good time so much that he neglects his work.

This was to become a familiar refrain !

Father, despite his occupation with World War I and politics, frequently became involved in our school problems. In a letter written to Granny just two days before the Armistice Mother reported that " Anna is way behind " in her studies, " and F. spent 40 minutes last evening coaching her in algebra & I fear will have to do it every night." The same letter also related how, after the algebra coaching, Father

> had to go to Mr. Creel's office [George Creel, President Wilson's chairman of the war-time Committee on Public Information] last night over the peace rumour of which there has been no official word. He got home about 2:30 & I hope it won't happen often as he will get very tired.

When I entered St Albans Father would sometimes drive me to school in the Stutz. We talked a great deal on those rides, but, as I recall it, our conversations were nothing very profound.

Mother's alarms over my scholastic shortcomings continued to be reflected in letters to Granny during 1919. On March 11 she wrote :

> His marks for two months past have been disgraceful. . . . I have been very severe & told him this Spring was his last chance as if this continued we'd have to take him away from school & all its fun & have [him] taught at home to get him into Groton. He wept but he just didn't try.

And two months later :

> James is worse . . . 12th in a class of 16. . . . I just told him I did not care to discuss it as unfortunately no one else could study for him. . . . He wept as usual & it will have about as much effect as

usual. . . . I think this Summer I shall have him work an hour longer than Anna daily.

By spring of 1920 I had bucked up ; by pulling up my average to over 80 and placing fourth in a class of fifteen I demonstrated that I was not a complete imbecile. Father personally took over the task of negotiating with Dr Peabody about getting his first-born son into the " old school." It came as quite a shock to Father when I took the examinations and came out with disastrous marks : I think my highest grade was something like 16 or 17 out of a possible 100. I didn't make the second form—the equivalent of tenth grade—and was set back to first form. In a letter sent to Father at the Democratic Convention at San Francisco in June 1920 I confessed : " Father—I failed my Groton exams for the Second Form my mark [sic] were all low and they were all dew to careless and thoughtless work."

Father took it philosophically and did not rant or storm at me. When he returned he asked me why I had done so poorly. I came up with the ingenious alibi that I was still upset because of the excitement of the previous June, when the anarchists tried to blow up Attorney-General Palmer.

My entrance to Groton was a rude shock. Although Mother's letters of this period displayed little sympathy—it was an accepted ritual at that time that children of " better " families entered schools such as Groton and " made the grade "—her thoughts in retrospect show a deeper realization of what it meant to dump an immature boy of twelve into a boarding-school. In *This I Remember*, her second autobiographical volume, Mother wrote : " I still believe it is too early an age and a loss both to the parents and to the children. The day I took each boy to school . . . was always a terrible day for me, and when it came to the last child it was particularly hard." And in her earlier book she recalled specifically how she felt when she took me to Groton for the first time :

> He seemed to me very young and very lonely when I left him, but it was a tradition in the family that boys must go to boarding school when they reached the age of twelve, and James would be thirteen the following December, so of course we had to send him. I never thought to rebel then, but now it seems to me too ludicrous to have been bound by so many conventions. I unpacked his trunk, saw

that his cubicle was in order, met some of the Masters, said goodbye to Mr. and Mrs. Endicott Peabody . . . and finally said goodbye to James and went back to Hyde Park.

Perhaps things are run better in private schools to-day but, in the process of getting me settled, no one bothered to orient me as to the location of the bathroom. I was too scared and embarrassed to ask. The result was that Father, who was campaigning in Colorado as the Democratic Vice-Presidential nominee, and Mother, who was making her first campaign trip with him, shortly received a wire from Groton advising them that I was in the infirmary with what appeared to be a " digestive disturbance."

Mother, in a flurry of her usual self-recrimination, was preparing to take the next train East when she received a second bulletin that good old Granny had come to my rescue. Granny removed me to Boston for a few days' recuperation, then returned me to Groton, and, incidentally, saw to it that I learned where the bathroom was.

I had played football at St Albans. I continued football at Groton, and I also rowed, went out for track, and played basketball. One of my cherished souvenirs is a summary of the basketball season of 1921 which states : " Roosevelt, the captain [of the second form team] . . . played well at forward." I went out for baseball one year, but was retired from the team because I was curiously unable to follow the ball in action. No one knew it at the time, but I was painfully near-sighted ; with all the medical attention I had, I was never given an eye test until 1935.

My athletic activities earned me a certain number of injuries. I acquired a heel infection which spread to my groin. I was hit on the head and knocked unconscious while playing football for the Monadnocks versus the Wachusetts.

Father would come to see me participate in athletic events. He loved the atmosphere of the old school, and always enjoyed getting back. He was there with Granny to see the football match against St Marks during my last year at Groton. On the opening play there was a pile-up, and every one got up except me. Granny wanted to run out on the field to succour me, but Father held her by the arm. He was quite annoyed with her for making a fuss, and kept telling her, " If you'll just sit still he'll he taken care of ! " Finally, I was carried off the field, and a short time later I was assisted back to the field, but only to sit on the bench. " See ! " said Father. " They wouldn't let him sit on the sidelines if anything was the matter." It turned out that my leg was broken. That ended my football career.

While he was interested in my progress, Father made no effort to guide me scholastically while I was at Groton ; that, he felt, was something best left in Dr Peabody's hands.

For that matter, everything at Groton was pretty much in Dr Peabody's hands. The founder and headmaster of the school could be a pretty awesome, even frightening character to a scared youngster away from home for the first time : as Averell Harriman, an old Groton boy, once commented to his father, Dr Peabody " would be an awful bully if he weren't such a terrible Christian." He knew—or seemed to know—everything that went on. From my own days at Groton I recall the headmaster's custom of coming each evening to Hundred House, where our dormitory was located, to say good night to the boys—individually. As each boy passed before him to shake hands, if all was well the headmaster would say, in his resonant voice, " Good night, George " or " Good night, Jim." If he said, " Good night, *boy* ! " and looked at you significantly you understood that he knew you had done something wrong, and that discipline was yet to come.

Yet occasionally Dr Peabody, just like any less exalted peda-gogue, was caught off base. For instance, on January 22, 1924, the headmaster informed Father that I had met " with an accident the other day which was startling but turned out not to be serious." Reading the letter in retrospect, one might say that the headmaster was a little less than candid ; in fact, he had waited several days to write, during which time Elliott had tipped off the folks as to what had happened.

It seems that I had gone to the infirmary " to be treated for a cold and the nurse put in his eyes what she thought to be argyrol but . . . turned out to be iodine." Dr Peabody went on to describe what was done immediately to attempt to save my eyesight, and how, after a couple of days—" the first day that it seemed prudent for him to move "—he sent me to Boston in his car, where an eye specialist diagnosed the damage as " a slight burn resulting from the iodine but . . . there is no doubt whatever it will be perfectly right in a short time." I was to be allowed to skip studying for a while, though I would attend recitations and the headmaster was going to " arrange, if it be possible . . . for one of the masters to tutor him."

Dr Peabody went on to say :

> This is of course a very serious event for us and I naturally feel it deeply. The nurse was almost overwhelmed by her mistake, and if she had been unknown to me I suppose we should have been obliged to let her go . . . but I have known Miss McLeod for many years. . . .
>
> I did not write to you at once because I thought that you and Eleanor would feel great anxiety until James had been examined by an oculist and we could not get him to Boston before this. Of course if there had been any check in his improvement we should have sent him immediately, notwithstanding his cold. . . . It occurred to me this morning with a sinking of the heart that Elliott might have written to you about this and that my intention of saving you worry might have been frustrated, indeed, you might have been all the more anxious because you had not heard from me at once. It is difficult in such matters to be sure that one is choosing the best way. I feel confident that you and Eleanor will realize that we were in constant attendance on James and had you in mind when we postponed giving you the information.

I have not been able to establish whether Father ever answered this letter, and Mother says she has no recollection of what he did. The Groton files, however, turn up a letter from Mother, in which she (a) revealed she had heard from Elliott, but had done nothing pending receipt of some word from Dr Peabody, (b) expressed concern for the nurse who had put the iodine in my eyes, and (c) went on to discuss my grades ! The letter read :

> I was thankful to get your letter for Elliott had written me but I knew if you didn't write or telephone there could at least be no grave danger and nothing that we could do. Of course I am very sorry about it but we are very grateful that it turned out so well and I know how poor Miss McLeod must have felt. It has always been one of my fears that I would do something of the kind myself ! Franklin and I are both very grateful to you for all you did for James. We are always sure that whatever happens everything that can be done is being done and we have, of course, entire confidence in your judgment.

I have a letter this morning from James himself and he is much upset at losing two Sundays in which he hoped to review for exams, so if there is anything that can be done to help him in the way of tutoring, please try to have it done. His last marks were better and I hate to have him discouraged.

This accident, incidentally, led to a unique letter—a complaint on my part because of not being able to study ! "With this sad eye of mine," I wrote Father, " all I can do is to write letters and dream. It's the dumbest feeling not having anything to do. I'd give anything to be able to study strange as it seems."

There certainly was no diminution of affection between Father and the headmaster as a result of this incident. When the first wedding in the family came around in 1926—Anna's marriage to Curtis B. Dall—Father personally took over the arrangements of getting Dr Peabody to perform the ceremony, writing him : " Naturally, I don't need to tell you that I would rather have you than anybody else in the world, marry Anna."

I hit my stride in my third-form year, when James Regan, a master and one of the finest educators and men I've ever known, took me in tow and spent hours with me, patiently straightening me out. He taught me how to study and how to get along with people. From that time on my work improved materially, and I even became the student prefect at Hundred House. Father and Mother could hardly believe the transformation.

Elliott was installed in Groton in the fall of 1923. I, a lofty fourth-former, almost immediately began playing the heavy-handed big brother, and Bunny, a rebellious soul, retaliated by tattling whenever he thought he had something on me. In one of his early denunciations he accused me of having " cast a damp blanket over [his] rowing." (There was a big family hassle at the time as to whether Elliott should be permitted to go out for the crew because of his health and his grades, neither of which were good.) " I really don't think that he can talk as he flunked at least two exams in the mid-years," Elliott observed. He also mentioned that I had been pretty busy chasing around after a certain young lady.

In another letter of that period our stormy brother took out after Anna, who was then taking a course at Cornell. " I don't know what the Alpha Phi is yet," he wrote, " but I understand

Anna got into [it] just so she could go to a certain dance. Pretty soft I think ! ! Several Yale boys have been up here and have mentioned her. They think she will probably get flunked out or something like that because she never seems to be at the college at all."

Father was always interested in these letters reflecting our adolescent problems. On the envelopes of some which have been preserved are notations in his handwriting : " Keep for me ! "

For his part Father wrote Elliott a number of cheerful, encouraging letters. " Dear Bunny," said one,

> . . . Jimmy says you are in the squad of which he is Corporal. Don't try to beat him up while you are a mere private in the ranks—you might get court-martialed and shot ! Do drop your old Daddy a line to tell him something about your activities. . . . Also, don't forget to step on the gas for those exams ! Start now !

An intimate sidelight on our relationship with Father is the fact that all of us felt sufficiently free to use him as our " legman " in gathering research material for school work. My younger brothers did this on occasions even after he became President. Early in Groton days I began using Pa as an idea man for essays and debates in which I discussed the then red-hot questions of naval disarmament and airplanes-versus-battleships—subjects close to the former Assistant Navy Secretary's heart—and other topics. In one letter I asked : " Send me as soon as possible some dope on why Moving Pictures do more good than harm. If you can get hold of some speeches or statements by some man of importance it would help a great deal. We won the first debate but we must win four more in order to win the season." Pa never let me down : he always came through with something.

There was always a terrible scene at home when it came time for Elliott to return to Groton in the fall, but I, after the shock of my initial adjustment, went back eagerly. Mother has written : " James . . . was always happy and conformed easily to the expected pattern."

As my Groton career drew to a close and Elliott's progressed Father was at the peak of his personal struggle to rehabilitate himself physically after his polio attack. Often he was off by himself in Florida or at Warm Springs. Yet, striving to maintain his father rôle, his interest in our progress was unflagging. During this period he exchanged a number of letters with Dr Peabody about our respective problems. These letters tell more than Father ever revealed elsewhere concerning his feelings towards us and some of his pet theories about growing boys—also his own assessment of a father's responsibilities.

In January 1926, for example, Father raised with Dr Peabody the question of holding out as an " incentive " to Elliott the possibility that he would be allowed to row if his grades improved.

> He is, I think, going through the period of wondering what all the work is about [Father wrote]! I went through it myself and can readily understand why he can see very little use in the daily grind at Caesar's commentaries and at learning certain parts of algebra, which seem to him of no possible use in after life.

Later that year, " upset " because Elliott was in danger of being set back a form, Father offered the headmaster an ingenious theory on what might be retarding Bunny. He wrote :

> In my judgment, Elliott's mental processes this year are slow— he loves to " sit and think " and from seeing him a good deal these holidays I think his cogitations are worth while and that he is making a mighty interesting psychological development.
> Perhaps his great physical growth has slowed up his mind—but he has stopped growing and will, I think, speed up mentally from now on.

In April 1926, after Elliott had been with him in Florida for two weeks, Father wrote Dr Peabody : " Elliott . . . is a much more individual boy than James—less cast in the common mould."

(Perhaps Father was right, and perhaps Groton itself had contributed to my conformity. In a letter to Mother just before the previous Christmas, by the simple act of itemizing what I wanted for Christmas, I unwittingly gave a pretty good portrait of myself as a rather unexceptional young man. I wrote :

> Here is my Xmas list. . . . Books [a Shaw and a good modern novel especially] ties [I only own two good ones and about sixty that are in threads] golf stockings and a Parker fountain pen. A bowler hat ! ! ! [dont laugh I mean it] and a subscription to either the Times or Herald Tribune for the next two terms ?

When school resumed Dr Peabody replied to Father :

> Elliott is all the better for having been with you on the boat. He seems to me more cheerful and up-headed than he was. . . . I can see in him what you describe. He is more original than James. The latter is a very good chap, however, and ought to become a useful man.

Father, Harvard, and I

The year I was to graduate from Groton Father and I began having discussions about where I was to go to college. These talks were significant for several reasons : first, it was the only time I ever knew Pa, torn between his newly developing liberal ideas and the tug of tradition, to waver even momentarily in his sentimental allegiance to his old Alma Mater. Second, it was one of the few situations in our relationship wherein Pa was just a little devious with me. Third, it was one of the rare instances in which he sought to influence me on a major personal decision— and the only one in which he actually induced me to do something against my wishes.

I had not wanted to go to Harvard : my choice was Williams College. Father heard me out, then started on a line of attack *against* Harvard—too much social falderal and all that. Next he set up a diversion by suggesting that a " liberal " Mid-western institution—perhaps the University of Wisconsin—would do me the most good. (At this point I, the young Groton gentleman who yearned for a bowler hat and a subscription to the *Herald Tribune* for Christmas, began having certain qualms.)

Then, nostalgically, almost hypnotically, Father began reminiscing about old Harvard, Hasty Pudding, and Fly Club. At this point, perceiving how obvious it was that Father really had his heart set on having his eldest son follow in his footsteps at the old college, I gave in and said I would go to Harvard. Remember, I was at heart a conformist ; furthermore, I loved Pa deeply and was almost painfully anxious to please him and win his approval in all respects. Also, I suppose, I did not feel strongly enough about the issue to resist him, though in later years I have wished that I had gone to another college. At Harvard I tried to do too many of the things which he did, and consequently was not my own man.

Having thus won his point, Father revealed his own inner conflict in a series of letters through which he sought to justify his position. To Dr Peabody he confided :

James and I had a long talk about Harvard. . . . I had up to lately inclined to sending him to the University of Wisconsin. However, we have agreed on Harvard under certain very definite conditions. He is to receive a very small allowance and he . . . [will] partially work . . . [his] way through college. . . . [I never did.] I really think that Harvard has improved during the last year or two, and there seems to be a different spirit in favour of good scholarship, as well as a decrease in the importance of social life.

Father's next major expression on the subject was a letter to Dean C. N. Greenough of Harvard. The dean had sent Father a form request, asking for a " confidential " appraisal which would assist the school authorities. Father, then at Marion, Massachusetts, undergoing treatment for the rebuilding of his leg-muscles, wrote by hand the following rather remarkable letter :

Marion Mass.
Aug 15, 1926

My dear Dean Greenough
This is a more or less personal note in reply to yours of Aug. 11th regarding my oldest boy James who is about to enter the Freshman Class—
He goes to Harvard with the usual advantages & handicaps of having spent six years at Groton— He did very well there in athletics & leadership—rather poorly in studies—lower half of the form—but passed all his College Board Examinations, two with honors.
He is clean, truthful, considerate of others, & has distinct ambition to make good. He has at the same time, I think, too much of a love of " social good times " (like the rest of his crowd)—& for that reason, although a former Overseer etc I hesitated for some time before letting him go to Cambridge at all— In other words I know enough of the club & Boston life of the average private school Freshman to fear the lack of individuality & the narrowness which comes to so many of them—
One of the principal troubles with most of these private-school undergraduates of yours is, I am convinced after a good deal of investigation, that their parents give them a great deal too much money to go through college on. To this is added in most cases, automobiles, and all sorts of expensive toys in the holidays—

Your people in authority have done & are doing a great work in aiming at greater simplicity of college life, & incidentally your fine efforts for higher scholarship, i.e. more work, is bearing fruit.

I, as one graduate among many want to cooperate with you in this. During this past summer my boy has worked as a laborer in a Canadian pulp & paper mill— Most of the Groton boys will have college allowances well over $2,000 a year. James & his room-mate, Harrison Parker Jr will have only $1500 or $1600.

I should like them in addition to find some sort of employment while at College so that they could earn part of their education— even if it covered only the $300 tuition— In my own days such a thing was rare & difficult— Waiting on table at Memorial was about the only method, & the College office made very little effort to encourage boys to find jobs— I hope this phase is better handled now.

Concretely in regard to my boy I feel that the following should be the objectives : 1. Better scholarship than passing marks. 2. Athletics to be a secondary not a primary objective. 3. Activity in student activities such as debating, Crimson, etc to be encouraged. 4. Acquaintance with the average of the class, not just the Mt. Auburn St [1] crowd to be emphasized. 5. Opportunity to earn part of his education.

I hope to get up to Cambridge this autumn & to have a chance to see you.

Very sincerely yours
Franklin D. Roosevelt

Having thus violated his own rule about not interfering in the affairs of his children, Father then reverted to his life-long principle of giving us a voice in our own affairs. Instead of mailing the letter to Dean Greenough, he sent it to me at Campobello via Elliott, who had been visiting him in Marion, inviting my " comment." My " comment "—flavoured with injury and anguish—was as follows :

Campobello N.B.
August 17th, 1926

Dear Father ;

Elliott has just given me your letter to Dean Greenough. I'm sorry I couldn't have talked with you before you wrote, especially

---

[1] Mt Auburn Street was the fashionable section where the more desirable and expensive dormitories were located. Father himself had lived in one of these, Westmorly Court. After my freshman year I too lived in Westmorly Court.—J.R.

on two points (1) the working the way through and two, " the social good times ". I know how you and Mother feel on the subject and to a certain extent I agree with you, but on one point in your letter I not only disagree but object very strongly. When you say " He has at the same time, I think, too much of a love of ' social good times ' (like the rest of his crowd) ". Now it seems to me that to say that strongly implies that " my crowd " is a wild, pleasure-loving crowd which is not so at all. Of course every boy and girl likes to have a good time, it is only normal to do so but boys from Groton, St Marks, etc, do not do so any more than any others, as you imply. . . . I think it distinctly unfair to tell Dean Greenough that we are a pleasure loving crowd. High school boys and all boys enjoy dances and " social good times " but I *know* and believe that you will come to see that a large majority of us know when to stop and behave as gentlemen in the true sense of the word, therefore I think it hardly fair to give the Dean the false impression that I and others from Groton are over social. We know and I will prove that work is foremost and that we really intend to get something out of college.

The second point about working ones way through seems to me to come down to this. If one intends to study, play games and participate too in hard extra curriculum activities such as the Crimson, there is really no time left to do the other. If on the other hand you feel that you can only afford to give me so much I will without hesitation give up debating etc. and earn my board. It can be done but I feel that I can get more out of college (by) taking part in outside activities but I know also that with the work (scholastic) it will be necessary for me to do, I cannot combine and do everything thoroughly. If you feel that by giving me $1800 I will be free to spend socially I will gladly give you an itemized account of every penny I spend and turn the surplus back to you at the end of the year.

I hope you will realize that I have written this because I really feel it and not because I am obstinate and trying to justify myself. It is frank and I hope you will understand what I mean because I do want you to understand and it is the only way isn't it to understand each other

Affectionately
James

On receiving this heartfelt protest from me Father put the letter away and never sent it. The original is in the library at Hyde Park, still with a George Washington two-cent stamp (uncancelled) on its envelope.

So I followed Father into Harvard. Far from putting any brakes on " social good times," athletics, and such, I went right along in the pattern of joining the same clubs to which he had belonged. By now I realized this was what he had wanted me to do all along. Father even talked to me tolerantly of maintaining " a gentleman's C " average.

I became a member of Fly, the Mt Auburn Street " eating club " (eating clubs are the substitutes for social Greek-letter fraternities at Harvard), just as Franklin, Jr., and John later became members. Father himself wrote a letter about getting me into Fly. I also joined, as Father had, the Hasty Pudding, familiarly known as " the Dicky." On the athletic side, I rowed in the freshmen crew (my poor grades kept me off the varsity), and only my bad knee, the result of my Groton mishap, kept me from playing football. It was a giddy, strenuous life, and, by the start of my sophomore year, with my grades already beginning to slump, I gave Father and Mother the following candid picture :

> Haven't written for an age but I've been so swamped that every-
> thing has just gone up in the air. Started running for the Dicky
> Monday and finished on Thursday. It was good fun in a way but
> terribly strenuous and hard on the nerves. I had to get up at 6:30
> and then until 9 o'clock run errands for Dicky members. Then
> run to classes (carrying my books in a coal scuttle and a pink and
> blue ribbon in my hair !) After lunch more crazy stunts, some
> pretty awful, I'll tell you about them sometime in private ; then
> rowing after which from 5:45 to ten the initiation went on in the
> club house. Its all rather hazy as we were drunk all three nights.
> The result was a complete cessation of all intellectual studies and
> pretty much of a physical wreck. I'm way behind in my work.
> I don't know how I'll ever catch up. . . .
>
> Just between you and me and for Heaven's sake don't let it out,
> I'll be pretty peeved if I don't get elected . . . because I've lost more
> time talking Fly . . . and going to " Campaign meetings " of the Fly
> than I can afford and the result is very poor scholastic work to
> date. . . .
>
> The initiation fee to the Pudding was $85, to the Iroquois [the
> Fly waiting club] fifty bucks which has made the bank account
> very shaky could you advance a bracer in the near future ?

Mother, who had told Father she hadn't wanted me to go to Harvard in the first place, reacted by immediately forwarding my letter to Father at Warm Springs with the following terse and biting comment : " 'l'oo bad James needs the money, you never can get away from your many gold diggers, can you ? I can't say 3 nights drunk fill me with anything but disgust ! " If Father commented at all I cannot recall it.

An early letter to Mother showed, at least, that I could appreciate a joke on myself. " It seems queer," I wrote, " but . . . my marks have gone up. . . . I'm trying to get on the Dean's list which amuses everybody greatly but maybe I can fool them yet." This optimistic bulletin, alas, was penned before the Iroquois, Fly, and Dicky " lost week-ends." I didn't make the dean's list.

In fact, as result of my frivolity, a letter went out from the assistant dean to Father at the end of November 1927 warning that my grades were unsatisfactory and that, if I did not improve by mid-year, I would probably be placed on probation. Father questioned me about this. Somehow some mistakes had been made in the grades forwarded to Father. He fired back at the assistant dean :

> My boy assures me that the enclosed list of marks were not accurate and that they were higher in everything except German, which he (in common I take it with others) finds a most difficult subject ! Would you be good enough to let me know whether any mistake in the record was made ?

Father went on to take another swipe at Harvard social life, stating :

> The great part of the difficulty in his case has been, I am very certain, this impossible club procedure, which seems to be even worse than it was when I ran for the " Dicky " and was " joining " various other social organizations in the autumn of sophomore year. I hope and expect that now the worst part of this social business is out of the way, he will do better next term.

The following month I was in the doghouse again with Mother over the high cost of " keeping up with Father " at Harvard. Having talked with me at Groton when I came over to take my younger brothers to Cambridge for the Yale-Harvard football game, she reported to Pa :

> James . . . looks very well & sports his Pudding tie with ostentation, he wanted me to beg you to come across however for he has

$250 in the bank & owes the University $210. I gave him $20 to pay for John & Elliott's game tickets & a car to Groton & back on Sunday but that was all I could afford ! He said he had to spend $50 the week he " ran " [for the Hasty Pudding] buying people's breakfasts ! I wonder what boys do who can't ! It all seems idiotic to me.

I was not the complete gay blade at Harvard, however. I was active in the Circulo Italiano, a serious-minded language club, and I became president of Phillips Brooks House, an organization devoted to social work, which at least made Mother happy. Curiously, Father advised me against going out for the *Crimson*, the college newspaper which he had edited in his last year at Harvard ; he thought it would cut too much into my time.

The spring of 1928 saw me on the probationary list at Harvard, and I had to curtail some of my extra-curricular activities. I wrote Mother a frank letter, which she passed on to Father with the comment : " He's taken it very well . . . tho' I'm sorry . . . I think it was the best thing that could have happened." I already had written Father about my troubles, and he had answered me with a long letter—unfortunately not preserved—to which I had replied : " I appreciate [it] *very very* much."

My letter to Mother, which indicated—on paper, at least— that I might be showing some signs of becoming dry behind the ears, was, in part, as follows :

> Of course as I wrote Father it is tremendously disappointing in many ways. I had to resign from the nomination to the Student Council and from Phillips Brooks House but I have learned what we talked about and perhaps it is better to learn it now when I can make the changes that I never realized until now were so necessary if I was ever to do more than drift along. You see Mother, things have until now luckily come my way rather easily, things that seemed to me to be of superior importance such as elections and what Pa calls " a gentleman's C " average in most things. Well, having to give them all up makes them all the more desireable [*sic*] but I do realize now that to have them should be the resultant of a solid foundation in the more lasting matter of learnings or studies, and that real success in the former can be based only on real success in the latter.

Part Two

HE WAS NEVER AN INVALID

8

Transition: Politics to Paralysis

UNTIL August 10, 1921, Father was our vigorous part parent, part playmate. After that date, when polio struck on Campobello, everything was changed. My tireless, energetic father-playmate was gone. The time of the second father—the father with the dead limbs—began.

At first I was crushed and scared and confused, full of pity both for him and for myself. After a while I learned that, while his legs no longer would pace us in strenuous pursuits, this new father was to develop his own method of romping and racing with us by means of his mind and his unconquerable spirit.

This middle phase of his life, when he was waging his fight back from the ravages of polio, was the period of Father's greatest personal humanity. In his physical weakness, I think, he made every one of us a little stronger.

Between the time he first went to Washington as Assistant Secretary of the Navy and the time that polio struck Father's political and business fortunes had undergone radical alterations. In 1914, as Assistant Secretary, he made one of the worst blunders of his political career when he sought the Democratic nomination for United States Senator from New York. Fortunately, he was not obliged to resign his Navy post to make the primary race. Tammany Hall, which had old scores to settle with Father, denounced him as a " renegade, meddler and bootlicker," and prepared to do battle. Louis McHenry Howe, the brilliant, sardonic newspaperman, who had become Father's chief lieutenant and political adviser, took a properly bleak view of the senatorial tilt. Even President Wilson was chilly about it, but Father was not to be dissuaded.

Tammany handed him a terrible licking, and the nomination went to James W. Gerard, then Ambassador to Germany, who lost to the Republican candidate in November. (Years later, as President, Father named Gerard special ambassador for the coronation of King George VI.)

In 1918 Father wisely sidestepped a boom to run him for Governor of New York. There was some talk that year about the Republicans nominating his kinsman, Theodore Roosevelt, Jr., but this move failed to materialize. Father was in Europe on Navy business when Granny, all agog over the exciting rumours, wrote him : " The papers today say buttons & pictures of you are being prepared to run for Governor, against TR. in case he can be persuaded to run ! ! ! " Granny had been just a bit chilly toward the Oyster Bay Roosevelts since young Teddy's father, the former President, had taken to attacking the Wilson administration, in which she felt a proprietary interest ; after all, her boy Franklin was a part of it. Some years earlier she had written Father that " T.R." [the former President] was hesitating about visiting her at Hyde Park because his onslaughts against the administration might make such a visit an " error from Franklin's standpoint." This was decent of him, Granny acknowledged, but " why he should go on a tour deliberately to attack the Administration is what I cannot see the wisdom of. I think no one gains by pulling others down—It is not a noble or high-minded view point."

At the Democratic convention in San Francisco during July 1920 Father was nominated as the Vice-Presidential candidate on the ticket with former Governor James M. Cox of Ohio. A stream of letters went to Father from Campobello, where Mother was languishing with " the chicks." Father had figured in an exhilarating tussle—it was the last time he would be able to perform such a physical feat in a political convention—in which he wrested the New York State standard from Tammany henchmen who wouldn't get up and demonstrate for Woodrow Wilson.

Mother wrote him : " Mama is very proud of your removing
the State standard from them ! I have a feeling you enjoyed it
but won't . . . [Tammany] be very much against you ? " Poor
Granny, I'm afraid, never became quite reconciled to politics
as an ennobling occupation : she wrote Father : " I . . . [hope]
that the time at San Francisco will be . . . ' elevating ' . . . but I
fancy that the last epithet is not very likely in a crowd of every
sort of politician."

Communications to isolated Campobello were primitive ; on
July 7, the day after Father had been nominated for Vice-
President, Mother still had not received the news and was writing
him : " I suppose you started to-night for the East. I heard in
Eastport Cox was nominated but am in the dark as to the rest.
. . . I do hope I shall hear from you soon, I long for a little more
personal account."

When the news finally did come to Campobello I was bursting
with pride and promptly wrote him : " Dear Father : It was a
great surprise when we heard *you* had been nominated to be
Vice President. Eastport is planning a great holiday for you
when you come up." Later I gave my stamp of approval to his
campaign tactics by writing : " I think all your speeches are very
good and I love to read them in the paper . . . the *World* praises
them and the *Tribune* condemns them I think the *World* is right."

In August of 1920 one of the strangest lines—in view of later
developments—to be found in any of the Roosevelt family
correspondence appeared in a letter received by Father. The
line was " Oh ! dear I wish I could see you or at least hear from
you. I hate politics ! " That sentiment was penned by Mother
in a letter addressed to " Dearest Honey."

The rest of the letter mostly dealt with news of " the chicks."
She had taken me and two friends on a successful salmon-fishing
expedition, as a result of which I was " feeling very grown up &
bumptious." Franklin, Jr., Anna, and I had all won prizes in
the annual field day on Campobello ; Elliott had won nothing,
and Baby John, too young to compete, " wept because he ' didn't
go up & be given a prize ' ! "

Early in the campaign I was a little jealous of Anna. A young
lady of fourteen, with long golden hair, Sis was taken by Father
to Governor Cox's mansion in Dayton, where Mother recalls

she was shown much attention. Anna's recollection to-day is :
" I haven't the slightest memory of being much made over.
What I do remember is that I was made to wear a Navy blue
alpaca dress, which the family thought was simply beautiful
but which I hated because it scratched, and that I had a private
bathroom at the Cox's place, which I thought was really something."

Later Mother hit the campaign trail with Father. After I
became sick at Groton she wrote Granny anxiously to inquire
about my condition and to report : " Franklin has certainly made
strides in public speaking and gets enough praise everywhere to
turn anyone's head." In another note, describing the rigours of
campaigning through West Virginia and Kentucky, she said :

> We have had a hectic day. F. made 2 speeches & drove 26 miles
> in a motor over awful roads before we got any breakfast ! There
> have been two town speeches since then & at least one platform
> speech every 15 minutes all day ! We had coffee & sandwiches for
> lunch & a very hurried supper & now he still has to get off at Bowling
> Green at 10:10 for a speech in a hall ! I never will be able to do
> without at least four large cups of black coffee again *every* day !
> . . . I really don't see that I'm of the least use on this trip !

The same letter contained a hurried note from Father,
apologizing for a tiff he had had with his mother. He wrote :

> Dearest Mama—I am still alive, tho' it has been about the most
> strenuous work of the campaign. It has been a great comfort to
> have Eleanor. Some day when this is all over I will regain my
> normal mode of life—& then I won't be horrid to you as I was
> last Sunday—& I will really try to do the many little things that
> do count ! It is too bad about James.
>
> > Your devoted
> > FDR

All the speeches, the expended energy, the bouncing over bad
roads, and the gallons of black coffee consumed by Mother went
for naught, and, as Granny's diary for November 2, 1920, noted :
" Rainy day—Harding and Coolidge elected, quite a landslide
for Republicans. Franklin rather relieved not to be elected Vice
President." Somehow, in retrospect, I doubt that a keen com-
petitor such as Father would be " relieved " at being defeated,

even though he knew before the campaign ended that the cause was hopeless.

So Father became a private citizen for the first time in seven years. He returned to his old law firm, Emmet, Marvin, and Roosevelt. He did not devote much time to law practice, however, for he also took on the vice-presidency—actively in charge of its New York office—of Fidelity and Deposit Company of Maryland, a large surety bonding firm. This post, offered Father through his friend Van Lear Black, Fidelity's board chairman, paid him twenty-five thousand dollars a year, which was five times his Navy salary and more money than he had ever made in his life up to that time.

In August 1921 Father went to Campobello to join his family on vacation.

Campobello : Father's Rugged Playground

Campobello was next to Hyde Park in Father's affections. It was his second home. In 1883, the year after Father was born, Grandfather James bought property on Campobello, a rocky, rugged island, nine miles long and three miles wide, just across Passamaquoddy Bay from Eastport, Maine, with the waters of the Bay of Fundy touching its outer shore. The island is part of the Canadian province of New Brunswick, but ever since I was a little boy I heard Father and various old salts on the island repeat the legend that if the commissioners had not had a few drinks too many the day they drew up the boundary Campobello would have been United States territory.

By 1886 Grandfather James completed a home for Grandmother and their young son, Franklin, and the Roosevelts became accepted as " permanent " summer residents. Father's love of the sea was born aboard the *Half Moon*, a sloop which was the predecessor of a later *Half Moon*, the sixty-foot, two-masted schooner on which all of us sailed. There are photographs of Father as a boy in short pants, tugging at the wheel of a neighbour's yacht. I was wearing short pants, too, when I began sailing on the *Half Moon* with Father. Unfortunately on one such cruise I split them. Mother turned me over her lap and, using a sailmaker's needle, sewed them up right on me without jabbing me once.

Every year until he was stricken—unless he was abroad—
Father went to Campobello, first with his parents, then with his
widowed mother, and finally with his own family. The summer
after his engagement to Mother became official he took her there
to become better acquainted with his Mama—her " Cousin
Sally." One of my favourite snapshots of Pa and Mother shows
them wading barefoot in the bay. Mother, of course, was
properly chaperoned by her aunt, Maude Hall—as if Granny
would not have been chaperon enough !

After Father and Mother were married and there became too
many of us to camp out comfortably in Granny's house Father
and Mother acquired their own place on Campobello, adjoining
Granny's " cottage." That too was a gift from Granny. A
Campobello neighbour, Mrs Hartman Kuhn, who was devoted
to Granny, directed in her will that her place and its furnishings
might be purchased by Grandmother for the modest sum of five
thousand dollars, provided that it be used by Father as his
summer home. Thus in 1910 Father fell into ownership of a
place containing, as I remember it, some thirty-four rooms, small
and large.

Mother came to love the island, but she never found it very
restful. An early letter to Father tells of how she had spent an
afternoon playing " croquet with the chicks . . . I assure you it
was very good exercise for the temper ! " She also found plenty
of exercise for her lungs, for when she wanted to summon us
from the dock, where we usually were, she had to yell to us
through a huge megaphone.

How well I remember the formidable physical task of moving
our family of seven to Campobello each summer ! Even in 1912,
when there were only Elliott, Anna, and me, the job was almost
too much for Mother. That summer Father, as usual, was off
somewhere when it came time to pack, and Mother wrote him :
" I wish you could see how much there is to go by express . . .
it takes my breath away . . . Nine express packages left this morning & we have 31 trunks & valises besides 1 more barrel & large
box ! "

First, we would proceed from New York to Boston by train—
six hours if we were lucky. We would arrive in Boston in mid-
afternoon, and go to a certain old-fashioned hotel to " rest "

until train-time. That hotel had been selected years ago by Grandfather James, and Granny always insisted that we continue to stop there, even after it had become rather down-at-the-heels. Occasionally we went by steamer from Boston to Eastport, but usually we took the 11 P.M. sleeper, arriving next morning at Ayers Junction, Maine. There we would change to an antique train—a real museum piece, heated by a coal stove—and ride through Indian reservation country to Eastport. The Indians would board the train with baskets and other handicraft to sell, and I always was terrified—I had more hair in those days than I have now—that I was going to be scalped.

We would reach Eastport at noon, more or less, then transfer to a carriage, which would take us to the dock. If the tide was right we could get off fairly quickly ; if not, we had to wait to board the " chug-chug," as we called the small motor-boat that took us to Campobello. We switched there to a rowboat, which took us to our own pier, then, on foot, made the almost precipitous climb to our house, while men brought up our hand-luggage in wheelbarrows.

Those mountains of baggage, boxes, barrels, and trunks which had been shipped by express came across separately on a larger ferry and were brought by horse-drawn dray from Welch Pool to the house on Campobello. The boxes and barrels, incidentally, contained all sorts of household items—even kerosene lamps. The Campobello place was non-electrified, and in later years I often thought Father drew part of his inspiration for the Tennessee Valley Authority and the Rural Electrification Administration from his memories of those eye-straining evenings on the island. For years, of course, it was one of Father's pet dreams to create electric power by harnessing the tides of Passamaquoddy Bay, a project that, as this is written, is being studied again by the Corps of Engineers. I never think of the Passamaquoddy project without remembering Pa's attempt one summer, before polio, to build a concrete swimming-pool that would be filled by the tide waters. Engineering-wise, it was a complete failure, and we kidded him about it for years. Father always insisted, however, that basically he had a sound idea.

In his own youth at Campobello Father engaged in many feats of derring-do on the rugged terrain of the island and in the waters around it. Many times I have heard him tell the story of how he and Lathrop Brown came from Harvard to Campobello one summer, and, on a sailing expedition, encountered a surly and belligerent Yankee skipper, who took it much amiss when Father brashly questioned him about his cargo and his destination. " The fellow was smuggling ' Chinese potatoes ' [illegal immigrants]," Pa would relate. " It wasn't very bright of me to accuse him of it—I think he would have done me violence if Lathrop had not been watching."

Stories of buried treasure, pirates' loot, and such always intrigued Father. Henry A. Wallace, Father's first Secretary of Agriculture and later Vice-President, recalled—and seemed surprised by it—that at one of their first social-business conferences, Father, then President-elect, talked at great length not about agricultural problems, but about treasure that was supposed to be buried on an island off the coast of Nova Scotia.[1] If Mr Wallace had known Father more intimately he would not have been surprised, for at least twice in his life—once as a youth and again after he was married—Father actually went out on treasure-hunting expeditions. All his life, I suspect—and perhaps some of his daring and ill-fated business ventures of the twenties proved it—Pa cherished a secret dream of finding a pot of gold buried somewhere !

Father sailed in both the *Half Moon* and our smaller boat, the *Vireo*—the one which our family offered to present to the United States Naval Academy at Annapolis a few years ago, but which the Academy " could not accept " because it would " cost too much " to keep her ! The *Vireo* now is on display at the Marine Museum at Mystic, Connecticut.

I never developed much interest in some of Father's pursuits, such as stamp-collecting, but love of sailing is one hobby which he definitely passed on to me. The straits and narrows around Campobello and close-by islands are treacherous, but Father knew them all ; he had a thorough knowledge of how the tides ran and the locations of all the snug harbours. He wanted all of us to sail, and he put more personal effort into teaching me

[1] Mr Wallace aired these recollections in a 1957 interview given Dr Rexford G. Tugwell under sponsorship of the Franklin D. Roosevelt Memorial Commission of Warm Springs.

the art of handling a boat than into anything I can remember. He made good sailors out of Anna and me, and even Franklin, Jr., and five-year-old Johnny were beginning to learn some yachtsmanship from Father when polio struck. Elliott—always a cowboy at heart—was never greatly interested in the sea.

Actually Pa turned us over to a Campobello skipper, Captain Franklin Calder, for our basic instructions in how to handle the sheets and lines and tiller. Then he took over the fine points, and taught us what he knew about the tides. Though he gave the impression of recklessness in his handling of a boat, the one thing he would not stand for in anybody else was any fooling around on the water. Over and over he hammered into me that a boat was no play-toy, and that sailing, while the grandest sport in the world, was serious business. He could be quite impatient at any demonstration of incompetence on my part.

When Pa took the *Vireo*'s tiller, despite his fetish for safety, his skill was such that he could sail her in a way that would scare the lights and liver out of any timorous landlubbers who might be aboard. He would take her through rocky passages, perilously close to jagged reefs, seemingly with inches to spare ; I suspect he would have kicked me off the boat if I had tried any such stunts, but he always insisted there was no danger when he did it because he knew his tides and passages so well.

Sometimes it was not just landlubbers whom he scared. As Assistant Secretary of the Navy, he occasionally came into Campobello on naval vessels. He would " persuade " the captain to let him take the helm—a most unusual privilege to bestow upon a civilian, but this civilian was the " AstNav "—and then would bring the ship through fog-bound narrows at full speed ahead. The hapless skippers didn't know whether to defy the Assistant Secretary then and there, or to risk court-martial later by allowing this wild man with the pince-nez and Harvard accent to pile up their ships ! Even to-day I occasionally meet a retired admiral who will regale me with a horrendous account of one of those mad sails into Campobello with Father giving the orders.

" Cliff walks " were another of Father's favourite pastimes on Campobello. The rocks there are as treacherous as they are picturesque, and Father would organize hiking expeditions, always along the most hazardous, slippery paths. He also dragooned all of us, our various governesses, and all but the few stubborn souls in the summer colony who had strength enough to resist him into equally strenuous and risky games of " hare and hounds," or " paper chases," along the cliffs and down by the shore. Father loved to be the hare, and, knowing the tides as well as he did, he took diabolical delight in dropping a paper trail that would lead us poor hounds on to rocks where we would be trapped by the rising waters. I have heard Mother, a long-suffering " hound," remark, with that wonderful talent of hers for under-statement, that " quite a number of persons really did not enjoy Father's games at all."

Polio Strikes

That August of 1921, when Father joined the family at Campo-bello, promised to be the most vigorous of our vacation summers. Father was in a mixed mood. On the one hand, he was feeling bullish over his personal business prospects. On the other hand, he was annoyed almost to the point of outrage by a petty Republican muckraking effort then in progress. (Towards the end of World War I there had been a vice investigation at the Portsmouth [Rhode Island] naval prison, and the Republicans were seeking to blame Father for allegedly questionable methods employed by the investigators.) When Father was mad his way of working off steam was through an outpouring of physical vigour—and Campobello was the place where he could do it. Immediately on his arrival we began having a wild, whooping, romping, running, sailing, picnicking time with him.

One day, while sailing in the Bay of Fundy aboard the yacht of his friend Van Lear Black, Father slipped and fell overboard into the numbingly cold waters. He thought it was a good joke that an " old salt " such as himself should be so left-footed ; yet he suffered a chill.

Next day he took Anna, Elliott, and me for a sail on the *Vireo*. We had a grand outing. Cruising off Campobello, Father spotted a forest fire on a near-by island. We landed, cut ever-green boughs, and spent several strenuous hours beating out the flames.

Then we sailed back to Campobello and docked the boat.

Hot and tired, Father suggested a plunge in a lake, about a mile and a half away. He led us on a dog-trot to the lake, then we ran to the shore for another swim in the cold waters of Herring Cove. In our wet bathing-suits we trotted back to the house.

At home Father found the mail and newspapers had arrived. Still in his damp suit, he sat down and read for thirty minutes or so.

Suddenly a chill—accompanied by stabbing pains—hit him. He went to bed. Next morning he was feverish and his right leg was weak. The local doctor was called, and pronounced it a " cold."

By the second morning both legs were affected. By the third day the paralysis had spread to practically all of Father's muscles from the chest down.

Little was known of the treatment of poliomyelitis then. A celebrated specialist was located at a near-by resort and per-suaded to come to Campobello to see Father. He diagnosed the ailment—incorrectly—as an involvement of the spinal cord, and prescribed vigorous massage of the limbs. Doctors since have informed us that this was a tragic error, as the massage actually caused further damage to the muscles. The distinguished specialist sent a bill for six hundred dollars.

As the paralysis and the fever set in Father's agony, both physical and mental, was acute. He could barely stand the pressure of the bed-sheet on his body.

Finally, some ten days later, after Father's legs had been punished daily by the harmful massaging, a Boston specialist, Dr Robert W. Lovett, was brought to Campobello and correctly diagnosed the sickness as infantile paralysis. Medical opinion seems to be that the virus had been working in Father and that the strenuous exercise and chilling exposures on August 9 and 10 had aggravated and intensified the force of the attack.

There was much concern as to whether the disease would strike the children too. Mother, who was working almost around the clock, with no rest, remembered how, during the polio epidemic in 1916, Father, then Assistant Secretary, had sent the *Dolphin* to Campobello to evacuate us ; this time there was to be no Navy rescue vessel. So far as we children were concerned, Dr Lovett advised Mother there was nothing to do but " pray " :

either we had the virus and would come down with the disease or we would escape. As it was, none of us was stricken with anything that could be definitely diagnosed as infantile paralysis, but several of us had symptoms of colds and slight fever, giving some credence to the possibility that we might have had mild cases of polio.

Father took the blow in a way that I still find incredible. His pain was excruciating, and the doctor warned that mental depression would most likely accompany the illness. We children were allowed only a few glimpses of him, a hurried exchange of words from a doorway. Yet from the beginning, even before the paralysis had receded fully from the upper regions of his body, Father was unbelievably concerned about how *we* would take it. He grinned at us, and he did his best to call out, or gasp out, some cheery response to our tremulous, just-this-side-of-tears greetings. Terrible as it was for him, he had the mental depth and the compassion to realize how overwhelmingly frightening it was for his children, and he tried to lighten *our* fears.

At the time of the attack Grandmother was in Europe. The news was kept from her as long as possible. When it came time for her to return—it was ritual that Father and Mother met her at the dock she found a letter awaiting her, which had been carefully composed by Mother, stating : "Franklin has been quite ill and so can't go down to meet you on Tuesday to his great regret." Granny came immediately to Campobello, and Mother recalls that she controlled herself remarkably in Father's presence, though there is no doubt that my proud, strong Grandmother, when she was alone, shed many bitter tears. It was later that she decided Father never would recover and that he must spend the rest of his life out of mind and out of sight of the world ; then it was that the arguments between Father and Granny began.

The dedicated Louis Howe, his Navy Department duties as Father's assistant over, had been about to take a position with an oil company. When the news of Father's illness reached him he dropped the job and set out immediately for Campobello. Mother told me once how she chided Louis, who had a family of his own, for remaining so long away from his job. He replied simply : "This is my job—helping Franklin."

In thoоc first days, befure a masseuse was brought up from New York to carry out the misguided instructions of that first " specialist," Mother and Louis took turns at massaging Father's tortured legs. Louis also became the generalissimo for releasing news to the Press of what had happened to Father—always seeking to minimize the seriousness of the situation—and of stage-managing his removal from Campobello in a way that would not attract too much attention.

I shall never forget that day—September 13, 1921—when four men from the island came to the house with a home-made stretcher to carry Father down to the dock to start the trip back to New York. We kids watched it solemnly, and that day, though I was going on fourteen, I was as young and scared as little Johnny.

Father left the house—I remember how he turned his head awkwardly for a last look at the place—with his favourite fedora on his head, a cigarette in his lips, and his Scottie of that time, Duffy, cradled in his arms. His chin was out like a bulldozer blade, and he managed a big, flashy smile and a wisecrack—that was for benefit of us kids. I said, " So long, Father," and bit my lip until it hurt, and I remember the irrelevant thought that crossed my mind as he was lowered down the front steps in the canvas sling : *Just the month before we came to Campobello*, I thought, *this big, wonderful father of mine had taken me to see the Dempsey-Carpentier world's heavyweight championship fight in Jersey City, and on the way out I got pulled away from him in the crowd and was scared to death until he found me. Would he ever*, I wondered, *take me anywhere again?*

There are just two sidelights to add to this chapter.

One comes from my brother, Franklin, Jr. He was recalling the paper-chases which the younger children continued at Hyde Park when Father could no longer participate.

" Pa was as keen about it as if he were out running himself," Brud recalls. " Whenever I was to be the hare and drop the paper trail for the hounds to follow, I'd go to his bedroom and consult with him. He knew the countryside better than any of us, and he would tip me off as to wonderful routes I could take that would completely confuse the hounds.

"Once, in freezing weather, he gave me a route that was a honey—it was across a little creek, and the hounds had to wade across, boys and girls alike. The hems of the girls' skirts got wet, and they came out frozen like hoopskirts. I told Pa about it later, and he thought it was a howl."

The second concerns Pa's return to Campobello. In letters and in conversation he often referred to his "homesickness" for the island. He did not go back until the summer of 1933, after he had completed his history-making first "hundred days" as President of the United States. That was twelve years after he left the island on the stretcher.

On that occasion he told the crowd that had gathered to welcome him :

I think I can only address you as my old friends of Campobello— old and new. I was figuring this morning on the passage of time and I remembered that I was brought here because I was teething forty-nine years ago. I have been coming for many months almost every year until twelve years ago, when there . . . [was] a gap.

9

After Polio—the Way It was

WHEN I came home to New York from Groton for the holidays that first Christmas after Father was stricken with polio I dreaded the thought of seeing him lying in bed, a cripple.

I needn't have. Pa saw to that.

I went into his room, striving manfully to assume an air of nonchalance, even gaiety, so as not to let him know how I really felt. Remember, I was a solemn, earnest young gentleman of fourteen—indoctrinated in the Groton code and brought up not to show emotions.

Pa read me like a book, and he worked a small miracle for me. He was propped up on pillows, and those trapezes and rings over his bed in which he was already exercising his upper body upset me a bit. Pa instantly made me forget it. His chin still stuck out and he was grinning and he stretched out his arms to me. "Come here, old man!" he said.

I rushed over and received his embrace, and I learned right then and there that whatever had happened to his legs had not affected the power in his arms. Then, even though I was a Roosevelt and a Grotonian, I cried a bit, but, with Pa squeezing me and slapping me on the back and carrying on enthusiastically on how "grand" I looked, I was soon chattering right along with him, telling him all about Old Peabody—only I didn't call him that—and the football team and prospects for spring baseball.

That very Christmas—only four and a half months after polio—Father was getting down on the floor to exercise. He had been Indian wrestling with Elliott, Franklin, and Johnny, and now with me home he had some competition nearer his size.

" You think you can take the Old Man ? " he challenged me.
" Well, just get down here and try it ! " His grip was so strong
he could make me yell, and he beat me every time. We went
from Indian wrestling to more vigorous forms of rough-housing.

I still don't know how he did it, but Father kept us almost completely at ease. Even that first Christmas when he could move
only the upper half of his body he gave the impression of mobility.
He cushioned the shock for us. I know he made it possible for
me to participate in various festivities that Christmas without
feeling any depression or guilt.

As Father progressed the subject of his disability was mentioned
less and less. There is evidence that in the beginning, when I
was away from his inspiriting influence, I was oppressed by what
had happened to him. Two of my early letters from Groton
contain the following comments : " It sounds horrible about
Fathers legs especially the wedges." And : " I hope Father is
getting along alright on his crutches."

Father was sensitive enough to know that the children were
going to brood about his condition, particularly as it became
obvious that the lower limbs had atrophied. He countered this
by making a sort of game out of the situation. He boldly pulled
back the covers, showed us his legs, and taught us the anatomical
terms for each muscle that was involved. We were just about
the best-posted kids to be found anywhere on anatomical names
for muscles. He would give us progress reports as a little life
returned to various areas, and we would cheer jubilantly, as if at
a football game, when Pa would report, say, a slight improvement
in the muscles leading from the *gluteus maximus*. How we loved
to talk about Pa's *gluteus maximus* !

Inside himself Father was fighting his own battles. It was
only as we grew older that we realized the significance of some
of the little ways in which he let his feelings show. His bed
was placed so he could see a certain corner from his window.
Elliott was allowed to skate to school, and Father would ask him
if he would cross at that corner : he wanted to see him skating.

Though he was only seven years old that first Christmas,
Franklin, Jr., recalls, as I do, that there never was any shock at
seeing Father. Brud was in a phase then of drawing pictures of
Abraham Lincoln, because he was fascinated with Lincoln's

A.F.D.R.—5*

beard He would take them to Father's bedroom—Pa always
was an enthusiastic sketcher—and Pa would work with him on
improving the lines.

It was a rougher time for Sis. She was in the adolescent,
emotional stage. Louis Howe, now giving full attention to
Father's affairs, had moved into our household. Louis was not
a well man, and, for his comfort, he was given Anna's commodious,
sunny front bedroom with its private bath, while she was
" banished," as she viewed it, to a smaller, bathless room in the
rear of the house. Granny despised Louis, and often provoked
Father to cold fury by calling him that " dirty, ugly little man."
(Louis *was* ugly and untidy, but his unwavering loyalty to Father
was clean and beautiful.) Granny played on Anna's resentment,
and there were some unpleasant times until Sis became more
mature and learned to appreciate Louis as all of us—except
Granny—eventually did.

Part of the reason Granny detested Louis Howe was because
she viewed him as a " dangerous " influence in persuading her
son to remain in public life, whereas she had it planned for him
to become a country squire. Just as determined in her way as
Father was in his, Granny did not give up this active struggle
for years : I think it took the Presidency to convince her that her
boy Franklin was not going to become a mummy in a wheel-chair
at Hyde Park.

In those first months after Father was stricken it was obvious
that Granny, though crushed by what had happened to her beloved
son, was struggling to contain her feelings. In a letter to her
brother, Fred, written from Campobello the day after she returned
from Europe and learned for the first time what had happened
to him, she said :

> I got here yesterday at 1.30 and at once . . . came up to a brave,
> smiling, and beautiful son, who said : " Well, I'm glad you are
> back Mummy and I got up this party for you " ! He had shaved
> himself and seems very bright and *keen*. Below his waist he cannot
> move at all. His legs (that I have always been proud of) have to
> be moved often as they ache when long in one position. He and
> Eleanor decided at once to be cheerful and the atmosphere of the
> house is all happiness, so I have fallen in and follow their glorious
> example. . . .
> Dr. Bennett just came and said " This boy is going to get all

right." They went into his room and I hear them all laughing. Eleanor in the lead.

As time passed Granny became increasingly protective towards Father and fiercely resented any criticism of him. In a March 1924 letter to Father, who was cruising in Florida, Mother comments : " Mama is wild over Nick L. [Nicholas Longworth, the Republican Speaker of the House of Representatives, who had married Mother's cousin, " Princess Alice " Roosevelt, daughter of Uncle Teddy] having called you in a speech a ' denatured Roosevelt ' but I tell her he was just trying to be funny."

Mother became a real rock of strength, both physical and mental. She sensed that Father would wither if treated as an invalid ; as soon as feasible she dispensed with the trained nurse and embarked on a determined policy of not treating Father as an invalid. That was the way it was, and it helped turn the trick for Father.

The day of the timid, fluttering, inept housewife, subservient to the whims of her husband and her mother-in-law, was over. Tracing Mother's transition into a self-reliant, independent personality, it is hard to believe that she was the same person who, only ten years earlier, was writing to Father in Europe : " Since the ' Titanic ' I think everyone is nervous & I don't think I shall ever let you go away again alone." Or who, in 1913, was confessing : " Dearest Honey. . . . My head whirls when I think of all the things you might do this . . . coming year, run for Governor, Senator, go to California ! I wonder what you really will do ! I hate your leaving any time "

It was several years before Father started making public appearances again. Meanwhile, with Louis Howe's encouragement, Mother, almost ruthlessly, suppressed her innate shyness, and began doing things to help Father's career. She appeared for him at civic and political meetings. Louis taught her to suppress her high-pitched, nervous giggle ; she even stood up in front of people—strangers—and made speeches for Father, though, in the beginning, she " died " every time she did it. She became a pair of legs for Father—and eventually she became a first-class thinking mechanism for him, too, bringing him her keen observations on personalities and on events from which he was physically shut off. Finally, in later years, Mother evolved even further : she became his determined goader, seeking—not always successfully—to stir him into action in a variety of causes in which she passionately believed.

On the surface Mother maintained her polite demeanour to Granny—most of the time, anyway. Granny would write Father letters full of gossipy trivialities, such as : " I met Dr. Wilmer the other day . . . he said *such* nice things about your being *brave*, & having *high standards*, & a *constructive* mind, & he was so pleased to see *your* ' ma.' " Mother, meanwhile, was writing him about politics, politicians, and world events. Her increasing independence of " Ma-*ma* " was reflected more and more in her letters, when her patience would give way and she would lash out against her mother-in-law's doings.

One can trace the changing pattern of Mother's and Granny's relationship through passages in their respective letters to Father. Granny's letters revealed an almost intangible but unmistakably patronizing attitude towards Mother, an attitude that seeped in even when she was being complimentary. In the first summer of Father's convalescence, when Mother came to join us at Hyde Park, Granny wrote Father : " I fear . . . [the children] were not very good yesterday when poor Eleanor was here. They do stand a *little* in awe of me." On a later visit she wrote : " It is such a comfort to have Eleanor and a few peaceful days with her beloved children will do her no harm ! She accomplishes so much in her quiet way, and is always so sweet and cheerful, never nervous or cross."

For her part, Mother became increasingly forthright. By August 1925 she was writing Father in Warm Springs :

> I wish you could read Mama's last letter to me. She is afraid of everything . . . ! Afraid of your going over bad & unfrequented roads, afraid I'll let the children dive in shallow water & break their necks, afraid they'll get more cuts ! She must suffer more than we dream is possible !

In April 1926 she wrote him :

> I think you ought to ask her down [to Warm Springs]. . . . She's dying to go & hurt at not being asked. I'll bring her if you want. . . . I'm trying to be decent but I'm so conscious of having been nasty that I'm uncomfortable every minute !

A month earlier Mother had been really upset by her discovery that her mother-in-law had arranged to give Anna and
Curtis Dall, as a wedding present, a lavishly expensive co-opera-
tive apartment, much above their means, and that Granny had
asked Anna " not to tell me as she thought I would dissuade
them from taking it." While conceding—somewhat incon-
sistently—that it was a " lovely thing " for Granny to do, Mother
wrote Father :

> I am so angry at her offering anything to a child of mine without
> speaking to me if she thought I would object & for telling her not
> to tell me that it is all I can do to be decent. . . . Sometimes I think
> constant irritation is worse for one than real tragedy. . . . I've
> reached a state of such constant self control that sometimes I'm
> afraid of what will happen if it ever breaks !

Mother can recall only one time when her self-control gave
way. That was during the first spring of Father's convalescence,
when she was attempting to do the work of a mother, father,
nurse, and companion combined, and she was close to physical
and mental exhaustion. In her autobiography she describes the
incident in her own words :

> One afternoon . . . when I was trying to read to the two youngest
> boys, I suddenly found myself sobbing as I read. I could not think
> why I was sobbing, nor could I stop. Elliott came in from school,
> dashed in to look at me and fled. Mr. Howe came in and tried to
> find out what was the matter with me, but he gave it up as a bad
> job. The two little boys went off to bed and I sat on the sofa in the
> sitting room and sobbed and sobbed. I could not go to dinner in
> this condition. Finally I found an empty room in my mother-in-
> law's house, as she had moved to the country. I locked the door
> and poured cold water on a towel and mopped my face. I eventually
> pulled myself together, for it requires an audience, as a rule, to keep
> on these emotional jags. That is the one and only time I ever
> remember in my entire life having gone to pieces in this particular
> manner. From that time on I seemed to have got rid of nerves and
> uncontrollable tears, for never again have either of them bothered me.

In addition to conquering her shyness, controlling her inner
feelings, and asserting her independence of her mother-in-law,
Mother also made herself learn to do things she never had
mastered before, in order to become father as well as mother

to the two younger boys She learned to swim, took them on
exhausting camping trips, and even came to grips with learning
to drive an automobile.

Mother's adventures at the wheel occasionally were rather
disastrous, as I'm afraid Mother was—and still is—one of the
world's least adept drivers. She had tried to learn to handle a
car in 1918, but more or less gave it up after an occurrence which
Anna, in a letter to Father from Hyde Park, described as follows :
" Mother drove the ' Stearns ' the day after she came and nearly
took off Grandmama [*sic*] back door step because she ran into it."
Her re-emergence as a chauffeur provided us with numerous
incidents about which to tease her, such as her knocking over
one of the big stone pillars flanking the Hyde Park driveway, or
letting the station wagon roll backward into a ditch. In fairness,
I cannot blame Mother too much for the last mishap, for all—or
most—of the kids were in the station wagon, each yelling instructions at her.

In one of my Groton letters to Mother from this period I
find the following needle : " I saw by the paper that you and
your party were arrested for speeding. So did everybody else in
school. It's rather a good way to get advertized don't you think ? "
I used this against Mother for years when she lectured me about
my fast driving.

Cars always have seemed to hold a fascination for members
of our family—and I suspect that the flame has burned brighter
for Franklin, Jr., than for any of us (to-day he even sells cars).
Certainly he was the youngest motor-owning Roosevelt. Before
his tenth birthday Frankie wrote Father a letter from " Campo-
below," asking if he might have a " Palm Beech Bug "—a sort
of motorized buckboard—as his gift that year. " It is the only
Birthday I would wish for," Brud pleaded, even offering to pay
twenty-five dollars of his own money towards it. He got it.
Some years later, as a Harvard undergraduate, Franklin, Jr., held
the unofficial speed record for driving from New York to Boston,
via Hartford, in his souped-up LaSalle—three hours and fifty-six
minutes.

There is a further adventure concerning the rough-riding
Roosevelts which concerns this period when Mother was attempting to do both her job and Father's. I am reminded of it by my

brother Elliott, himself no old lady at the wheel. Franklin, Jr., and Johnny, though both considerably under age, had somehow talked Mother into allowing them to drive our Model T Ford over a back road in the vicinity of Hyde Park. They set out with her secretary, the late Malvina Thompson. Frankie had the wheel, and Johnny thought his turn to drive had come, but Franklin wouldn't give it up. So Johnny started slugging him. Frankie, without even slowing down the car, began slugging back. The Model T careened madly down the road with the two boys exchanging blows and with poor Miss Thompson almost suffering a heart attack.

Learning to Live with It

As time went by Pa mentioned his legs less and less. It was as if he was determined to ignore them and to proceed as if the affliction did not exist. He continued to discuss, without diffidence, what he was doing to strengthen his legs, and occasionally he would betray his irritation when political opponents sought to make capital out of his disability.

For instance, in his 1928 gubernatorial campaign Pa laced into the " sob stuff " which he said was being spewed out by Republican editors. In one speech, after detailing the man-killing schedule he had been keeping, Pa was greeted with cheers when he jibed : " Too bad about this unfortunate sick man, isn't it ? " In another, after again describing his heavy schedule, he asked : " Do I look to you good people like an unfortunate, suffering, dragooned candidate ? " In the same speech he made one of his rare humorous allusions to his condition : " I hope you will pardon me if my voice is a little bit frayed tonight. That is the only part of me, except a couple of weak knees—physically but not morally ! "

Never to my knowledge did he rail or rant against the blow fate had dealt him in making him a cripple. Actually, his self-control, always rather remarkable, increased rather than decreased, once he got over the first shock of polio. Except on the few occasions when he felt it necessary to strike back at partisan misfortune-mongers, Father's infrequent references to his disability usually were oblique ones, such as his note to me in 1929

about the Harvard-Yale game : " I won't be able to go unless
arrangements can be made for me to motor to the field and watch
the game from the players' bench." Or, much later, his rejoinder
to Mme Chiang Kai-shek at the White House, when she thought-
lessly told him not to rise as she left the room : " My dear child,
I couldn't stand up if I had to."

To me, one of the most unwittingly poignant letters he wrote—
only forty-nine days after he was stricken—was to Walter Camp,
who had coached Father's " physical fitness " group in Washington World War I days. To Camp, one of hundreds—friends and
strangers alike—who had written to buck him up, Father replied
cheerily :

> There were days in the old " Flying Squadron " when I felt that
> " double-quicking " around Potomac Park came very near [the]
> classification of hard work, but 1 can assure you that if I could get
> up this afternoon and join with Messrs. McAdoo, Davis and Delano in
> a sprint for the record, I would consider it the greatest joy in the world.
> However, the doctors are most encouraging and I have been given
> every reason to expect that my somewhat rebellious legs will permit
> me to join in another course of training sometime in the future.

To his 1920 running mate, Governor Cox, Father, on December
8, 1922, wrote :

> It is mighty nice to get your note. . . . I am just back in New
> York after a very successful summer in the country at Hyde Park.
> The combination of warm weather, fresh air and swimming has
> done me a world of good ; in fact, except for my legs I am in far
> better physical shape than ever before in my life, and I have
> developed a chest and pair of shoulders on me which would make
> Jack Dempsey envious. The legs are really coming along finely,
> and when I am in swimming work perfectly. This shows that the
> muscles are all there, only require further strengthening. I am
> still on crutches but get about quite spryly, and, in fact, have
> resumed going to my office down town two or three times a week.

His helplessness did give Father one phobia, or, rather, intensified one that always had bothered him—a fear of fire. Fire
was the only thing I ever heard Father confess—either before or
after polio—that he feared physically. There had been several
tragic blazes, taking lives of close relatives in both the Roosevelt
and Delano families. Father frequently lectured us on the

dangers of carelessness with fires, and sought to impress us by describing how Algonac, the old Delano homestead, had burned. After he lost the use of his limbs he admitted to Mother—and later said the same thing to me—that the one thing which caused him some sleepless nights was the fear of being caught in a fire and not being able to help himself. This fear was one of the reasons he forced himself so early after his illness to begin his attempts to learn to crawl, propelling himself across the floor, inch by inch, with his powerful arms. " If I ever get caught in a fire," he once told me, " I might be able to save myself by crawling."

As he learned to live with polio and finally managed to get about with the aid of his steel braces, a cane, and a strong arm on which to lean, Father taught himself many ingenious techniques for minimizing the appearance of his physical helplessness. My brothers and I—and later his aides and Secret Service men in Albany and Washington—became adept at matching our pace with his slow, stiff-legged gait, or at helping him in and out of an automobile with the least fuss. The braces, even when orthopædic technicians had learned to lighten them, were always a source of discomfort, and he couldn't wait to be rid of them. Often when I was travelling with him on campaign trains I have seen him go to the trouble of taking off his shoes and trousers in his compartment between whistle stops, just to be rid of his braces even for a short period.

In addition to the true things that have been written about how Father learned to live with polio, a lot of legends—interesting but questionable—have sprung up. For instance, one journalist has described in detail how Father, at his first inaugural,

picked up his silk hat the wrong way so that, if he put it on, it would be backward on his head. He was walking on the arm of his son James, and could not stop, so laboriously, little by little, he worked the brim of the hat around with the fingers of his free hand until it was in the right position.

This is a perfectly fascinating story ; the only trouble is that it did not happen. For one thing, if he was holding on to my arm with what would have been his left hand he would have been gripping not his hat but his cane with his right hand. Even if he

could grip both hat and cane while walking, how did he work
the brim of the hat around " with the fingers of his free hand " ?
Some extravagant admirers have attributed superhuman traits
to Pa, but I never heard anyone claim he had three hands !

I have also read that I sometimes experimented by putting
on Father's braces to see if I could walk in them, and that I
fell sprawling. I never did such a thing in my entire life : the
idea to me would have seemed repugnant, and disrespectful to
Father.

Exaggerated stories have been written about falls which Father
was alleged to have taken in public. I have tracked down some
of these stories and found them to be untrue.

Actually, after falls in the privacy of his home during the time
he was teaching himself to stand and walk again, Father, to the
best of my knowledge, only had one bad accident in public, and
I was a witness to that. That was in 1936, when he went to
Franklin Field in Philadelphia to deliver his renomination acceptance speech. He was using my arm for support, and just as he
started his slow walk to the platform he saw and recognized the
distinguished poet Edwin Markham, an elderly man with a full
white beard. Father reached over to shake the poet's hand,
and at that moment his left brace became unlocked. The sudden
lurch and Father's weight threw me off balance, but Gus Gennerich
and Mike Reilly of the Secret Service moved in swiftly, and the
three of us managed to keep him from falling. Father snapped
instructions for us to straighten his disarrayed clothing, lock his
brace, and pick up the scattered pages of his speech. He took an
instant to compose himself, and, to my amazement, completed
his handshake with the by now thoroughly unnerved poet, who,
incidentally, would have been in real danger had some quick-
shooting Secret Service agent jumped to the erroneous conclusion
that the man with the white beard had something to do with the
President's mishap. Then Father went on to the platform, faced the
throng smilingly as if nothing had happened, and made his speech.

Did Polio Help Father ?

Much has been written in speculative vein about whether
Father would have become the humanitarian that he was—
indeed, whether he ever would have become President—had he

not been stricken by infantile paralysis. A popular theory is that polio gave him " character," taught him patience and broadened his understanding of human suffering.

I have no doubt that these things in some measure are true—particularly in reference to his understanding of human suffering. Yet I cannot accept the theory that Father would not have been a great man and a great public figure had he not gone through his personal Gethsemane. Indeed, I believe that it was not polio that forged Father's character, but that it was Father's character that enabled him to rise above the affliction. I believe his path would have led him to the White House regardless of polio : everything I remember him saying, everything I have read of what he did and said in early life, convinces me he was headed in that direction.

It is true that Father knew how to surround himself with creative persons, capable of generating exciting ideas. But he also knew how to absorb the exciting dreams that others might conceive, but could not possibly execute, and how to bring these dreams to fruition. More than that, he was in his own right a creator of exciting ideas, as well as a doer of dynamic deeds.

I go back to Granny again for what, to me, is striking proof that Father, long before polio struck, was well on his way to evolving from Franklin D. Roosevelt, the Hyde Park gentleman, to F.D.R., the humanitarian.

Long ago—in October of 1917—Father and Mother came from Washington to spend a week-end with Granny at Hyde Park. A discussion—one of the endless discussions which could be generated when Granny and Father got together—arose. It dealt with concepts of social responsibility. As Mother remembers it—and this was long before there ever was any thought of Father becoming President and the home place becoming a national historic site—Grandmother wanted Father and Mother to promise her that the Hyde Park estate would be kept in the family " forever." She viewed it as a home for generations of Roosevelts, just as Algonac for many years had served the Delanos.

Mother demurred, and Father came in strongly on Mother's side. He said he would make no such promises, and then, as Mother recalls, he took off on a vigorous exposition of his social and political philosophies that were far afield from Granny's.

Already Father was moving towards the ideas which later became
the foundation of his New Deal.

That same Sunday night—October 14, 1917—a few hours after
she had seen Father and Mother off on the train for Washington,
Granny sat down and started a letter to " Dearest Franklin &
Dearest Eleanor." She mailed it next day when she herself
returned to New York. It is a rather significant letter ; it not
only discloses a good deal about how Father's thinking was
developing, but it also provides a revealing picture of Granny herself. In it she expressed—and, whether she was right or wrong,
she did so with dignity, conviction, and eloquence—the views of an
honourable, old-fashioned lady on the sort of world she preferred.

This is the letter which Sara Delano Roosevelt wrote on that
long-distant October Sunday :

> I am sorry . . . that Franklin *is* tired & that my views are not
> his, but perhaps dear Franklin you may on second thoughts or
> *third* thoughts see that I am not so far wrong. The foolish old
> saying " *noblesse oblige* " is good & " *honneur oblige* " possibly ex-
> presses it better for most of us. One can be democratic as one
> likes, but if we love our own, & if we love our neighbour we owe
> a great example, & my constant feeling is that through neglect or
> laziness I am not doing my part toward those around me. After
> I got home, I sat in the library for nearly an hour, reading & as
> I put down my book & left the delightful room & the two fine
> portraits, I thought : after all, would it not be better just to spend
> all one has at once in this time of suffering & need, & not think of
> the future for with the *trend* to " shirt sleeves ", & the ideas of what
> men should do in always being all things to all men & striving to
> give up the old fashioned traditions of family life, simple home
> pleasures & refinements, & the traditions some of us love best, of
> what use is it to *keep up* things, to hold on to dignity & all I stood up
> for this evening. Do not say that I *misunderstood*, I understand
> perfectly, but I cannot believe that my precious Franklin really
> feels as he expressed himself. Well, I hope that while I live I may
> keep my " old fashioned " theories & that *at least* in my own family
> I may continue to feel that *home* is the best & happiest place & that
> my son & daughter & their children will live in peace & happiness
> & keep from the tarnish which seems to affect so many. . . .
> When I *talk* I find I usually arouse opposition, which seems odd,
> but is perhaps my own fault, & tends to lower my opinion of myself,
> which is doubtless salutary. I doubt if you will have time dear
> Franklin to read this, & if you do, it may not please you.

10

"... The Water has to bring Me back"

BETWEEN the time he was hit by polio in 1921 and his return to public office following his election as Governor of New York in 1928 Father had three main concerns—to learn to walk again, to earn a living for his family, and to avoid obscurity. The first two were struggles ; the third came easily.

He also had two collateral aims : one was to maintain contact with his family and not surrender his father rôle while exerting the time-consuming effort to regain use of his limbs. The other, which came later, was the development of Warm Springs, Georgia, as a health centre where " polios "—the flippant term which Father came to use—could be helped back to health.

Looking back on this period, I must say in all honesty that neither Anna, my brothers, nor I had the guidance and training that I think Father would have given us had he not been involved in his own struggle to re-establish a useful life for himself. Yet he managed to do a good job or not losing touch with us, and of making us feel that, even though he had to be away from us, we were not out of his mind.

Pa also paid us the compliment of wanting us with him as much as possible. We were invited to join him to fish, swim, play, and later work with him at various stages of his journey back to health and public life.

He also encouraged us—though perhaps he could not have shut us off had he tried—not to be vegetables of the " yes, Father " type. He always wanted us to argue with him and, if we felt so inclined, to express our opinions on public issues just as vehemently as we pleased. Later all of us travelled with Father at various times on Presidential trips. I can recall how certain local political stuffed shirts, who came aboard our train, listened with obvious amazement when they heard the " Roosevelt brats," as they must have regarded us, telling off the Old Man in loud, impolite language. But Father enjoyed these free-wheeling discussions, and never can I recall his shutting us up peremptorily or arbitrarily. Sometimes, if the argument showed signs of getting completely out of hand, he would deftly turn it off with a mocking " Papa knows best ! " He didn't necessarily feel that Papa knows best, but that was our tacit signal to slow down.

I never heard Father seek to place the blame for his paralysis on any special circumstance, but subconsciously he must have linked the severity of his case with the chilling plunges he took on the two days preceding his attack. He learned early that his crippled limbs could be exercised more freely in warm water, and as soon as possible he began using water as a means of therapy. One of his first experiments in 1922 was in Vincent Astor's heated indoor pool at Rhinebeck, New York. While swimming there one day Father suddenly called out to Granny's chauffeur, Louis Depew, " The water put me where I am and the water has to bring me back ! "

Between 1923 and 1926 Father pursued a number of avenues in his quest for recovery. In 1925 he spent part of the summer with Louis Howe at Horseneck Beach, near Westport Point, Massachusetts. He took treatments at Marion, Massachusetts, late that summer and early fall with Dr William McDonald, a neurologist, who was experimenting with rehabilitation of polio-wasted muscles by a combination of swimming and exercises, which included crawling.

For four consecutive winters—1923 through 1926—Father took to the water. He rented a craft the first season ; then he purchased a down-at-the-heels houseboat, spruced her up, and sailed in Florida waters, seeking out deserted beaches where he could strip to the skin, crawl in the sand, and swim in the warm currents, keeping an eye out for sharks which sometimes circled within striking distance.

It was one of the strangest interludes of Father's life. While maintaining a tenuous contact with public affairs—partly by sporadic correspondence, but mostly through Louis Howe's indefatigable public-relations activities back East—Father "lost" himself from the world almost completely. In his outlook and his pastimes he reverted to a mood approaching that of his undergraduate days. Mostly he sought out sailing companions who would be light-hearted and attractive and would not burden him with intellectual discussions.

The houseboat—a seventy-one-foot craft, christened the *Larooco*—was purchased by Father in partnership with a friend of Groton and Harvard days, John Silsbee Lawrence, of Boston. Lawrence, who had cruised with Father aboard the rented craft, also had some difficulty with his legs, and he and Father both thought that sun and exercise on the beaches might be beneficial for them. Father found the houseboat, and they closed the deal in September 1923 for $3750. The name *Larooco*—pronounced "La Roe-co"—for Lawrence-Roosevelt Company—was Lawrence's suggestion. Lawrence, however, became involved with business affairs and never even saw the craft of which he was half owner until March 1926, the month they put the *Larooco* out of commission for ever.

The "Log of the House Boat Larooco," for the most part in Father's handwriting, is a fascinating record of Father's frame of mind during those three rather aimless winters. In writing his log entries Father indulged his weakness for atrocious puns, and he reverted to the rather unsophisticated humour of his college days. Hinting at unprintable high jinks, he decreed in the "rules" at the beginning of the log that "all references to 'community life' must be written in code." On February 2, 1924, the day he commissioned the *Larooco*, he noted : " Library of the World's Worst Literature placed on shelves." A few days later he noted : " Painted ¾ of a chair—booful blue." Washington's Birthday (1925) was entered as " Birthington's Washday," and the marathon Parcheesi tournament that ran throughout the cruises was referred to as " Ma & Pa Cheesy."

The *Larooco*'s crew consisted of Captain and Mrs Robert J. Morris—Mrs Morris serving as the cook and housekeeper—and an engineer. Miss Marguerite A. (Missy) Le Hand, who had come to work " temporarily " for Father during the 1920 Vice-Presidential campaign and remained as his secretary for the rest of her life, was along on most of the cruises to handle his correspondence. Elliott and I joined him on separate occasions, and Sis visited him in Miami at the end of one cruise. Mother came down only twice during the three years ; she had her hands full taking care of Franklin, Jr., and Johnny, and she didn't care much for houseboat life anyway. Mother's loneliness during this period is reflected in a line from a letter she wrote him during his first cruise : " I miss you very much & want your advice so often but . . . it is as well you are far away from all entanglements."

One of the *Larooco*'s most regular guests was Maunsell Schiefflein Crosby, Harvard '08, a noted amateur ornithologist ; he and Father had much hilarity together and wrote some awful verse about birds they spotted or dreamed up, the favourite being a " Pink Bazoo," to rhyme with " Blue Laroo," as the houseboat was dubbed. Another early guest was Livingston Davis, also a Harvard chum, who had been Father's special assistant during Navy days. Davis, however, offended Father's sense of propriety on the second day of his visit, and there is no indication in the log that, despite their long and close friendship, he was ever invited back. Father's own description of the incident was as follows :

Mon., March 17th—[1924]
Water too cold to swim & wind too high to go to reef—L.D. went to the R.R. bridge to fish & came back minus trousers—to the disgust of the two ladies. Earlier he had exercised on the top deck a la nature. Why do people who must take off their clothes go anywhere where the other sex is present ? Captain Morris remarked quietly that some men get shot for less.

Over the three-year record of the cruises there are references to " grog," bridge, poker parties—also much fishing and exercising. Early on the first cruise Father went ashore at Palm Beach, which he had not seen since 1904, and he did not like what he saw. " I found the growth of mushroom millionaires' houses luxuriant. The women we saw went well with the place—and we desired to meet them no more than we wished to remain in the harbor even an hour more than necessary."

The second year's cruise started badly when Father, after catching a thirty-five-pound barracuda, was thrown to the deck of the launch when a heavy squall blew up. " Had to be passed in through galley window," he wrote. The ligaments of a leg and knee were torn, and he was immobilized for several days.

The gaiety resumed as his leg healed, but soon he had to take time off briefly to work on his income-tax returns. A guest, whose handwriting is not identified, took over the log entries for a few days, and noted that " Our Admiral . . . took to his accounts and had a glorious time planning to cheat the U.S. Government." I can take oath that this was pure inventive facetiousness, as all his life Father detested tax-dodgers, and, after he became President, he spent considerable time thinking up schemes for detecting and socking them. He felt the same way about expatriate Americans who preferred to live abroad—even though there were several of these in his own family—and rich Americans who registered their yachts under foreign flags to dodge taxes.

Mother's arrival for her first visit to the *Larooco* was noted in the log by one of Father's guests, Julian Goldman, a New York businessman, as follows :

Sunday March 8th [1925]
Could we commence the Sabbath in any better way than to proceed to the Station to greet the Heavenly Mrs. Roosevelt. . . . Mrs. Roosevelt upon her arrival at the *Larooco*, vindicated my high opinion of her by seizing the Heavenly deck for her sleeping quarters. Mosquitos, flies etc. mean nothing to her so long as the Citronella holds out.

The lunch was delightful. Bowing to the latest arrival from the civilized world . . . we listened with much interest to charming stories about the Roosevelt children. . . .

The afternoon was spent by FDR . . in catching a Fish—with Mrs FDR . . . knitting & reading. . . . After the usual evening meal Mrs. FDR . . . joined Capt. Charley in Evening Services which were concluded by all singing " Onward Christian Soldiers."

A Rubber of Bridge, a hasty retreat by F.D.R. who with his big boyish smile found it was time to retire as he was about to lose concluded a perfect Day.

That March I came down on holiday from Groton, and Father noted my arrival with the log entry : " James & I fished the trestle in the morning, went outside and got a mess of bottom fish including a Turbot." I had a delightful time with Father on that visit. A number of his Eastern friends were cruising in Florida waters that season, and there was much company. I enjoyed listening to the lively conversations and watching Father and his friends play poker in the evenings. Pa treated me not as a schoolboy, but as one of the gang—though I did sit on the sidelines for the poker games. One day I went ashore with him for lunch with William Jennings Bryan, who had been Secretary of State in Washington during part of the time that Father served in the Navy Department. Bryan, the old Chautauqua orator, then was helping boost real-estate sales by lecturing to crowds of prospective buyers on the wonders of Florida palm-trees, sand, and sunshine.

On the sunny days I would swim with Pa, and it seemed to me that he was making some progress towards recovery, though I still winced inwardly when I saw how difficult it was for him to manœuvre his wasted limbs.

We also had a good deal of bad weather, which always seemed to catch us when I was fishing with Father. " Sea too much for JR'S breakfast," Father noted in his log after one rough expedition. Later, in typical fashion, he made the incident the subject of a much-embroidered bulletin to the family. This led me, after I had returned to Groton, to write him protestingly : " No fair telling people where I got sick, especially when John and F.D.R., Jr. bring it up before a large luncheon party ! ! "

Before the end of the second cruise Father's disenchantment with the houseboat had set in. It was an expensive operation, and he realized it was not doing him as much good as he had hoped. Furthermore, the previous fall he had discovered Warm Springs.

In April 1925 he wrote his absentee co-owner, John Lawrence, from Warm Springs, proposing that they try to sell the *Larooco*.

> The sharks make it impossible to play around in deep water for any length of time [Father noted], and the sand beaches are few and far between. . . . There is now no question that this Warm Springs' pool does my legs more good than anything else. Last autumn I added at least 10 pounds to the weight I could put on my knees, and already this spring I have . . . gained another 10 pounds.

Lawrence was agreeable, but before the *Larooco* was put out of commission Father took her out once more in 1926 on her final cruise. Mother began this cruise with him on February 2, and returned to the East on February 12. Three days later Father's prize guests arrived—Sir Oswald Mosley and his wife of that time, the beautiful former Lady Cynthia Curzon, daughter of Lord Curzon, ex-Viceroy of India. Mosley at that time was a Member of Parliament : he was not to become the leader of the British blackshirts until later. Father found the Mosleys fascinating, and when they left him after a four-day stay he noted in his log : " The Mosleys are a delightful couple & we shall miss them much." As an historical curiosity, it is worth noting that one of the routine entries in Father's log is written by Mosley, whose later aims Father did so much to smash in World War II.[1]

Most of the broad humour was gone from Father's entries by 1926, and already he was receiving business callers to discuss his plans for buying Warm Springs and making it into a health resort. There was to be one more family interlude on the *Larooco*, however—Elliott's visit during March. In the March 18 log entry Father wrote that he and Elliott had a swim in a spot known as the " Bath Tub," and that Bunny's " ' tan ' came off under the application of soap ! " Later, on a fishing expedition, Elliott created considerable excitement by hooking an enormous jewfish which required the combined efforts of the captain and two other hands to land. It was more than seven feet long and weighed close to five hundred pounds. Father also noted—rather unkindly, I thought—that " Elliott beat Jimmy's record by retaining his insides."

The *Larooco*'s last cruise ended on March 25, 1926. She was laid up at Fort Lauderdale, but efforts to sell her were unsuccessful. In September of that year a violent hurricane hit the area and carried the old tub four miles inland, where she settled in a pine forest, a mile from the nearest water. Father conceived the idea of selling her as a hunting lodge, but that didn't work either. In 1927 the " old *Laroo* " was sold for scrap. Always sentimental about sailing vessels of any kind, Father inscribed her epitaph in the last paragraph of the log : " So ended a good old

[1] A query was addressed to Sir Oswald Mosley in London, asking if he could explain the significance of a photograph from *Larooco* days which it was intended to publish. In his response he wrote : " I have very happy recollections of the voyage with Mr. Roosevelt [*sic*] on his house-boat off Florida. He was a very kind host and we had a very pleasant time. He wrote to us on occasions in subsequent years. But ultimately as you know our political paths diverged very considerably. Those were happy and peaceful days which I recall with pleasure."

craft with a personality. On the whole it was an end to be preferred to that of gasoline barge or lumber lighter."

Though the houseboat interval did not do much for Father physically, it proved a valuable catharsis. He learned that, while frivolity and aimlessness were enjoyable in small doses, he could not take the life of a dilettante as a steady diet. Every now and then he would absent himself from the social routine aboard the houseboat and would go off by himself to ponder the future, or to start some serious writings, none of which he ever finished.

At the end of three winters he had had enough. He was ready to get back to the world of important affairs.

" Please Send Me What You Can . . ."

During this period of Father's long absences in the south family problems—mostly on Mother's head—went right on, particularly in regard to our always strained budget. In February 1924 I wrote Mother from Groton : " Please write Father that he still owes me $202. I don't know his address so I can't."

But Mother had her own financial worries. On February 24, 1924, she was writing Father in Florida : " I find after paying all the household bills up to date & cash for food . . . I have $151.46 which I can put in my account & deduct from your Xmas check to me. . . . You owe still on Xmas, weddings, etc . . . $398.54. . . . Please send me what you can . . . but in any case be sure to send me the house $1,000 so I will *get* it on the 1st. There, that is all the disagreeable part over ! "

The following month Father cut the household budget by $300 on the theory that his absence meant smaller food bills and one less servant. Mother philosophically wrote him : " Of course I haven't $80 to pay . . . [the servant] or you two to feed, but you hardly eat $220 worth of food & the regular expenses go on the same as ever. . . . I just pray I will have enough with your $700 & my $300 this month ! "

At one point cash was so low that Father had to sell off some of his beloved marine and naval prints to raise a thousand dollars.

In April 1925, when he was at Warm Springs after completing a cruise on the *Larooco*, there was an exchange of unusually lengthy letters between Pa and me, covering a variety of matters. Among other things, I told him that, since he had become national director of the fund to raise ten million dollars for the Cathedral of St John the Divine in New York City, I wanted to contribute some of my War Savings stamps. I advised him that my team had lost a " close " debate with Middlesex. We took the affirmative side of the subject, " Resolved, that the Airplane has Supplanted the Battleship as Our First Line of Defense." Father commiserated with me on our defeat, but at the same time, as an old Navy man, he was writing a column for the *Macon Daily* (Georgia) *Telegraph*, taking a more or less opposing view on the same subject. I also asked Father if he would get me tickets to a Harvard boat race and take it out of my allowance : he replied that he already had done so and that " you owe me nothing for them ; they are on me ! "

" I am staying on until May 14th," he added. " The legs have really improved a lot. There is no question that this place does more good than all the rest of the exercising etc. put together."

All of us wrote Father frequently during this period. The letters were not always complimentary. In February 1925 our little brother Johnny sent Father a complaint, complete with unflattering caricature, which is herewith reproduced :

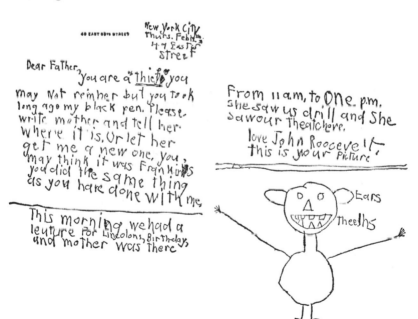

The family scattered during the summer of 1925. Father was at Hyde Park, supervising the building of a swimming-pool and Mother's cottage at Val-Kill ; Anna was spending the summer at the State Agricultural Experimental Station at Geneva, New York, prior to enrolling in Cornell University for further agricultural studies that fall ; Elliott and I went to a ranch in Wyoming, and Mother took Franklin, Jr., and Johnny back to Campobello for their first visit there since Father was stricken with polio. "Everyone . . . asked after you," Mother wrote him from Campobello.

> I adored being here & the quiet is heavenly but even though I know you couldn't enjoy it I can't help wishing all the time you could be here. If you & the boys have a schooner next summer you might cruise up & just stay on the boat & be here for a little while.

On the family front, it was Sis for a change whose personal problems were foremost on Mother's mind. "Just now I am more worried about Anna than anyone," she wrote Father. " I do hope at Cornell at least her name will mean little and she'll get some of the foolishness out of her." In his next letter to Sis, Father, in mock seriousness, lectured her : " By Golly, if I have to call you up next Saturday for failure to hear a line I will jolly well reverse the charges ! " Sis apparently reacted in good style, for Mother, in her next letter to Pa, said : " I am so pleased at her letter to you. She has evidently not resented whatever you wrote her the way she did my letters and I'd rather have it that way for then you can be sure she'll take your advice on anything important."

The Western trip which Elliott and I took was to a ranch near Dubois, Wyoming, owned by Charles and Dorothy Moore, who were friends of Mother's. Elliott reminds me that I got awfully sore at him on one stage of the trip, which was by bus across the desert, when he managed, in a manner which I shall refrain from describing, to get cactus spines in his rump. I was utterly humiliated at having such a tenderfoot for a brother !

We spent the Fourth of July watching a parade and rodeo in Lander, Wyoming, a town which I described in a letter to Father and Mother as " very quaint and simply crammed with Indians . . . and Cowboys, to say nothing of a lot of dude Easterners like ourselves." The cowboy in Elliott bubbled to the surface, and he advised Pa :

> Father, I think that I will get a pair of cowboy boots . . . they say you can use them forever. They will cost about $16 or $18. . . . It's lucky we bought those chaps as everyone has them and wears them. . . . P.S. If I do get the cowboy boots I won't have much more than $10 left.

Father apparently was unmoved by Elliott's financial distress, and I had to come to my brother's aid. When we both were back at Groton that fall I wrote Mother :

> Do you remember that Elliott lost a watch belonging to a boy out west ? He didnt ever do anything about it so two weeks ago I wrote him a check for twenty-five dollars and told him to send it to the boy with apologies. As I also lent him twelve dollars to buy his " chapps " with out West he now owes me some thirty-seven dollars. What had I better do about ever getting repaid as that is quite a sum for me ? Dont tell him anything about my writing you, as he might be hurt and do something crazy in order to pay it back.

Despite her inherent softness for Elliott, Mother handled this situation firmly. To Father, who had gone south again, she reported :

> I . . . sent . . . [James] $37 but told him Elliott must pay him every month & he refund to me. I think you should start Elliott on a $100 a year allowance . . . payable quarterly. . . . He has no idea of money & this seems to me the only way to give it to him. Tell him he must pay all presents, car fares, trips (outside of school & summer or with us & planned by you) & make him keep an account for you. I've only been giving him $1 a month & it isn't enough to give him a sense of values.

As I am trying to make this a candid chronicle, I must confess that, just as the cowboy streak in Elliott emerged, the city boy in me remained rampant, even in the wilds of Wyoming. A letter from Mrs Moore to Mother reports : " Jim . . . [is] charming, the winner of all the girls' hearts at the Ranch ! "

Before the summer was over the city boy in me came out again, and, as I wrote Mother : " We went up to the Hotel to dine. . . . I met a boy and two girls I knew there and we had a pretty good time." I added that it felt odd " getting back into a blue suit and white shirt but it was rather a nice change." Mother promptly wrote Father : " What's he doing with a blue suit, dining in hotels, well, I suppose it is his age like Anna's."

As our vacation drew to an end Father wrote us, offering to be helpful about arranging our train and hotel accommodations for the trip home. " It is perfectly grand that you are getting so much out of the trip," he wrote. " I have an awful feeling that neither of you took trout rods and that you are needing them in the Yellowstone country." Of his own activities he added :

> I am having a very busy summer . . . lots of work at both offices [he had returned to his law practice and his position with Fidelity and Deposit Company] and I hope some of it will be profitable. The swimming pool is done and the foundation for the cottage is poured.

The strain Mother was feeling in attempting to control her children of assorted ages is indicated again in another letter to Father that fall, pertaining to Franklin, Jr., and Johnny. She wrote : " The chicks seem to be beginning to realize that Mlle. has to be obeyed, which is a great relief to me as I have had to be very severe & there have been many tears ! " (She also let him know in the same letter that he had not put the ten-cent special delivery stamp on his last special-delivery letter to her !)

Around this period of his convalescence Father, when he was at Hyde Park, picked up the hobby of making model racing sailboats. He and Louis Howe began competing with each other, and Father came up with some radical designs. We would have regattas on the Hudson, and Father, as keen as any youngster about the sport, would go out on the river in a rowboat to watch the progress of his entry. The prize was the Krum Elbow cup, and it was one of Louis Howe's proudest moments when he captured the cup one year. Father would allow us to race his older boats, but he held back his most advanced models for himself.

Poor Elliott was the victim of another activity dreamed up by Father and Louis Howe. Louis had a son named Hartley, about a year younger than Elliott. Hartley was a perfectly nice chap, but Elliott, who liked to pick his own companions, didn't get along with him. The two fathers, however, conceived the idea that it would be perfectly grand—educational, too—for Elliott and Hartley to become real pals and to take up together the hobby of making lead soldiers.

Elliott, in his own words, " didn't give a damn about lead soldiers," but Pa and Louis thought it was a fascinating pursuit. As Granny's hostility towards Louis extended to all Howes, Hartley couldn't come to visit us at Hyde Park, so Elliott every now and then had to go to Hartley's house and spend a couple of days pouring molten lead into moulds and painting the little military figures that emerged. Even to-day Elliott says with real feeling, " Oh, how I hated lead soldiers ! It was one of the few things he made me do that I really held against Pa."

11

My Canadian Ordeal;
Other Family Problems

IN the summer of 1926 Father, for the first and only time in his life, took a major, positive, forceful action to guide and prepare me for the sort of rude world in which I eventually would have to live. To me it was so positive that I felt as if I were being shanghaied !

By this time Father had lived with polio long enough to have a pretty good idea of his own situation, and he felt it was time to give more personal attention to his children's problems. As I, the eldest son, about to embark on my college career that fall, was going to be the first fledgling to leave the gold-plated, feather-bedded nest, Pa decided he should do something about teaching me to fly.

Accordingly, some time early in the year Father hinted to me that he was going to get me a job that summer—a tough one. He gave me no details, and I began to churn inside with anxiety. Long before my graduation from Groton I was writing him : " I'm not quite straight yet on the job. . . . Could you drop a line about it when I begin, where it is, the work etc some time. It's rather important as I must arrange about . . . other plans soon."

Thus prodded, Father wrote a business friend of his, who, in turn, arranged for me to get a job with a Canadian paper-mill operated by the Metabetchouan Sulphite and Power Company. It was in the wilds of Quebec near a primitive village called Desbiens. Pa paved the way for me by having word sent ahead that " Franklin Roosevelt would certainly want his son to rough it [and] would not want him treated in any other way [than] any of the laborers." None of the lumberjacks in Desbiens, of course, had the faintest idea who Franklin Roosevelt was, and, if they had, they could not have cared less.

A few days after the job was set up for me Father wrote me from Warm Springs that " the inclosed [*sic*] from the Canadian Paper Company sounds mighty interesting." So, trustingly, with the ink hardly dry on my Groton sheepskin, I set out in my best Eastern clothes for Desbiens. I was met at the company depot by the pulp-mill foreman. He took a look at my city clothes and sent me to the commissary to draw some overalls and work shoes. Then I was routed to the bunkhouse to meet my future colleagues. I noticed (*a*) that I was the only youngster in the lot, and (*b*) that no one seemed very happy to see me. I later found out why : they all thought I was a company spy.

The job was as rugged as Pa had promised. We were up at 5 A..M, had breakfast at 5.30, and were on the job at 6 o'clock. There was an hour out for lunch, then we went back to work until 6 P.M. The pay was eighteen cents per hour and keep.

My first job was at the log-sorting pond. With a lumberman's cant hook I separated the logs which were marked for our mill, and let the other pass down the river. Gradually I worked in every phase of the pulp-making operation.

In the evenings there was nothing to do in camp except to play cards, sit around singing loggers' songs, or do a little whisky-drinking. For the first time in my young life the lack of recreation didn't bother me, for, until I toughened up, I was too dog-tired to do anything after dinner except flop down on my bunk and fall asleep. Not even the snores of my thirty-nine room mates in the bunkhouse bothered me.

The low point of my summer was when an acid line exploded near me, filling the pulp-mill with noxious fumes that left me sick for days. It was like being gassed.

The summer was a rough experience for me—the roughest I ever experienced until years later when I became a combat Marine officer in the Pacific. I have since come to realize, however, that it was a valuable one, though I would not admit it at the time. I remember staying mad at Father almost every moment of the summer, and, to the best of my recollection, I wrote no letters at all to either of my parents. The only good thing about the summer, so far as I was concerned, was that there was so little to do in the way of recreation that I came home with enough money saved up to buy an automobile.

On being liberated from Desbiens I headed straight for Granny and Campobello for a wonderful, luxurious let-down. Granny made much over me, as she never had approved of sending me up to that awful place. When I was finally reunited with Pa before entering Harvard that fall my " mad " disappeared as soon as I saw him. I was too proud to tell him how much I had disliked it. Father must have suspected, however, how unhappy I had been, for he never attempted to repeat the experiment with me. He never duplicated it with any of the other boys either, although Elliott, Franklin, Jr., and John each had summer-work experiences on his own.

Those Eternal Family Complications !

Anna's wedding to Curtis Dall, at which I served as an usher, was the big event in the spring of 1926. Again, just before the wedding, Father was away and Mother was left to cope with all the arrangements. As the date drew near she sent him a reminder : " Aren't you going to have a new suit for the wedding ? If you want anything from England you'll have to cable ! "

As a new bride, Anna wrote Father a letter which reveals how remarkably free and close she—and the same was true of all of us—felt to him. Relating how she and her husband had dropped in unexpectedly to spend the night at our New York town house " without any pajamas or underclothes," Sis told him :

> So I stole (borrowed !) your best pair of pajamas from one drawer, and a pair of B.V.D.'s from another ! The pajamas were a good fit,—but Heaven help the B.V.D.'s ! They wouldn't stay on so I spent a good half hour tying him into them with tape !

In the fall of 1926 it was evident once again that the strain of living for long periods apart from Father, managing the family problems, and coping with her mother-in-law was telling on Mother. In a rare admission of indecision she wrote Father :

> I'm glad you enjoyed your holiday dear, & I wish we did not lead such a hectic life a little prolonged quiet might bring us all

together & yet it might do just the opposite ! I really don't know what I want or think about anything anymore !

With Father at Warm Springs in the spring of 1927, spending much time—and money—on developing the resort, Mother, back in New York, continued to be plagued by financial problems. In various letters she disclosed that she was having difficulty paying our long-suffering chauffeur, William ; that the garage had sent Father a bill and " asked you please to pay it " ; that Elliott was pining for a car to drive out West that summer ; and that I was agitating to go abroad. I was sweet on an English girl named Lucy Archer-Shee, whose parents had been Dutchess County and Campobello friends and neighbours of ours, and I was yearning to get over to England to see her. Apparently, though I was just a college freshman, I had marriage on the brain, for Mother wrote :

Mama has not offered to finance Jimmy as far as I know for his trip. . . . I think he just took it for granted that he'd cost you $600 in summer & you'd be willing to give it to him. . . . I told him he should have written you before making definite plans & I hope even if you send him you'll make this point clear ! He only plans to bicycle in England and . . . see as much as possible of Lucy Archer-Shee but of course she or he may have changed a number of times before he is earning $5,000 a yr. which is the minimum I told him he could marry on much to his dismay !

I made the trip, with the aid of an advance from Father, but nothing came of the romance.

That summer Elliott drove the family car to Maine instead of out West, and Pa composed this typical fatherly letter of warning about his driving :

Dear Bunny—

Sorry not to see you before you go. Do please wire us when you get safely to Maine & also when to expect you back. Do you realise that your license is only good for driving on my business & that no police officer would construe this trip as such !

Be *very* careful—if you smashed up I could not collect my insurance aside from any question of injury to you !

Affectionately,
Pa

The year 1928 would have been an easier one financially for the family except that Father was putting so much of his own money into development of Warm Springs. His half-brother, " Uncle Rosy," had died the previous year, leaving Father about a hundred thousand dollars in securities, and his late father's estate was in excellent shape, although that money was controlled by Granny.

Nevertheless cash remained short, and, in March 1928 Mother, discussing the furnishing of Father's new cottage at Warm Springs, was writing wistfully : " If Mama doesn't give you a sofa I may if my cash holds out which is always a question ! " In April she wrote : " *Please* send me my checks. I've advanced so much money I am now penniless & can't provide food or pay William [the chauffeur] next week." Mother was beginning to become a breadwinner on her own, for in the same letter she reported :

> I've just got another article to do for *McCall's* for $500 & only 2500 words . . . it . . . is to deal with the achievements of women in politics. . . . I suppose James will tell me he " wouldn't write for such a magazine " as he did about the *Red Book* but I am glad of the chance !

Throughout his convalescent period Father exerted rather urgent, almost desperate, efforts to make money quickly by various business enterprises and promotions. A few made money ; others were disastrous. He had formed a new law partnership with Basil O'Connor, which yielded him some income, and he also retained his connexion with the Fidelity and Deposit Company. He had played the stock market earlier, but had retreated in 1923 because he was apprehensive of a slump. He speculated in German marks ; he was active in various banking and promotion schemes, in a Western oil wild-catting venture, in shipping, in an automatic vending machine company, and—with Henry Morgenthau, Jr.—in a quarter-in-the-slot automatic picture-taking machine. Some of his wilder gambles included promotion of dirigibles, and a scheme, into which he was wheedled by a spell-binding promoter named Arthur Homer, to corner the lobster market. The latter cost him some $26,000.

The Summer When Bunny Got " Lost "

Although I was in Europe again in 1928, I still remember that summer as the time in which my brother Elliott got himself " lost " out West, and Father, then under terrific pressure to decide whether to run or not to run for Governor of New York, had to take steps to have him found.

Bunny, then seventeen years old, was in one of his unhappy moods. Father arranged for him to go to Houston, Texas, where he served as Father's page at the Democratic convention which nominated Al Smith for President. From there he was to proceed to the White Grass Ranch in Wyoming.

What happened after Bunny left Father in Houston was a comedy of errors, though it was not particularly funny at the time. Two months went by in which Father and Mother did not receive a single line from him. " He was lost—we could not find him," Mother said recently in refreshing my memory on the story.

At last Mother, who had been enduring it in her customary silent, stoic fashion, could stand it no longer.

" I went to Franklin," she related, " and said : ' Franklin, we must do something about finding this boy.'

" ' Oh,' he said, ' do you think so ? '

" ' Yes,' I told him, ' I think so.' "

So Father sent a discreet inquiry to the New York State Police, and Elliott finally was tracked down, not at the place where he was supposed to be, but at the Bar BC Ranch near Moose, Wyoming.

Some time later there arrived from Elliott an eleven-page letter relating his summer's adventures. " I've been rather awful so far but I'll attempt to make it up just a bit . . ." he began. " Well here is the story."

After the convention adjourned Bunny departed by train for Phoenix, Arizona, where he was " to catch the aeroplane over Grand Canyon for a connection with the train for Salt Lake City." The arrangements for the plane trip had been made—or presumably had been made—by Mother's brother, G. Hall Roosevelt, who had some sort of connexion with the one-plane aviation outfit with which Elliott was supposed to fly, and Father had given Elliott seventy dollars for his fare. But when Elliott

arrived no one knew anything about him or the supposed arrangements. There wasn't even any plane.

Bunny wandered around Arizona for a while, finally caught up
with Uncle Hall's aviator friend somewhere, and was told it
would cost him not $70, but $240, to fly to Salt Lake City.

> If I didn't go by aeroplane [Bunny wrote] the only way I could get
> to Salt Lake City would be to go back to Phoenix and then take the
> train to Los Angeles and then to Salt Lake. As this was not in any
> way cheaper I went by the first way [plane] the next morning and
> if Father's mad about the money I'm sorry.

Elliott finally arrived in Victor, Idaho, where he was to have
been met by a cowboy friend called Freddie, who was supposed
to have run the White Grass Ranch that summer. " On arrival
at the doohinky little station," Bunny related, " I found not a
soul to meet me." So he piled into a convenient truck, which
happened to belong to the Bar BC Ranch, and went on out there.
At the Bar BC the ranch boss knew the missing Freddie. He
was able to tell Elliott that Freddie wasn't taking that job at the
White Grass Ranch, where Father and Mother thought Elliott
was going to be ; instead he was going to run a junior " dude "
outfit for the Bar BC, which, unfortunately, wasn't quite built
yet. " I was cordially invited," related Elliott, " to stay . . . [at
the Bar BC] for a few days."

Finally, Elliott located Freddie. " I can tell you I was a bit
tired and mad," he said. But he decided to stick around, instead
of proceeding to the White Grass Ranch, where letters to him
from Pa and Mother were piling up.

His letter continued :

> I got a job tutoring a boy in algebra for two dollar [sic] and fifty
> cents an hour which may help a little toward paying off all the money
> I had to spend on that trip to get here. You needn't try offer [sic]
> to pay for any of it either as I realize that I've been rotten about not
> writing and you giving me the trip and everything. Oh well I guess
> it was just because I was so lazy and always thought I had something
> more importent [sic] to do.
>
> Well pretty soon part of the ranch went on a pack trip and I
> waited to go on the second one when I got an infected leg . . . and
> couldn't go. It went up to my groin from my foot and then I got
> an absess [sic] on my rear end from it and that has just started to

get well. Aside from such little things as that though I have had a carefree summer and I can't say how swell I think you were to give it to me. . . .

Do you think I could have a little money to come home on as Father never did pay me the seven hundred to the bank that he owes me and I'm afraid I haven't a cent. I've managed to last out by selling one by one my articles of clothing so I'd have some money on hand. . . .

I hope you really will forgive me for no [sic] writing before. Of course I suppose you told everybody how terrible I was and that I hadn't written so I suppose there is no use in asking you to keep my defects and faults quiet, but I do hate to have . . . that sort of thing told to people whom it doesn't concern.

Lots of love
Elliott

Eventually Bunny got home. He expected to catch the devil ; instead he .was received like the Prodigal Son. Pa's annoyance had simmered down, and he even began chuckling over the " humorous " side of Elliott's misadventures. That was typical of Pa : he never could stay angry at any of us for very long.

12

Father's Warm Springs

DURING the spring holiday in 1925, after our cruise on the *Larooco*, I made my first visit with Father to the run-down, old-fashioned resort at Warm Springs, Georgia, which had captured his enthusiasm. On returning to Groton I wrote him :

" DEAR FATHER : Warm Springs certainly is a peachy place and the water simply wonderful. . . . I can't tell you how much fun I had with you." With the full nobility of my seventeen years, I added : " Now I can go back to School really rested and well and not a danced-out creature like most of my other friends."

Warm Springs was a very special, very intimate part of Father's life. Anna, my brothers, and I visited him there as often as possible, and we loved it, for we always enjoyed being anywhere with Pa. But Warm Springs really is his story, not ours, for it was Father's personal bailiwick.

Mother, strangely enough, has family ties with Warm Springs. Up until a few months before October 1924, when Father first went there, part of the present village of Warm Springs had been known as Bullochville, after the Bulloch family, to which Mother is related. Her kinswoman, Miss Minnie Bulloch, as this is written, still operates a bonafide dry goods and " notions " emporium in Warm Springs, where a lady can find herself a pair of high button shoes or a gingham sun-bonnet. During the Civil War Mother's " Uncle Jimmy " and " Uncle Irvine " Bulloch were rabid Confederate blockade-runners. In fact, they not only ran the blockade, but preyed on Yankee shipping to the extent that the United States Government regarded them as "pirates" and refused after the war to grant them amnesty, whereupon the Bulloch brothers fled to England. Mother remembers seeing Uncle Jimmy when she was a little girl ; he had returned to the United States for a visit under an assumed name.

Father, as might have been expected, took great pleasure in reminding Mother about her Confederate "pirate uncles," just as he doted on teasing Granny about the lurid characters among our Delano and Roosevelt forebears.

Despite Uncle Jimmy, Uncle Irvine, and Miss Minnie, Mother, in the early days when Father was developing Warm Springs, never felt at home in the town. The pattern of life in the small Southern village was alien to her. In February 1928, when Mother was faced with the necessity of deciding whether she would take on extra work as associate principal of the Todhunter School in New York City or spend more time in the South with Father, she wrote him frankly : " I ought to plan to be freer . . . yet . . . as you know I'm not keen to get into W.S. [Warm Springs] life at all as one would have to do if one stayed long or often. It is very hard to decide, so please write me at once how you feel." Their joint decision was that Mother would pursue her activities in the East, and Father would spend as much time as he could in Warm Springs, striving towards the physical recovery he wanted so desperately to achieve.

Often I have heard Mother comment on how out of place she felt in Father's Georgia domain. All of us have howled with glee at Mother's dead pan description of how, on her sporadic visits to Warm Springs, she would unhappily accompany Father when he drove to town to buy what he called " chickens on the hoof." Pa would have the live chickens dumped into his car, and would take them to the backyard of his cottage, where they would roam, squawking and clucking, until Daisy Bonner, the cook, who was an institution in Pa's kitchen, needed one for the stewpot or frying-pan. Then Daisy would capture one of the chickens and wring its neck—a process which my tender-hearted Mother always found highly distasteful.

At Warm Springs Father was many personalities. He first came there as the polio victim in search of recovery ; people meeting him for the first time were prepared to pity the big, strong figure, cut down in his prime by the crippling disease, but were completely diverted from such sentiments by the irrepressible optimism which bubbled from him like the warming waters of the springs in which he sought to swim to health. In the pool of the rococo Meriwether Inn Father became not just a " polio," but " Doctor " Roosevelt, a persuasive, confidence-inspiring figure, who was delighted to teach other victims how to do the restorative exercises he had painstakingly learned, including some he had developed on his own. At the same time, an aura of glamour attached itself to him—wasn't he that " rich " Eastern fellow who was somebody important in politics and whose uncle or father or something had been President of the United States a while back ? The Warm Springs folks were pretty certain he was going to do something about reviving their decrepit inn, and that he would accomplish great things for their town.

And Father did do something. He put a great deal of his own money—more, in fact, than he could afford—into acquiring the property, at a stiff price, from his wealthy New York banker friend, George Foster Peabody, who held an option on the place. At one time Father had more than $200,000 of his funds loaned to the Georgia Warm Springs Foundation. This original loan was gradually repaid by the Foundation, part of it after his death, but Father's own outright contributions and family gifts amounted to nearly $55,000—not counting substantial grants made by others because of Father's personal interest in the foundation.

So in Warm Springs Father became a hotel-keeper, then a health-clinic operator. For a while he was a newspaper column-ist, taking over the spot in the Macon *Daily Telegraph* ordinarily filled by his ailing newspaperman friend Tom Loyless, who was lessee-manager of the inn. He was also a farmer, buying several thousands of acres of land, part of which he put into cattle and crops.

And he was a friend and good neighbour to the community. It was at Warm Springs that Father first had Tom Bradshaw, the local blacksmith, rig up an old Model-T Ford—later followed by other makes and models—with ropes and pulleys, so he could drive it. Pa in his hand-driven Tin Lizzie became a familiar sight. That unorthodox vehicle became his substitute for a horse. (Pa actually rode horseback a few times after polio, but gave it up because he could not use his legs to control his mount.) In his flivver he raced around the countryside, visiting with every one he knew and introducing himself to those he didn't know. Occasionally he even poked into that locally hallowed region known as " the Cove," where—in those days, at least—certain spirituous beverages were said to have been obtainable. I have talked with old-timers, who swear they have seen Pa sample some of these beverages, drinking right out of a fruit jar along with every one else.

One of Father's earliest letters mentioning the possibility that he might invest in the Warm Springs property was written to Granny as he was finishing up the final cruise of the *Larooco* in March 1926. " I had a nice visit from Chas. Peabody [George Foster Peabody's brother] & it looks as if I had bought Warm Springs," he said. " If so I want you to take a great interest in it, for I feel you can help me with many suggestions & the place properly run will not only do a great deal of good but will prove *financially* successful." In a letter the following month Mother was cautioning him : " It was good to hear about you from Louis [Howe] and you seem to be moving along in Warm Springs. Don't let yourself in for too much money and don't make Mama put in much for if she lost it she'd never get over it ! " Later Granny endowed a cottage, which was her sole gift of any consequence to the foundation.

Father's cottage, which in later years became the " Little White House, was built on a spot personally selected by Pa and known locally as " Gambler's Den." The area's leading crap-shooters used to gather in this particular wooded spot ; this was a bit of lore that Father particularly relished, and he often joked about the appropriateness of the name in relation to the eventual owner of the site—*i.e.*, himself.

Even before he built his own place Father stayed in rented cottages rather than at the ramshackle inn, which was a fire-trap of the worst order. He utilized the inn's old swimming-pool, however, and an Atlanta newspaper reporter, sensing a human-interest story, came to Warm Springs to interview him. The result was an article relating how the former Vice-Presidential candidate was " swimming back to health " at the obscure little spa, and how the waters warmed by Nature seemed to be effecting an improvement. The article was picked up and reprinted widely throughout the country. Soon other polio sufferers, in search of a cure, were flocking to Warm Springs.

The inn in those days was still patronized—in a desultory fashion—by persons not afflicted with polio. Their " sensibilities " were offended by the sight of the " polios " and their awkward struggles to hobble about on crutches ; in their ignorance, they especially objected to swimming in the same pool or eating in the same dining-room with the " cripples," lest they somehow contract the disease. No polio sufferer, of course, ever came to Warm Springs until the communicable period was long past.

I remember how Father would describe his cold anger over this intolerant attitude. His reaction was to buy the place—even though he could ill afford it—and make it into a haven where " polios " such as himself would not be regarded as pariahs, but would be given non-discriminatory treatment. After Father made it possible for the " polios " to move in as " first-class citizens " the " able bodies," as polio victims sometimes call non-afflicted persons, gradually disappeared entirely as patrons.

In his development of the Foundation Father was aided enormously by two of his closest associates and friends, Louis Howe and Basil O'Connor, his new law partner. " Doc " O'Connor, a tough-minded, professedly unsentimental Irishman, came into the picture protestingly at first, complaining about the time and effort that would be " wasted." His devotion to the cause grew to rival Father's, and now he is the much-honoured president and treasurer of both the Georgia Warm Springs Foundation and the National Foundation.

The Little White House to-day is maintained as a public memorial to Father, administered by the Franklin D. Roosevelt Warm Springs Memorial Commission, an autonomous agency of the State of Georgia. The commission's chairman and guiding spirit, Charles F. Palmer, has seen to it that, so far as is possible, the cottage is kept just as it was when Father died there on April 12, 1945. The most frequently voiced comment from visitors is one of amazement at how " simply " Father lived. It is an unpretentious, pine-panelled cottage, plainly furnished and crammed with the odds and ends of memorabilia with which Father invariably surrounded himself.

Visitors often exclaim over an exhibit of table utensils which Father used at the cottage : it is genuine dime-store " silver."

I was always intrigued by the old-fashioned (non-electric) icebox which Father insisted on using at the cottage : it is still there. I can hear him say, " A long, tall, cool drink always tastes better with *real* ice." Pa was also partial to the old-fashioned ice-cream freezers—the kind with a crank that you turned by hand ; many times he told all of us that the only really decent ice-cream was the kind made in such a freezer.

In setting up the national—now international—centre for the treatment of polio Father had a definite dream of the spirit and environment with which he wanted Warm Springs inculcated. " Let's make it the *best* medical institution of its kind in the world, but as much *un*like a hospital as is possible," he said.

From innuendoes Father dropped from time to time I know that, even after he took over Warm Springs, he still was irked by the intolerant and uninformed attitude of some " able bodies " towards " polios." This made him even more determined to create an *esprit* at Warm Springs, which would brook no condescension, no mawkish pity. If there was anything infectious at Warm Springs it was the virus of insouciance and indomitability spread by " Doctor " Roosevelt. Following his example, the " polios " actually began poking the broadest sort of fun at themselves. Sometimes, conscious of my own healthy legs, I found it hard to laugh at the sort of jokes they made. I remember once trying to grin, but suddenly getting choked up, when Father told me of a hopelessly crippled youngster who spotted some " able bodies " staring at him in his wheel-chair. In embarrassment they turned to walk away, but he sang out to them, " Stick around ! They're going to feed us after a while."

I am told by L. Duncan Cannon, business administrator of the Foundation, that Father himself coined the name for those irrepressible, strong-limbed characters who roll the Warm Springs patients through the corridors and around the grounds in their wheel-chairs. He called them " push boys," and the name has stuck.

On the sweeping lawn at the foundation is an ornamental fountain which visitors sometimes mistake for the springs. Until Father—with secret reluctance !—had a halt called to the little game the off-duty push boys would loll near the fountain in wheel-chairs, posing as " polios." Wistfully, they would remark —loudly enough to be heard by visitors—how " wonderful " it would be if only they could raise enough money to pay for the miraculous bath in that fountain that would restore them to health. Sometimes a good actor could collect as much as sixteen dollars in an afternoon from gullible visitors.

One day a couple of push boys went too far. One represented himself to visitors as a " cured polio," and attributed it all to a dip in the fountain. The other boy moaned how desperate he was to start his treatments and be cured. " Well, why don't you start right now ? " said the " cured " boy, picking him up and throwing him in. The immersed lad floundered around for a while, then jumped out, shouting, " I'm cured, I'm cured ! " and went leaping all over the lawn. It was so startling that some of the spectators almost fainted.

News of this incident—as well as a report on the collections by the push boys—reached Father. When he was able to stop laughing over the ridiculousness of it he passed along a " suggestion " that put an end to such games. He wanted things to be relaxed at Warm Springs—but not that relaxed.

Father confined his own pranks to jokes played on his physical therapists and the Secret Service men who guarded him after he became President. He had a special trick he loved to play on a therapist named Helen Lauer, an earnest, bespectacled young woman with unusually long hair. There was an exercise in which Father would stretch out on a treatment table in the spring-fed pool with his legs hanging in the water. While Miss Lauer pulled down on his legs, Father would pull in the opposite direction. Whenever anyone in the know saw Father wink they knew what was coming : he would suddenly relax the pressure he was putting on his legs, and the therapist, thrown off balance, would plunge under the water like an anchor whose rope had been cut. Pa's laugh could be heard throughout the pool area as poor Miss Lauer came up spluttering, her hair streaming in wet strings down her neck and her glasses hanging off one ear.

After he became President Father pulled another stunt one time that almost gave the S.S. men heart-failure. The swimming facilities had been enlarged, and there were now three pools, side by side, with connecting channels. One day Gus Gennerich and another agent took their eyes off Pa for a few seconds. He instantly ducked under the water—he was a tremendously powerful swimmer—and swam through the channels, coming up for air momentarily only a couple of times. Gus couldn't find him, and was just about to jump fully clothed into the water and start grappling for him when Pa came up in the pool at the far end, a good 180 feet away.

It was standard operating procedure for Father, both at Warm Springs and Hyde Park, to get into his hand-operated automobile and whisk off on to wooded trails where the Secret Service detail, in its huge, armoured limousine, could not follow. At both places Father knew all sort of little nooks—quarries and clumps of woods—where he could pull off the road and watch the Secret Service men come racing past, frantically looking for him ; he loved to do this, particularly if he had an amiable companion with him. When he was ready to reappear he would emerge from his hiding-place and drive home leisurely—or as leisurely as Pa ever drove. The late Colonel E. W. Starling, then head of the White House Secret Service detail, would come simmering over to his car, and Pa would inquire blandly, " Is anything wrong ? " The harassed colonel finally added a little car to the S.S. fleet, so his men could pursue Pa on the back roads.

On another occasion Father thought up some convincing excuse to get Gus Gennerich to climb a ladder to the roof of one of Pa's farm buildings. Then he had a hired man remove the ladder, leaving Gus stranded while Father waved cheerily and drove off to visit in the village.

Father's social contacts at Warm Springs were what one might call all-inclusive. He made friends with every one—the " polios," the villagers, the farmers, a few moonshiners, the wealthy Easterners who began coming to the health resort after Father publicized it, and the well-to-do folk of the Warm Springs area.

One of Father's best friends among the " polios " was Paul Rogers, a Milwaukee engineer, who as a young man was stricken with polio and, like Father, was left with loss of mobility in his legs. He read about Father's " discovery " of Warm Springs, and was one of the first of the " polios " to arrive there.

Father, Rogers, and a few other friends—both " polios " and

" able bodies "—had a regular poker-game which floated from
cottage to cottage. If I was in Warm Springs I would tag along.
I always have regretted that I was not present at Paul's cottage
on the night during Father's first term as President when the
episode occurred which I always think of as " F.D.R. and his
Famous Disappearing Act." I have heard Pa and others who
witnessed it describe it many times.

Some seven or more players were gathered around a dining-
room table, with Pa sitting in a spindly-legged antique chair.
There was an interesting pot on the table, and Pa moved to hitch
himself forward.

Suddenly he began sinking—slowly, inch by inch, like a drowning character in a slow-motion movie. Finally he got down to
the level of his cigarette-holder, and all the others could see
was the top of his head. As Rogers says, it was so startling and
" looked so damned ridiculous " that for a moment or two no
one could figure out what had happened, and no one went to
Pa's aid. What had happened was that the chair-legs gave way
and, as the chair gradually collapsed, Pa went down with it.

Finally, a couple of the " able bodies " in the game came to
and helped him up. At first Pa was as startled as anybody, but
almost immediately he let out his loud laugh, and the game went
on.

Springboard Back to Politics

Warm Springs was the springboard for Father's return to
public life. Many of the conferences leading both to his race
for the Governorship in 1928 and his later decision to run for
President took place there. After he became President it became,
in effect, a second capital. Statesmen, both national and international, and a host of lesser, politically ambitious men swarmed
to Warm Springs, either at Father's invitation or in the hope of
capturing his ear. The little village soon became clogged with
opportunists and importunists.

This is not the place in which to trace all the behind-the-
scenes political events that took place at Warm Springs during
the years of the New Deal. However, there is one little known
anecdote which, with the permission of former Vice-President
Henry A. Wallace, I cannot resist recording. Father was then

President-elect, and Wallace, destined to become his first Secretary of Agriculture, had been summoned from Iowa to Warm Springs for their first conference.

On arriving Wallace found what seemed to him a sort of " carnival atmosphere." One plenipotentiary to the Warm Springs " court "—the late Eleanor Medill (Cissy) Patterson, the temperamental lady newspaper publisher—had even come into town in a private railroad car.

Wallace was met by Raymond A. Moley, then a prominent " brain-truster," but later a severe critic of the New Deal, who escorted him to the meeting with Father. Moley, Wallace recalls, " seemed to be full of remorse " about something, and Wallace asked him if anything was wrong. Moley confided that there was something wrong indeed, and that it was tied in with a " lively party " he had attended the previous evening in Cissy Patterson's private car.

" He felt he had done things which were quite unforgivable, and had hurt the President's cause by his behaviour," Wallace relates. " It seems that he had gone into the toilet on the private car and had discovered that the handle of the flusher was gold-plated. He had somehow managed to detach it and had brought it back in fun to the party, indicating it was no wonder that there was unrest in the land with gold-plated toilet flushers in the hands of the wealthy. It made Cissy Patterson enormously angry, and Moley left the party in disgrace. That accounted for his strong feeling of remorse the morning after. Well, this made a deep impression on an Iowa boy ! I wondered what I had got into there ! "

Wallace's impressions of his first conference with Father did little to dispel his bewilderment. Pa was in the bathroom shaving himself, and Wallace was asked to sit just outside the bathroom door. As Father shaved they talked in a general way about agricultural problems.

After finishing with Father Wallace conferred for an hour and a half with Moley and Henry Morgenthau, Jr. He reported finding Moley the " clearest thinker " of the three—Father included. Morgenthau's participation made the proceedings " quite exhausting," Wallace observes. " While I didn't know it," he adds, " Mr Morgenthau wanted very much to be Secretary of Agriculture, and he must have looked on my being there as very, very annoying. I didn't know how deep his resentment was until his memoirs came out."

Wallace came away from Warm Springs with the feeling that the new President-to-be was a " daring adventurer." However, he regarded him as " a godsend to this country at the time he came," and he felt the same way about Father's capabilities when World War II broke out. He sums it up : " F.D.R. had just exactly the qualities that were needed—this *élan* which gave him the lift of the imagination to do things that a more plodding type of mind wouldn't conceive. I found repeatedly in the agricultural world that he would have some insights that would vary from those of the scientists, and he would come as close to being right as the scientists would."

He Loved the Youngsters

Father loved children, and his heart particularly melted when he was in the company of youthful polio victims. He would spend hours playing with them, telling them stories, and teaching them how to exercise in the pool. When one of his favourite little girls died in 1928—at the height of his personal involvement in the 1928 Democratic convention that was to mean so much to his personal career—he found time to write his mother : " We had a tragedy at Warm Springs just before I left. That dear little Pattison girl, ' Tishy '—the younger—died very suddenly after being ill for only a few hours—acute acidosis—& we were all much upset."

After he became President he would have his Thanksgiving dinners at Warm Springs, and would show off his turkey-carving prowess. The patients would draw lots to determine who would sit on either side of him, and it was an unwritten rule that at least one of his partners must be a youngster. Some of the patients could not even sit up—they were rolled in, flat on their backs—and some who could not use their hands had to be fed. On this day Pa was not the President—he was " Rosy " or " Uncle Rosy," as some of the youngsters called him—and his face took on a grin as big as Stone Mountain, Georgia, when he heard this greeting from the kids.

At the Thanksgiving dinners, when he pulled himself to his feet to speak, the patients, young and old, watched him carefully and critically, much as one pro golfer watches another take a swing ; if he made an awkward movement that was likely to upset his balance the dining-room became bedlam as they yelled advice to him.

Medical men will tell you there is nothing miraculous about the water at Warm Springs. It has no special qualities, no secret ingredients, that " cure " polio. What it does have is a natural warmth and possibly a bit more buoyancy than ordinary spring-water. Both these qualities make it felicitous for the exercising of wasted limbs. The " secret " of the Foundation's success in the treatment of certain types of polio cases lies in the carefully worked-out therapeutic exercises and other factors, of which the water is just one.

In his heart and mind Father knew this, but he never quite admitted it. Once Prime Minister William Lyon Mackenzie King of Canada came to Warm Springs to confer with the President, and was invited to come down to the pool while Father took his swim. While Father was getting into his bathing-suit the Prime Minister asked Duncan Cannon if the water had any special qualities. Cannon answered that, outside of the warmth and buoyancy, it was the same as any other water. Behind the canvas curtain of his dressing-room Father heard him.

" He came out," Cannon recalls, " and, right in front of Mr William Lyon Mackenzie King, said to me, ' Dunc, dammit, you're wrong ! You sound just like all these doctors—they're wrong, too, and they just don't know what they're talking about ! Why, I can do things here that I never can do in the White House pool or any other water. Watch ! '

" And with that he eased himself into the water and gave the Prime Minister, me, and every one else who was watching a demonstration of what he could accomplish with his legs in the Warm Springs pool."

Perhaps the above story is the clue as to why Father poured so much time, effort, and money during periods when he was desperately short of cash into building up Warm Springs as a haven for polio victims.

If it had been just a question of swimming in warm water

Father certainly could have built his own indoor, year-round swimming-pool at Hyde Park, where he could have exercised with much less expense and grief. But he *believed* in Warm Springs, and he wanted passionately to provide a place where others, who could not afford to build their own swimming-pools, might, in the words of that old newspaper feature story, " swim back to health."

The significance of Father's decision to leave the congenial, healthful life of Warm Springs in 1928 in order to run for the Governorship—a stepping-stone to the Presidency—should not be discounted. I am no doctor, and I doubt that any cautious medical man could or would say with finality that Father would have recovered the use of his limbs to a larger degree had he devoted the rest of his life to continuing his exercises at Warm Springs. But I know that Father himself felt he was improving, slowly but steadily, and that, even though he continued to exercise as much as he could at Warm Springs and later in the White House pool, his condition did not improve from the time he returned to public life. As the strain of the Presidential years wore upon him he definitely regressed.

It is my considered opinion that Father—optimist though he was—knew in his heart that, when he made his choice to return to a full-time job of public service, he was turning his back on what he believed were the possibilities of continued improvement. But that was how he wanted it. Much as he loved Warm Springs, engrossing as the work of doing something for his fellow " polios " was to him, he no more could rusticate there the rest of his life that he could have succumbed to Granny's entreaties that he retreat from active living to become the Squire of Hyde Park.

13

Back in Politics

IN the fall of 1928 Father returned to active politics, while I, a Harvard sophomore, made my debut as a political campaigner.

The Democratic candidate for President, Alfred E. Smith, had persuaded Father to run as his successor for the office of Governor of New York. He thought Father would be a good vote-getter for the whole ticket, not only in New York, but nationally. As it turned out, Father was elected by a narrow margin, while Governor Smith lost—even in his home state—to Herbert Hoover.

Meanwhile I had bought myself a brown derby and an old Ford touring car and, in company with some other Harvard men, was having a glorious time stumping the state of Massachusetts on behalf of the Al Smith-Joe Robinson ticket. After Father's election as Governor I sat down and wrote my grandmother a letter, into which I poured all the sage judgment of my nearly twenty-one years, on the perils of politics as a profession. Granny preserved the letter in its original envelope, marked " from dear young James." Sometimes, when I read my early letters to Granny, I wonder why they didn't stuff me and put me under glass as a specimen of purest *Grotonaria Harvardiana Cantabrigensis*, but I shall quote from the letter just the same :

Dear Grandma,

I haven't seen you since election except in various poses in the newspapers ! I'm tickled that Father won as long as he ran and we must all hope and pray that he has the most successful administration possible. Public office is a dangerous place, for discredit may come to a man through no fault of his, and in a way, I hate to see Father risk his well deserved reputation of the one example of the successful scholar, gentleman and statesman-politician. However, "nothing tried nothing gained," and there is every reason for hope not fear !

Though there had been the four-year hiatus during the *Larooco*-Warm Springs period, Father had gone before the 1924 Democratic convention in Madison Square Garden, New York City, to make his famous " Happy Warrior " nominating speech for Governor Smith. That had been his first major public appearance after polio.

I was Father's page and " prop " at that convention. I was sixteen, tall and strong, and I was excited and elated beyond description when Father one day asked me, " Jimmy, would you care to come along and lend me your arm ? " By this time— slightly less than three years after that day on Campobello—Pa had learned to walk, painfully and awkwardly, by propping a crutch under his right arm and gripping a supporting arm with his left hand. His legs were locked rigidly in steel braces, and his movement actually was achieved by pivoting with his powerful arms and torso and propelling his body by brute strength. I had learned to match my stride to his slow movements, and had taught myself not to look anxious, but to smile just as he did when he forced himself forward.

At that 1924 convention Father not only made the nominating speech for Al Smith, but also attended the sessions as a delegate, sitting with the others on the crowded floor. I was fearfully worried that he might be hurt when the inevitable wild demonstrations began. If it bothered Father he never showed it. He was absolutely determined that he would not be wheeled on to the convention floor, and it was my job to get him in early—by means of the crutch and arm procedure—before the floor became too clogged. It was a far cry from the 1920 San Francisco convention, when Pa had yanked the state standard from the hands of a resisting Tammany delegate.

The process of getting into his seat was an ordeal for Father. We practised the awkward business of standing together by a chair, with me supporting him and taking his crutch from him as he lowered himself into his seat ; he became quite proficient at it. There was a woman delegate who was so enormous that a special oversized seat was installed for her. She was a friend of Father's, and I remember her suggesting to him that he too should have an oversized chair. He smilingly rejected the suggestion. He wanted no accessories that would emphasize his disability : the only concession he would make was to allow arms to be placed on his chair, so he would have something to grip as he lowered himself into it.

Once he was seated, it was my task to stand by, run errands, deliver messages, and help Father off the floor when he wished to leave. I was kept so busy, in fact, that I hardly had time to further a ' crush ' I developed at the convention for the pretty young niece of the chairman, Senator Tom Walsh of Montana.

The galleries came to know Father, and it became apparent to the spectators that it took a certain measure of fortitude for him to make this effort. After his first few entrances he was greeted regularly with applause as he entered the hall.

Father's big effort was to be exerted in the nominating speech. He had made up his mind that he would walk—by himself—to the rostrum. Together we proceeded to the rear of the platform. Outwardly he was beaming, seemingly confident and unconcerned, but I could sense his inner tenseness. His fingers dug into my arm like pincers—I doubted that he knew how hard he was gripping me. His face was covered with perspiration (he had a good excuse for that, however, for it was sweltering in the Garden). Before " taking off," he called out in a stage whisper to Joseph E. Guffey, then Democratic national committee-man from Pennsylvania, and later United States senator, to go over and " shake the rostrum ! " Joe Guffey looked puzzled, and Father whispered again, almost fiercely this time, that he wanted to be certain that the speaker's stand would support his weight. He was going to have to lean on it—heavily.

Then came his moment to walk alone. I was standing there, trying to look as untroubled and confident as he did, but when he released my arm, took his second crutch from me, and started off I was sweating and shaking. As he slowly swung himself forward he saluted the crowd—since he could not lift his arms from his crutches—with his big smile. Then, as he reached the rostrum, came the tremendous, roaring ovation. At that moment I was so damned proud of him that it was with difficulty that I kept myself from bursting into tears.

During and after the 1924 convention there were a number of newspaper editorials suggesting that, if it were not for Father's disability, *he* would be the Democrats' best Presidential candidate. Anna and I held a strategy council to consider these comments. In our youthful wisdom we decided that, while it was all very flattering, Father was absolutely through as an active political candidate.

In the 1924–28 period, when he was striving to regain use of his limbs, Louis Howe and Mother kept the political home fires burning. Mother made speeches for Father, and Louis operated the publicity mill. Meanwhile Father was active in various civic undertakings, and was making his views known on public issues.

As the 1928 convention in Houston approached pressures from the Smith camp began to build up for Father again to make the nominating speech. More important, Smith wanted him to run for the Governorship. Father was delighted to take on the speech assignment, but for various reasons—both personal and political—he was genuinely loath for quite some time to undertake the race.

As early as April—the convention was not until midsummer —Mother was writing him in Warm Springs : " I'm telling every-one you are going to Houston without crutches so mind you stick at it ! F. Jr. [Franklin, Jr., had just returned from a Warm Springs visit] said you walked 17 steps without anything so your balance must be coming on well."

The same month Father firmly rejected his mother's pleas that he accompany her to Europe. " If Smith is nominated, as he probably will be, I shall have to do a lot of organizing work," he wrote her. ". . . I cannot see the object of sitting around hotels in Europe while the others ' sightsee '—and I can get more good out of Warm Springs than any place."

I went to Europe with Granny that summer, and Elliott went with Father to Houston. Again the convention was a personal triumph for Father. He wrote Granny : " The nominating speech went much better than I had anticipated & seems to have

been approved by both Dem. & Repub. papers, & there have
been a lot of really nice editorials, & flocks of letters & telegrams."

Soon the pressure was on Father to take the gubernatorial
nomination. In September he wrote Granny again : " I have
had a difficult time turning down the Governorship—letters—
telegrams by the dozen begging me to save the situation by
running—but I have been perfectly firm—I only hope they don't
try to stampede the convention tomorrow—nominate me and
then adjourn ! "

One such telegram was from Sis. She took time out from
her duties with a new baby to wire him in Warm Springs : GO
AHEAD AND TAKE IT. MUCH LOVE. ANNA. Father wired back :
YOU OUGHT TO BE SPANKED. MUCH LOVE. PA.

Once Pa yielded and took the nomination, he campaigned
with a vigour that amazed those who had wondered whether
he was physically up to it. I returned from Europe in time to
help him on some of his trips, and I recall vividly how Pa would
rip into Republican taunts that he was too feeble either to run
or to serve, and that the Democrats were using him as a sacrificial
goat.

I was with Father on an occasion during that campaign when
he had to be carried up a fire-escape in order to make an in-
conspicuous entrance into a building where he was to speak.
He was not trying to conceal his physical disability—he simply
did not want to seem to be playing for sympathy by rolling
through the front entrance in a wheel-chair. There were several
times when those of us travelling with him saw him patiently
accept what must have been the humiliating and physically uncomfortable experience of being lifted up and over obstacles like
a sack of potatoes. Whenever I saw this and remembered that
the big, smiling, physically helpless man was the same father
with whom I once ran and rough-housed at Hyde Park and
Campobello, the emotion was almost more than I could endure.

His two terms as Governor were Father's warm-up for the
big job that was ahead—the Presidency. Even before he took
office the *New York Times* was commenting :

> It is too early to select the new leader of the Democratic party
> or to predict nominations for a date so remote as 1932. . . . Yet by
> a most extraordinary combination of qualities, political fortunes

and diversified associations, Governor-elect Roosevelt is within reach of the elements of party leadership.

To this and other " premature " Presidential booming Father replied with the classical political gambit—a disclaimer. " I want to step on any talk of that kind with both feet. That is colloquial but clear," he said. I do not think, however, there was any serious doubt in his mind that the Presidency was exactly where he was heading.

He performed his duties as Governor energetically, demonstrating not only his administrative ability, but his physical capability to stand up to the job as well. Just as he was to scrap zestfully with many Congresses in future years, he tangled with the State Assembly repeatedly—and loved it. In February 1929 he wrote me : " I am getting into a grand little fight with the Legislature and from now on, for five weeks, it will be a general row." More vividly, the following month he described both his family and his political situations in a letter to an old friend, to wit :

> This family is going through the usual tribulations. James is getting over pneumonia ; Elliott is about to have an operation ; Franklin, Jr. has a doubly broken nose and John has just had a cartilage taken out of his knee ! Anna and her husband . . . are taking a short holiday in Europe and their baby is parked with us at the Executive Mansion. Eleanor is teaching school two and half [sic] days a week in New York, and I am in one continuous glorious fight with the Republican legislative leaders. So you see that it is a somewhat hectic life.

My Marriage to Betsey Cushing

During most of the gubernatorial period I was off on my own— finishing up at Harvard, getting married, raising a family, and establishing myself in business. I was never too far away, however, to be available to serve as Pa's " arm " on special occasions when he wanted me at his side, or to participate in our robust family celebrations. Pa's being Governor made little difference in the perennial Roosevelt family crises—financial, educational, and emotional.

I was a Harvard sophomore when I became engaged to Betsey Cushing, one of the three daughters of the late Dr and Mrs

Harvey Cushing, of Brookline, Massachusetts. It was Mother who broke the news to Father, and as many times as I have read her letter I have never failed to be amused by the casualness with which she did it.

The letter is dated November 22, 1928, and was sent to Father, then Governor-elect, at Warm Springs. Mother began it on a familiar theme—the chauffeur's cheque was overdue again, and she had paid William out of her own funds, so would Pa please reimburse her ? Next she advised him that the garage where we kept our car had gone into bankruptcy (I hope we weren't entirely to blame !). Then came some more data on family finances, and an enclosure of a proposition from a firm which wanted to present us with some sort of home laundry contraption, worth approximately a thousand dollars " if we will let them photograph it here & use as ad." " Please wire me if you are willing," Mother asked, but she hasn't the faintest recollection to-day of what happened.

The next item for discussion was : " James wants me to ask you if you will lend him his $50 initiation to the Signet ? I am also giving him $50 to cover car expenses during the campaign."

Finally—almost as an afterthought—Mother got down to another piece of news :

> He is engaged to Betsy [sic] Cushing & took me to meet Dr. and Mrs. Cushing last Friday p.m. after leaving Groton. She is a nice child, family excellent, nothing to be said against it but I regret that he wished to tie himself down so young, however perhaps it will be a good influence & in any case we can do nothing about it. He tells me they expect to be married about 2 years from now —It is to be a secret ! I have spoken neither to the Cushings nor to her about it but you & Anna were to be told.

Four days later I wrote Father, and my letter was almost as circumlocutory and disingenuous as Mother's. I started off by remarking : " I wish there was time to write you about all the many happenings such as victory over Yale at last." Then I got around to saying :

> I'm engaged to Betsey Cushing and terribly in love of course. I hope this isn't too great a shock and I want you to feel that we're both of us quite sane and sensible. We realize that we can't be married and don't plan to be until a year from next September.

If Father's reply to my little bulletin has been preserved it is in hands other than mine. I remember that he seemed to take it calmly and philosophically : it was grand, he was delighted, and he hoped he would soon meet my bride-to-be. If he gave me any warning concerning the responsibilities ahead for a college undergraduate with no guaranteed income and no definite career in mind, who wanted to get married and raise a family, I cannot recall it.

The general plan was to keep the engagement quiet and for us to be married in 1930, after I was through at Harvard. The long engagement became irksome, especially the secrecy business. It is indicative of my close relationship with Father that I felt at liberty in March 1929, which was a busy period for him in Albany, to write him an exceedingly lengthy letter, pouring out all my unhappiness over the delay in announcing the engagement, and asking if he and Mother please would drive over to Boston so we could make the announcement earlier than scheduled. Father could not come, but we announced the engagement anyhow.

During the summer of 1929, with financial help from Pa, I visited my fiancée in Ireland, where her family had taken a house. That was the summer in which I distinguished myself by falling in love with a horse—specifically, a fine-looking colt that was being auctioned at a horse-show. A persuasive Irishman named Lavery assured me that if I would buy the colt he would train it for me ; it would win all the races in Ireland and England, and I would become quite rich. I bought the colt for $450, and suddenly realized that was just about all the money I had left, and was supposed to have been for my passage home. I sent Father a cable—collect—telling him in glowing terms about the wonderful horse I had bought and asking would he please advance me passage money ? I would repay him out of my prize money on the Irish sweepstakes, which I surely would win with my new colt. He cabled back, in effect : SO HAPPY ABOUT THE HORSE. SUGGEST BOTH OF YOU SWIM HOME. He meant it, too. I sold the colt at a loss, made a touch from Granny for the rest of my passage money, and, mourning my lost opportunity to get rich quick, came on back to home and Harvard.

A delightful relationship soon sprang up between Father and my prospective father-in-law, an outstanding brain surgeon.

One of the doctor's first letters to Father spoke of the increasing frequency with which he was noticing a tall young man, who seemed to bump his head on chandeliers, around the house. He observed that he had only himself to blame for moving his family from New Haven, where there were so many nice Yale Republicans, to a town where his daughter would be exposed to a Harvard Democrat.

Father immediately replied :

My dear Doctor :

I am worried about that chandelier ! That youngster of mine is a persistent " Cuss " and I am reasonably certain that with the connivance of Betsey and your better half you will some day discover either that the chandelier has been removed, or that you are living in another house. You and I might as well be philosophical because this younger generation not only knows what it wants, but just how to get it !

. . . I honestly think that it is time for you and me to form a union and I do hope that if you are passing through Albany on a " cutting up " party you will stop over (after parking your knives in the parcel room) and discuss a permanent organization with me.

This easy relationship continued between the conservative surgeon and the liberal political leader, and soon they were on a " Dear Franklin " and " Dear Harvey " basis in their correspondence. When our second daughter, Kate, named after Mrs Cushing, was born in 1936, just about the time the Supreme Court upheld the constitutionality of the T.V.A., Dr Cushing wrote a facetious letter, reporting that some of his rich Boston friends were inquiring if the child would be named " Tennessee." Father replied :

I think Tennessee would be a splendid name for our new grandchild, provided her fond parents give her " authority " for her middle name. That is only fair to her future husband ! Notwithstanding, I prefer Kate—and so do you.

The doctor also had commented disapprovingly to Father on the fact that my exuberant brother, Franklin, Jr., had been photographed in a night club with Betsey's younger sister, Barbara. Father replied :

When will you ever become old enough to realize that the new generation goes to a Night Club instead of Sunday School and that being photographed there is the modern parallel of the pretty colored card you and I used to get for good behavior and perfect attendance ?

As our wedding date approached I began to experience some of the difficulties of attempting to live like a Rockefeller on a dime-store budget.   Father was being ultra-generous ;   yet my ideas were too big for my bank account.   Unfortunately, with twenty-three years of pampering behind me, I had no capacity for a realistic approach to the problem, so I did what I always had done : I turned to Granny for a " loan."   Father heard of it, and wrote me a long letter, giving me a bit of unaccustomed advice on how I must learn to get along on my own.   This is another of Father's letters that has slipped out of my possession, a loss which I regret deeply, because it is one of the few in which he sought to give me detailed counsel on financial matters.

I replied to Father contritely.   " I do realise you are absolutely right about borrowing and the lesson is well learned and will be remembered," I wrote.   " It's an all too easy habit to get into." I added :

> You are swell to pay for my ushers' presents and outfits.   I'm having the huge number of fourteen and the total for presents, ties, gloves, collars and spats would be more than $600. . . . I hope that isn't too much.   Also if it's convenient would you send me my last quarterly $500 about April 1st.

At the same time I was complaining to Mother that it was " unfair " of Granny to tell Father that she had let me have the extra money—I definitely planned to pay her back out of my next allowance, I said.   In retrospect, I realize it was only the hotheadedness of my youth that made me write such a bad-tempered letter, for Granny was giving us a two-thousand-dollar wedding cheque, which would pay for our honeymoon to Europe, and she intended to give me an allowance until I became established as an income-earner.

Father kept his good humour.   After all, it was the father of the bride who footed the heavy bills, so Pa was able to get off a typically jocular letter to Dr Cushing :

> My better half has made a demand that within three days I give her a complete list of all political and business associates whom

The " Nourmahal Gang," 1933

Left to right : Lytle Hull, Dr Leslie Heiter, William Rhinelander
Stewart, Father, Vincent Astor (owner of the yacht), Kermit
Roosevelt, George St George, and Justice Frederic Kernochan

The Campobello House

This picture was taken in June 1933 on the occasion of Father's visit

Associated Commercial Photographers, Ltd

Father and I in Washington about 1936

Harris and Ewing

The King and Queen attend Church

King George VI and Queen Elizabeth with Father and Mother outside St James's Episcopal Church, Hyde Park, June 11, 1939

Associated Press

I have shaken hands with during the past twenty-five years, in order that they may be invited to your wedding ! I want to go on record as expressing my gratitude to you for paying for the event ! I think you will find it better in the long run to hire Mechanics' Hall. Perhaps Jim Curley can introduce you to a good caterer. A shore dinner should prove the least expensive but for heaven's sake get the best brand of beer.

I am making arrangements with the New Haven for two special trains leaving New York the week before the wedding and have told them to bill you.

On June 4, 1930, the wedding ceremony was performed, with Dr Peabody from Groton officiating at his third Roosevelt wedding—Father's and Mother's, Anna's, and now mine. For the first time I began to realize the magnitude of the problem of living in the limelight as the son of a famous man. Father was the Governor, a glamorous figure, and already a much-talked-of Presidential possibility. He was guarded by state troopers and dogged by reporters and cameramen on his arrival, and the affair took on a little of the atmosphere of a Roman carnival. Politicos fairly beat on the doors for invitations, a breach of good manners which to me, with my Groton-Harvard ideas of etiquette, seemed strange. It was even stranger to my politically inexperienced new in-laws.

Later I kidded Father about stealing the show.

" Oh," said Father, " that was nothing ! When your mother and I were married her uncle, President Theodore Roosevelt, gave the bride away. After the ceremony, when T.R. moved into the library for a sip of punch, the crowd followed him as if he were the Pied Piper, leaving your mother and me standing all alone and forlorn."

From the first stage of our honeymoon—a stop-over in Campobello before we sailed for Europe—I wrote Father : " I hope you have recovered from the wedding, we both feel sorry that Elliott found the *heat* so exhausting but no one was hotter than the bride and groom ! "

I Spurn the Law and Pa is Disappointed

The post-honeymoon letters cast additional light on how Father attempted to maintain his position as head of the family while performing the duties of Governor and girding himself—tacitly, at least—for the big political effort in 1932. He was most anxious for me to follow his example and study law. Even if I did not pursue law, which he had not, he felt it would help me in either business or politics.

Our discussion over law as a career was another of the few occasions when Father attempted to sway me on a major decision. Just as I had acceded to his wish that I go to Harvard, instead of to the college of my choice, I tried once more to go along with what he wanted. But this time my effort to be a dutiful son got off the track.

As early as 1927 I had written Father :

I have decided that I do not want to go in for law as a profession. To begin with I'm not sufficiently attracted to the actual practice of it and the study of it for three years would finish me. I do want however to get a fundamental grounding in International, constitutional and state government and law, and so I have arranged to concentrate in Government at college. . . . I talked it over with Mother and she said that probably Mr. Black [Van Lear Black, head of Fidelity and Deposit Company] would be willing to give me a start at the bottom. . . . What I really want of course is to go in for politics.

Again, Father's reply to me is lost, but he did not do anything for me with Van Lear Black. (Always Father was loath to intervene for any of us—though there were some exceptions when he did—in job or business capacities.) I, of course, went to Europe that summer and the succeeding two summers, so I did nothing about pursuing the job hunt on my own.

Just before my marriage I brought up the subject of law again. Because of my lack of a diploma (because of flunking German) I was ineligible to enrol in Harvard Law School. I told Father I wanted to go to work and support my wife, and that meanwhile I would make up the language credit, earn my diploma, and consider entering law school the following year. Father, however, was pulling for me to enter Boston University Law School, which would accept me on the basis of the credits I had earned at Harvard. From Warm Springs he sent me the following persuasive telegram :

I DO VERY MUCH HOPE YOU WILL MAKE THE LAW SCHOOL THIS
AUTUMN STOP AFTER BEING OUT A WHOLE YEAR YOU WOULD FIND IT
FIFTY PER CENT HARDER STOP TAKE THE ADVICE OF AN OLD AND
EXPERIENCED BIRD.

So, on our return from our European honeymoon, we settled
down in a cottage in Cambridge, which was the gift of my father-
in-law, began housekeeping on the allowances from my father
and my grandmother, and I enrolled in Boston University Law
School.

But I stayed there less than a year. I got out—Father's wishes
notwithstanding—because of my basic lack of interest, my pride
(I was impatient to become self-sufficient), and a tiff with Granny.
Granny had come to visit us, and had informed me—not asked
me—that I was going to take her to visit a relative in a near-by
suburb. Betsey and I had previous plans, and I told Granny
I couldn't do it. She became angry and told me, rather tactlessly,
that I had best do as she said, because it was her money that was
making it possible for me to go to law school. I stood up on my
hind-legs—I was a grown man now, no longer the " Jamesie-
boy " of old—and told Granny that if such were the case I would
get a job and support myself.

Just about this time the dean of the law school had been
talking to me about the desirability of my working along with
my studies. He had pointed out to me that I was only one of a
handful of the students in my class who did not have a job. He
recommended me to a graduate of the school, the late Victor de
Gerard, who had come to the United States as an immigrant,
educated himself, and was making a fair success in the insurance
business. I went to see de Gerard, and made an arrangement
whereby I was to work for him at fifty dollars a week on a schedule
that would permit me to continue my studies.

Mother was delighted. She had visited us about this time—
Betsey was expecting a child—and I told her what I was planning
to do. I had even asked Louis Howe to investigate my prospective
employer, and Louis did so, giving him a clean bill of health.
Mother wrote Father a glowing account of my enterprise, beginning with the enthusiastic statement, as if hailing the millennium :
" James has got a job ! "

Father, however, was fit to be tied. First, he wanted me to

finish law school, and he sensed—rightly—that I would use this as an excuse to drop out. Second, he never had heard of Victor de Gerard, and suspected, despite Louis Howe's favourable report, that he was going to try to capitalize on the Roosevelt name. Third—and in this regard Father, untypically, was being just a little stuffy—he felt that if I had to go into the insurance business I should do it with some old-line company such as the one he had joined. He did not put his foot down, however, and say firmly that I should not and could not work for de Gerard. So I took the job.

Father was not completely wrong about de Gerard; yet, at the same time, he was somewhat unfair to him. I would be naïve to try to argue that in 1930 an inexperienced youth, unless his name carried some weight, would be worth fifty dollars a week for part-time work to an insurance broker. On the other hand, I found de Gerard, though ambitious and aggressive, a reputable man, and he never asked me to become involved in any " influence " deals or to do anything that was not ethical.

In any event, the experience brought me another of Father's rare " warning " letters. I had written him, asking him if he would see some job-hunter who was pestering me for an introduction to him. On January 24, 1931, he wrote me, agreeing to give the man an interview, and he went on to say :

> By the way, when I see you in New York, I will tell you all about the insurance company and you will be able to realize some of the reasons for the great willingness of some people to be awfully nice to you.
>
> Incidentally and confidentially, I wish you would impress upon Mr. De Girard [sic], politely but firmly, that he must not use your name in seeking business. Also, the more I hear, the more certain I am that you should not have anything to do with any form of bonds or insurance connected with any governmental agencies— state, city authority, or any other division of government, or any people who have been in influential political positions either in New York or Massachusetts.

This, of course, was impeccable advice. In fairness to myself, I must say that I was attempting to steer just such a course, and to avoid active solicitation of political business, but there were times when the line inevitably was drawn pretty close. Possibly

I should have been sufficiently mature and considerate enough of Father's position to have withdrawn from the insurance business entirely. But I was young, ambitious, spoiled—in the sense of having been conditioned to require a good deal of spending money —so I went right ahead in pursuit of what seemed to me the easiest solution.

After I had been married a little more than a year and was getting established in business I wrote Father to express my hope that an allowance cheque which he had just sent me would be the last I'd ever take from him. I added :

> I want you to know that it will be always one of the things that will stick with me how swell you've been about making it possible for me to go to college, school, law school and especially to marry Bets. It's made everything very perfect and I really plan and hope in my own peculiar way to make you feel some day that it was all well spent.

Elliott Again !

It was Elliott—not I—whose problems posed the biggest dilemma for Father at this busy period of his career. Elliott graduated from Groton, but absolutely rebelled against going to Harvard—or to any college. Father attempted to take a hand, but soon discovered that his second son had plenty of " Roosevelt Dutch " in him. In May 1929 Elliott wrote Father the following stiff note :

> I am under the impression that I owe you $120.55. Enclosed please find check for that amount. . . .
> I had no chance to tell you before you went South that I thought over what you said . . . and I hope that in future you won't bother " to lean over backwards to please " me. I'll do my best not to give you any chance to do that. In the future I will be perfectly frank so you won't have to feel that I'm hiding anything. All I ask you to remember is that you asked me to be frank. Maybe I have been " selfish " in my decisions but I must say that I am not intentionally so as seems to be your opinion. I have regretted only a *few* actions so far in my life. . . .
> Instead of " leaning over backward " for me, do it for Jimmie ; we all ought to give him every help in the next few years.

That summer Mother took the two younger boys to Europe,

leaving it up to Father to work out the college problem with Elliott. For a while Elliott talked about Princeton, but when he took the college board examinations he deliberately turned in blank papers.

When Mother returned from Europe and discovered what Elliott had done she showed herself to be a sterner parent than Pa ever was. She insisted that, whether Elliott went to college or not, he must demonstrate that he could pass the exams. So, protestingly, he was enrolled in Hun School, a " cram " preparatory institution, did well enough to satisfy Mother, and then *didn't* go to college.

For a period of several months Elliott, his dignity and sense of independence outraged, would not even speak to Mother. Before he consented to " make up " Mother found it necessary to complain to Father that she had discovered Elliott had been skipping school for stretches of several days, during which time no one knew where he was. " If anyone had died I could not have reached him," she wrote. " I think you must take drastic measures. He must be at school or we must know where he is. . . . Please act at once ! "

When the news got out that the Governor's second son was not going to college letters, pro and con, began swamping Father's office in Albany. Father commented : " I feel that a college education is a tremendous help but my son Elliott preferred starting out on his own and Mrs. Roosevelt and I feel he is the one to decide."

To his credit as a parent, Father refused to use his influence to get Elliott a cushy job. For a while Elliott floundered from one job to another, and drifted pretty much away from the family. However, the special sort of affection that existed between Bunny and Father—a deep, sympathetic bond—never wavered. In 1931, when Father had to make a hurried trip to Europe to see Granny, who had become ill in Paris, he took Elliott along. " I never had so much fun or travelled with a better companion," Elliott says.

" I had only one complaint against Father on this trip," my brother recalls. " I had met a perfectly delightful girl, and was interested in devoting as much time to her as possible. Father, on the other hand, was using me to be gallant to a number of charming persons who were making the crossing. One night, when there was dancing on deck, Father insisted that I substitute for him in at least one dance with Mme Rosa Ponselle, the opera diva, who had a lovely voice, but who outweighed me considerably. The ship took a sudden roll; we crashed against the rail with Mme Ponselle on the outside track, and I almost sustained a broken back."

Elliott also tells a typical story of Father's generosity and thoughtfulness in connexion with this trip. He helped Father shop for prints in a number of Paris art shops. Elliott himself fell in love with a little bronze statue of a mare and colt which he could not afford. Father merely said—rather unsympathetically, Elliott thought—that it was too bad Bunny didn't have enough money to buy it, and the subject was dropped. The following September 23—Elliott's birthday—the statue arrived as a gift from Pa. Wherever Elliott has gone since—and he has lived in a lot of places—the little bronze statue has gone with him.

Johnny and Franklin, Jr., at least, presented Father no major problems during the gubernatorial years (their time was yet to come !). Johnny was still young enough to be writing about crises at Groton—*i.e.* :

> The school has been stinking from the girls who are up here for the weekend for the dance. . . . Exams are over. . . . I did lousy and expect to be bounced any day . . . I guess my intellectual mind is degenerating if I ever had one.

Franklin's problems were somewhat livelier. He recalls one day when Pa came home from the Governor's office for luncheon and, when every one was assembled at the table, pulled from his pocket a letter on baby-blue stationery, fragrant with perfume, and tantalizingly waved it in the air. " I received this most unusual letter at the office this morning," Father began, opening the envelope and commencing to read the letter aloud. " It begins, ' Dear Rosy. . . .' "

" At this point," Brud relates, " I realized that Pa had got by mistake a letter from one of my crushes of the time. I jumped up and practically knocked over the table snatching it from him. It was one of the few times in my life I was sorry I was Franklin D. Roosevelt, *Junior* ! "

14

Campaigning with Father; the 1932 Victory

AT this point in Father's life every one of us, consciously or otherwise, was beginning to take stock of what lay ahead. We began to realize—and the feeling, while exciting, was not exactly a comfortable one—that this many-faceted Pa of ours was on his way to becoming a figure of history, and that more and more we were going to have to share him with the public.

However, even after Father was elected President and went on to become not merely the nation's leader, but one of the most powerful men in the world, I don't think any of us ever was overwhelmed by him. We were his enthusiastic rooters, we admired extravagantly what he was doing, but always he remained our familiar Pa. We continued to love him and kid with him in the same spirit of bantering affection that had always existed between us.

Among the many reasons for this was that Pa was no superman, and he never pretended to be one. Skilful as he was in politics and public utterances, he was just as capable of putting his foot into his mouth and perpetrating a classic boner as any tyro politician starting out in the sticks. He didn't do this often, but when he did, in the words of Mayor Fiorello LaGuardia, it was a " beaut."

For example, approximately eighteen months before he went after the Democratic nomination for the Presidency in 1932 Father pulled a boner that might have complicated his political future considerably had it not been for some fast footwork. Father, then the Governor of New York, but an " adopted son " of Georgia because of his association with Warm Springs, was guest of honour at a " possum-and-yam " dinner at White Sulphur Springs, Georgia. That was the night when some staunch supporters arranged the famous " possum hunt " in which three possums were tied to convenient tree-limbs so Pa could be photographed, seated at the wheel of his little car, peering up at one of them. The dinner was good ; the company was like-wise ; there may have been a little moonshine circulated, and Pa even may have sampled a drop of it.

In any event, when it came time for him to respond to his gracious hosts with a few brief remarks he came out with the observation that this was the sort of evening's entertainment he really enjoyed. The rest of the country, he went on, certainly could take a lesson from the South on how to throw a party. Then he added the fatal words : " If we could cut out the banquets in *that great sink of iniquity called New York* I'd be happy ! "

When the Press Association stories were printed in the early papers Pa's political advisers back East almost choked on their first editions. The telephone-wires began crackling between New York and White Sulphur. Somehow, before the final editions appeared, a toned-down version had been put on the wires, making it appear that the Governor was talking about how *some* persons—not *he*, of course—felt about New York. The *New York Times* was kind enough to note that the Governor's " great sink of iniquity " crack " was made smilingly and obviously was facetious."

In later years, when I began to get my foot wet in politics, Pa mentioned this incident to me as a painful illustration of the trouble one might get into by opening the mouth without opening the brain.

As Father's pre-convention activities got under way in 1932 I found myself considerably involved in his campaign. He had a serious problem in Massachusetts, where most of the important Democratic machine politicians—all but the late, inimitable James Michael Curley were for the defeated 1928 candidate, Al Smith. Ex-Governor Smith, a now unhappy warrior, was peeved with Father for moving forward while he moved back-ward, and above all for running the Executive Office in Albany as he saw fit, without advice from his predecessor. He regarded

Father as an ungrateful " protégé," and, while Smith had little chance to secure the nomination for himself again, he was determined to block Father's chances if he could.

Father appointed me as his official representative to work for him in the Massachusetts delegation. I still regard it as a high compliment that he would entrust such a responsibility to me, a politically inexperienced youth just two years out of college. Some political commentators have criticized Father's judgment for delegating so much to me in Massachusetts, and for accepting the alliance with Jim Curley, a machine politician—albeit an engaging one—of the most callous sort. (Curley at that time had served as mayor and congressman, and later was to become Governor of Massachusetts ; he was, at least, a frank politician, who once began a speech : " Fellow pickpockets, doormat thieves, lush rollers, baby-snatchers, and bottle-robbers—you see, I know you all.") Certainly the results of our efforts were not brilliant : we were swamped by the Smith forces in the Massachusetts primary, though later we carried the state handsomely over Hoover. Father took it all with equanimity, however, and told me that at least I'd " learn a good deal about practical backroom politics from Brother Curley ! "

After Father's election Curley turned on him, claiming that he had been double-crossed on promises of a choice of appointments. Among those he mentioned were the posts of Secretary of the Navy and Ambassador to Rome. Father actually offered him an Ambassadorship to Poland, which Curley refused. Later he became vitriolic when Father would not intervene to head off a Federal investigation which led, after Father's death, to Curley's imprisonment on mail-fraud charges. For the record, I must say this, based on conversations I had with Father on the subject : Father was not ungrateful to those who helped him, but he had a sense of propriety and fitness. Much as Father, as a connoisseur of rococo political bravura, might have admired James Michael Curley's showmanship, he no more would have considered naming the flamboyant Boston political brawler to head his beloved Navy Department that he would have appointed the Grand Wizard of the Ku Klux Klan as Ambassador to the Vatican.

I was in Chicago in 1932, doing my small bit for Father at the convention. When the nomination went to him he gave the delegates—and the country—a taste of what sort of personality the Democrats had picked as a candidate by flying to Chicago in a chartered plane to deliver his acceptance speech. No other nominee had ever used a plane in this manner, and the custom up to this time had been for the candidate to acknowledge his nomination weeks later.

I met Pa at the airport. Mother and John had flown out with him. I noticed that my sixteen-year-old brother looked awfully green. Despite the general excitement, I was curious enough to inquire what had happened, and I learned that, while Pa had worked serenely on his speech in the bouncy plane, Johnny was huddled in the rear of the cabin, sick as a pup.

I squeezed into the car which carried Father to the hotel. Louis Howe rode in the back seat next to Father, and immediately there began one of the most incongruous performances I have ever witnessed. Louis had strong objections to parts of Father's proposed acceptance speech, and he began arguing with him even as the car was rolling in from the airport. Pa listened to him with one ear, argued back out of the side of his mouth, all the while smiling and waving at the wildly cheering crowds. Finally—and it was one of the few times I ever heard him get really rough with Louis—Pa suddenly exploded : " Dammit, Louie, *I'm* the nominee ! "

Louis Howe and Gus Gennerich

Louis Howe was probably the most loyal man Father ever had around him. It was Louis who had the early dream that Father one day would occupy the White House, and he never stopped dreaming it, not even after polio did its job on the legs of his friend and chief. As early as 1912, when Father was a relatively unknown young politician working for the nomination of Woodrow Wilson, Louis was writing Father as " Beloved and Revered Future President."

This choleric little man was also one of the few persons who dared to tell off Pa. Lela Stiles, Howe's long-time secretary and biographer, tells of hearing Louis in Albany days explode on the phone, calling Father a " fool," a " pighead," and, on being told Father was going for a swim, expressing the hope, " I hope to

God you drown ! " I well can believe it, for during the 1932 campaign, when I made a speech prematurely pledging Father to outright repeal of prohibition, Louis gave me the worst bawling out I've ever had. Even after Father became President and Louis, by then a semi-invalid, had moved into the White House, he would still dress down Father when he thought he had it coming.

Father's affection for Louis was boundless, and he rarely lost his patience. Once he sent me to Louis' bedroom in the White House to smooth over a row which he thought might have gone too far. I expected to find Louis simmering, but he was sitting up in bed sort of smiling when I entered.

" The Old Man thinks you're kind of mad at him," I said.

" No," Louis answered. " He knows me better than that."

Then, temper rising all over again, he shouted, " He also knows, by golly, that I'm right, and that I'll be back to-morrow to argue with him some more, and that, dammit, I'll win ! "

And, if my memory is correct, Louis *did* return to the fray on the next morning, and he did convince the President, by golly, that he was right, and he did win.

During that first campaign another loyal aide, who helped Father enormously in personal ways, was August Adolph (Gus) Gennerich. Gus had been a New York city policeman, and a brave one. As a rookie he had entered a burning tenement and rescued a number of persons who were about to be burned to death. In 1925, as a motor-cycle officer, he singlehandedly captured several " wanted " gangsters, members of the so-called " Cowboy " Tessler mob, after a gun battle in which he was wounded. For this feat Gus was promoted to detective. In the 1928 gubernatorial campaign Gus was assigned to Father's security detail. Pa liked him enormously, and arranged for him to take leave and come to Albany with him. Gus never went back to the police force ; he went right along with Father into the White House, becoming a member of the Secret Service and a familiar figure to the millions of citizens who saw Father during that campaign and over the ensuing years.

Gus was more than just a pair of strong arms and legs and a bulky body to intervene between Father and possible harm, such as a would-be assassin's bullets. Father trusted him completely.

He liked to try out ideas on Gus. Father regarded him as his " ambassador " to the " man-in-the-street," for the big ex-cop had a knowledge of, and an insight into, many types of people with whom Father ordinarily would have little or no contact. I have heard Father refer to Gus as " my humanizer." He would have Gus bring all sorts of persons—merchants, tavern-keepers, workmen—to see him.

Gus was a good friend to Franklin, Jr., and me. He acted as our discreet guide—though none of us went out of the way to tell Pa about it—to certain speakeasies during the days of the " noble experiment." One of the problems of being the Governor's sons was that we could not get into the slightest scrape without its reflecting on Father. The thought of being caught in a speakeasy raid was a nightmare. Yet all our friends went to them, and we wanted to go, too. So we counted on Gus to pick " safe " places, which he did.

The relationship between Father and his gum-chewing body-guard was remarkable. Gus was awed by no one, not even the President. In the privacy of the family circle he took to calling Father " Pal." At first Father was a bit startled ; then he decided that he loved it, and *he* began calling Gus " Pal."

One week-end in 1933, when Father was at a hot-dog roast at Hyde Park, an urgent call came in from Havana from Sumner Welles, who had been sent as Ambassador to Cuba to attempt to head off a threatened revolution. Gus and another Secret Service agent made a " fireman's sling " with their hands in order to get the President to the phone as quickly as possible. On the way Gus began swaying Pa gently and singing *London Bridge Is Falling Down*, throwing Father into such laughter that it took him a minute or so to compose himself before talking with Ambassador Welles.

Gus also had a firm hand with our obstreperous little brother, Johnny. There is the story of how, just after Father became President-elect, a group of Democratic Congressional leaders, including Senators Cordell Hull and Joe Robinson, Representative Sam Rayburn, and others, were awaiting an audience with the President-elect at our New York City home when they heard a terrible crash in another part of the house. They rushed down-stairs, and found Gus sitting heavily on Johnny's stomach,

growling, " There, damn you, that'll teach you to stop ' prepping '
with me ! "

Gus had a few blind spots. He was a sucker for " natural
medicine " remedies, and he was a hard man to resist when he
began urging you " for your own good " to try some of his pet
nostrums. During Father's first term, when my ulcers were
acting up, Gus was insistent that I try some wonder pills he had
discovered, which were going to " mineralize " my body (whatever that means) and cure my ulcers without surgery. I finally
took a few of the pills to pacify him, then found myself receiving
batches of the medicine—plus requests for payment—from the
medicine-man. It took a lot of letter-writing to get that one
turned off.

Much more serious than his efforts to pour nature pills into
me were his efforts to get Father to take them. He just about
had Father convinced when Rear-Admiral Ross T. McIntire,
the White House physician, got wind of it, and threatened all
sorts of drastic measures unless Gus ceased practising medicine
without a licence.

Whistle-stopping with Father

Father was in fine physical trim and in jubilant spirits as the
campaign began. He had taken a one-week cruise in July, with
John, Franklin, Jr., and me as his crew, on a rented forty-foot
yawl called the *Myth II*. We sailed from Port Jefferson, Long
Island, up along the New England coast, to Portsmouth, New
Hampshire. Frankly, I was nervous during the whole trip,
because the *Myth II* leaked, and I was afraid if heavy weather
came out we might be losing ourselves both a father and a
Presidential candidate. Besides, I didn't see how Father could
relax much because there were two other vessels tagging along—
one loaded with reporters and another, the yacht *Ambassadress*,
carrying Democratic fat cats and money-raisers, who kept wanting
to talk with Father about financing the campaign. Father,
however, took everything serenely, and told reporters that the
cruise was " great fun," that he loved it, and that he was happy
afloat in anything except a steam yacht.

Quite early in his campaign—this was when Presidential

candidates travelled by railroad train and the whistle-stop was in full flower—Pa developed a little family act. He would come out on my arm, smiling at the crowd, then take his stance at the rail. If Mother was along she would be introduced. Then Pa would present the two blonde glamour girls—Anna and Betsey.

Finally, Pa would turn to me, cocking his head upward a bit—I was a couple of inches taller than Father, as polio had shrunk his legs—and say, " And this is my little boy, Jimmy." He would pause for effect, then add, " I have more hair than he has ! " The crowd's roar of laughter was my cue to grin, as if I were hearing a virgin gem of repartee, but to me the joke got pretty thin—as thin, in fact, as my hair.

Pa had a knack for easy give-and-take with the whistle-stop crowds and with the larger audiences at the meetings in stadiums and halls. I " spooked " easier than he did—in fact, he didn't " spook " at all—and I would get awfully nervous when people would start pressing in, trying to reach up and touch him, and shouting what seemed to me outlandish requests for souvenirs and such. Once a woman yelled at him that she wanted him to give her his shirt. I think Pa was startled, for those were depression times, and he wasn't sure for a moment whether she wanted it as a souvenir or whether, after four years of Mr Hoover, her husband might be in need of a shirt. He met the situation by calling out that if she would come to the train he would give her a clean one. She, of course, never got to the train.

One of my campaign chores was to appear on the rear platform at the midnight to 6 A.M. stops and try to explain to the faithful few who gathered even at those hours that Father had to sleep some time. One morning in Seattle, after coming out at 2 A.M., I decided to stretch my legs on the platform. I was accosted by a tall, thin, determined female, who said :

" You're that Roosevelt boy, ain't you ? "

" Yes, ma'am ! " I admitted, flashing her my best eager-beaver campaign smile and extending my hand.

" Young man," she said, ignoring my hand, " I came here to see your Paw. Now you just go right in that train and fetch him out ! "

I tried to explain how weary Father was and how cruel it

would be to awaken him. The more I talked, the madder she got, and finally she began hitting me on my naked head with her umbrella. I turned tail and ran. She was in hot pursuit, still whamming me with the umbrella, when Gus Gennerich came down the platform and rescued me. Pa had the story from Gus before I even awoke that morning, and thought it was the funniest incident of the campaign.

All in all, we had a lively, high-spirited, optimistic campaign caravan. Father got along famously with the correspondents. I was aboard for almost the entire campaign ; Anna was with us a great deal of the time, and both of us enjoyed the excitement and the feeling of trying to be useful to Father.

The mood, however, was by no means entirely light-hearted. The country was in the grip of a horrible depression. We saw some grim-looking people—men who obviously were out of work, and had been out of work for some time. In Detroit the tenseness in the atmosphere was a thing one could almost reach out and feel. We received reports that President Hoover had experienced some almost ominous receptions in several economically paralysed industrial centres where he appeared. In some places we were apprehensive about how Father would be greeted. In those days he was still an unknown quantity, another candidate after a big job, and we were not certain how he would be received by people whose pants were ragged and whose belts were pulled in. But, while there were meetings at which enthusiasm was less than overwhelming, there were no outstandingly unpleasant incidents. We began to pick up confidence that the people liked our Pa as a person and as a candidate, that they felt he was going to try to do more for them than Mr Hoover had, and that they were going to take a chance on him.

Which is how it worked out.

Father followed the election returns in New York City. I was with him at campaign headquarters when Mr Hoover conceded. When we finally got home that night I helped him into bed— the same bed in which I had seen him, an almost helpless invalid, that first Christmas after his polio attack. He was still Pa, only now he was not just Pa : he was the President-elect of the United States of America.

We talked a long time that evening.   We talked about a number of things.

As I kissed him good-night he looked up at me.   I shall try to reproduce his words of that evening as faithfully as my memory will permit, and I think I remember them well.

" You know, Jimmy," he said, " all my life I have been afraid of only one thing—fire.   To-night I think I'm afraid of something else."

" Afraid of what, Pa ? " I said.

" I'm just afraid," he said, " that I may not have the strength to do this job.

" After you leave me to-night, Jimmy," he went on, " I am going to pray.   I am going to pray that God will help me, that He will give me the strength and the guidance to do this job and to do it right.   I hope you will pray for me, too, Jimmy."

I stood there a moment, unable to say anything.   Then I left Father alone in his room, about to embark on the great loneliness of the Presidency.   I went to my room and did as he had asked me.

15

Pa—in Fun and Anger

FATHER'S personality had taken on a definite pattern by the time he prepared to enter the White House. Maybe I'm prejudiced, but I've never known anyone with a sense of humour quite like Pa's. He was addicted to practical jokes, and some of his badinage at Press conferences could be pretty heavy-handed, but he also could deal in rapier-strokes when the occasion demanded. His humour could be dry, bubbling, and delicious, like a good champagne—and the effect was just as deadly. He had become a master of the art of undercutting an adversary, a critic, or—if necessary—even a friend. He usually accomplished this with the plainest and fewest possible words.

For instance, in September 1932, when he was making his first Presidential race, he received a letter from Mary Willis Roosevelt, widow of James Alfred Roosevelt, a distant cousin from the Oyster Bay, or Republican, side of the family. " Cousin Mary " wrote him from Paris ; she apparently was one of those Americans who preferred to live abroad, which irritated Father, and she addressed him as " My dear Franklyn," which I am sure irritated him further.

Her message was :

> I shall not sail under any false colors, but tell you, that, because of your running mate, and your silly attitude, about that " forgotten man " and all the rest, that you have said about the President, in your very bad political strategy, in attacking him, a thing that has always been considered bad form in politics, I am unreservedly against you—

James [her late husband] who saw hundreds of men a week in his work, said, there were no " forgotten men " but plenty who thought they were owed something for *nothing*, was dead against such ideas of socialistic patting them on the back, as you are handing out. You have only belittled yourself by talking like this, and I know many people who, because of it, have decided they will *not* vote for you—

I am, sincerely yours

Mary W. Roosevelt

In his reply Father first evened up the score for that " Franklyn " by addressing her as " Dear Marye." Then he simply wrote :

Thank you very much for writing to me. It is good to hear from you. I am sorry that you feel as you do, but I must tell you quite frankly that it really never occurred to me that you would vote for me.

In January 1936, when Hitler was flexing his muscles, Italy was invading Ethiopia, the London Naval Conference was in progress, and the Spanish Civil War was about to erupt, Mother sent a typed memo to Missy LeHand, Father's secretary, as follows :

THE WHITE HOUSE
WASHINGTON

January 8, 1936

MEMORANDUM FOR MISS LEHAND :

This bill is for Franklin Junior's treatment for piles. He went eleven times but apparently it does not depend upon how many times you go, it depends entirely on the cure. I know F.D.R. will have a fit !

E.R.

At the bottom of this memo, in Father's bold handwriting, is written :

Pay it.
Have had the fit.
FDR

Pa sometimes solved his gift problems by (*a*) passing on something that had been presented to him or (*b*) writing a cheque. The memos with which he accompanied his cheques were delightful. The one all of us enjoyed the most was his note to Mother (with a two-hundred-dollar cheque attached) on their twenty-eighth wedding anniversary, as follows :

THE WHITE HOUSE
Washington

Mar. 17th, 1933

Dearest Babs

After a fruitless week of thinking and lying awake to find whether you need or want undies, dresses, hats, shoes, sheets, towels, rouge, soup plates, candy, flowers, lamps, laxative pills, whisky, beer, etchings or caviar

I GIVE IT UP
!

And yet I know you lack some necessity of life—so go to it with my love and many happy returns of the day !

F.D.R.

Father was not much on telling funny stories just for laughs. He was more given to reminiscing about his personal experiences —and some of these stories improved with age !—or to relating parables to illustrate some point, political or otherwise. Often he would make sardonic quips that were misunderstood by literal-minded persons, even some who knew him well. Mother frequently warned him that this habit might get him in trouble. Indeed, his broad jests were often taken seriously, with the result that some fantastic opinions and remarks were attributed to him. For example, I know of a private memorandum, drawn up by a person who was not an intimate, who talked with him after Father returned from Yalta. The person asked Father how Stalin had impressed him. Knowing Father, I am sure he had no intention of discussing Stalin with this particular person, so he remarked airily that he had " heard " Stalin had " poisoned his wife." The person did not know whether to take Father seriously. The result is the existence of a document, which some day might be released and taken seriously by some who see it, indicating the possibility that the President of the United States put credence in a rumour that the head of the Soviet Union was a wife-poisoner.

Pa took a rather Olympian attitude towards his right to jest as he pleased, and, when Mother or others who felt close enough to do so chided him on his " careless levity," he replied that he didn't give a hoot if some persons couldn't tell when he was joking. The trouble was that Mother herself was not always certain how to interpret some of Father's remarks !

Although most people thought of Father as an extroverted, gregarious person, Mother has a theory, which she has discussed with me, that basically he was a shy, reticent person. I disagreed with her at first, but the more I think of it, the more I feel she is right. Certainly Father had very few " soul-searching " conversations with any of us—Mother included—on matters other than public issues. Mother says, " His was an innate kind of reticence that may have been developed by the fact that he had an older father and a very strong-willed mother, who constantly tried to exercise control over him in the early years. Consequently, he may have fallen into the habit of keeping his own counsel, and it became part of his nature not to talk to anyone of intimate matters."

This almost hidden quality of Father's is what made it so difficult for him to be a stern disciplinarian with any of us, or even to be firm with subordinates.

Dear old Irvin McDuffie—now dead—was Father's valet. He had been an Atlanta barber in pre-Presidential days when Father began going to Warm Springs. Father had hired him, and they had been through a lot of experiences together. But Mac often tried Father's patience.

Mother relates how, at the White House one night, Mac let Father down badly. He was on night duty to answer Father's bell. Mac went to sleep under circumstances that were unpardonable, and there was no one around to help Father to bed. Not wishing to make a scene, the President of the United States sat in his office, pushing the bell futilely for his sleeping valet.

After Father had been ringing for a considerable time my brother John happened to come in. It was John who, after checking on Mac's condition, helped Pa to bed.

Next morning Mother told Father that Mac would have to go. " Yes," he said sadly, " I know." But, because he regarded McDuffie as an old friend and could not bear to fire him personally, he asked Mother if she would help him. He was going on a cruise shortly and would take Arthur Prettyman, who was to become Mac's successor, with him. Would Mother please break the news to McDuffie ?

" But don't tell him," Father asked her, " until I have gone." And that is how it was done. Father, in the meantime, arranged for Mac to have a comfortable, dignified job with the Treasury. He really wasn't mad at Mac at all.

That White House Menu !

Pa couldn't even bring himself to insist that Mother fire Mrs Henrietta Nesbitt, the White House housekeeper, who was responsible for serving him the uninspired meals which he disliked so passionately. As Robert Sherwood once noted with admirable restraint, " It ill becomes a guest to say so, but the White House cuisine did not enjoy a very high reputation." Sherwood goes on to describe one particularly repulsive salad— I've shuddered at the sight of it many times—" which resembled the production one finds in the flossier type of tea-shoppe." It was offered to Pa repeatedly, but he inevitably shook his head " and murmured sadly, ' No, thank you.' "

Pa once remarked to Anna—ostensibly in jest, but actually (or so all of us suspect) with a lot of real feeling—that one reason he wanted to be re-elected for a fourth term was " so I can fire Mrs Nesbitt ! " He made the fourth term all right, but the housekeeper stayed on.

Everybody was against Mrs Nesbitt—everybody except Mother,[1] whose discovery she was in the first place. Mrs Nesbitt was a Hyde Park woman whom Mother met through their joint participation in local women's political clubs. For some reason unfathomable to all of us Mother decided that she would make a fine housekeeper for the White House, so she brought her to Washington. Now, Mother is a wonderful woman, and I yield to no one in my admiration for her, but, as she herself will tell you, she has no appreciation of fine food. Victuals to her are something to inject into the body as fuel to keep it going, much as a motorist pours gasoline into an auto-tank.

Father, on the other hand, until he became discouraged after years of being subjected to indifferent viands, fancied himself a

[1] See letter from Eleanor Roosevelt to James Roosevelt on p. 341.

gourmet. He had a keen taste for such things as terrapin, venison, and duck—and he liked his duck hung until it was quite high. Periodically, he would yearn for such delicacies as oyster crabs with whitebait, and once he titillated a Press conference by lyrically describing a wonderful way of baking whole, fresh-caught fish in mud—" the most delicious thing in the world ! " he exclaimed. Of course, whether he ever actually ate any fish baked in mud, or whether he was just having a little fun with the reporters, is a matter for conjecture : none of us ever heard him mention such a thing.

Over the years Pa made valiant efforts to educate Mrs Nesbitt to cater to his tastes. He sent her memos on how his favourite foods should be prepared. " Feathered game should never be plucked until just before it is eaten," he once instructed her. " Taking off the feathers dries up the meat."

On another occasion, early after the United States became involved in World War II, he sent Mother a humorous but rather touching memo, as follows :

> Do you remember that about a month ago I got sick of chicken because I got it . . . at least six times a week ? The chicken situation has definitely improved, but " they " have substituted sweetbreads, and for the past month I have been getting sweetbreads about six times a week.
>
> I am getting to the point where my stomach positively rebels and this does not help my relations with foreign powers. I bit two of them today.
>
> F.D.R.

It was a losing battle for Father, however, and eventually he just gave up. On occasions when he wanted a meal to be just right for some special guest he would import an outside chef. After Granny died he brought her old cook, Mary Campbell, from Hyde Park, and installed her in the family kitchen on the top floor of the White House. He enjoyed his food more from then on, but Granny's cook was no trained dietician, and her meals were a bit heavy on the calories for Father.

Father's loyal staff—Grace Tully, Bill Hassett, and the rest—would become furious at the housekeeper when she failed to provide the few simple things that Father wanted and needed, particularly in the latter years, when his strength was waning.

Hassett has written feelingly of how Mrs Nesbitt rationed the coffee and oranges, even beyond the point of reasonable food conservation, during the War years, and Grace Tully recalls that she once went to Mother to complain that Pa really should not be deprived of butter at both lunch and dinner. Miss Tully also reminds me how Pa, when miserable with a bad cold during the War, was yearning for some fancy canned white asparagus, which, he said, Mrs Nesbitt had told him was " unobtainable." Grace yelled " Spinach ! "—one of Pa's favourite expletives. On her own she directed one of the office girls to get busy on the telephone and find Father some asparagus ; on her first call she turned up a whole case of it.

He Didn't Love His Enemies

Despite his distaste for involvement in unpleasant scenes, Father was no softie. Unlike some Presidents, Father did not try to butter up the opposition by lavishing personal courtesies and fulsome praise upon Republicans—or even Democrats— who were attempting to cut his political throat. He definitely did not believe in rewarding his enemies. Often he would take violent dislikes which warped his ordinarily keen political judgment—to wit, the attempts at " purges " of antagonistic Democrats in Congress. If he came to feel that it was he who had been wrong or hasty in his judgment Father could forgive a man who had riled him. On the other hand, he could bear a grudge for a lifetime. For example, he never quite forgave Jim Farley, who had the Presidential bee in his own bonnet, for leaving him in 1940.

Yet Father was not an angry man. The occasions when he would excoriate a person who had aroused his anger were few. When he did cut a man down in anger it was a deadly—but deliberate—act ; he had prepared himself for it, and usually had even rehearsed what he intended to say. Also the scene, once it was finished, usually left Father badly shaken.

All of Father's wrathful scenes were not rehearsed : some were spontaneous outbursts. The one which I remember most vividly hearing him discuss concerned the time he became angry with Dean Acheson. Acheson has confirmed for me my recollection of the way Father told me the story.

As Under Secretary of the Treasury in 1933, Acheson, always a man of strong convictions, had infuriated Father by refusing to sign an order devaluing the dollar. He told the President to his face that this was a matter for the Attorney-General to pass on, and simply wouldn't do it. Father almost had " apoplexy," Acheson relates.

Soon after Acheson was told by the late Will Woodin, then Secretary of the Treasury, that the President was about to fire him, but that Woodin had interceded and persuaded Father to let him resign instead. Woodin told Acheson he'd better write a letter of resignation, and, implying that the suggestion had come from my irate father, told him he was not to make and keep a carbon of the letter for himself.

The imperturbable Acheson wrote his letter of resignation, but told the Secretary, in effect, that he was damned if anyone was going to tell him he could not keep a copy of his own letter.

Some time later Woodin himself found it necessary to resign because of poor health. A loyal and friendly soul, he asked Dean Acheson to come along with him to Father's office to witness the swearing in of Woodin's successor, Henry Morgenthau, Jr., Father's old friend and Dutchess County neighbour. Acheson accepted. Father told me he was absolutely " flabbergasted " when the man whom he had virtually thrown out of office under such stormy circumstances urbanely appeared at the ceremony. Then the situation tickled his fancy, and he flashed Acheson a cryptic half-grin. After the function was over he called Acheson over, put out his hand, and complimented him on his " good sportsmanship." The rest of the story—how Dean Acheson rejoined the administration and eventually became Secretary of State under Father's successor—is history.

This incident, by the way, effectively disproves the legend that one had to be a " rubber stamp " in order to get along with Father.

Other Facets ; Pa and the Press

I have made the point that Father was a sincerely religious man ; yet he could be irreverent over what he considered unnecessary pomp and ceremony. Once, when he felt obliged in August of 1934 to attend the funeral of Congressman Henry T. Rainey, of Illinois, who had succeeded Vice-President John N. Garner as Speaker of the House of Representatives, Father wrote to his friend Vincent Astor : " I am on the train in East Saint Louis on the way to the Speaker's funeral. The only decent thing for public officials to do is to die at sea and get put overboard without fuss or feathers ! "

He dearly loved to squelch Granny whenever he felt she was getting unreasonably stuffy. Once, when the family was gathered around the swimming-pool at Hyde Park, Granny suddenly noticed that Elliott, just back from the West, had acquired a small tattoo on his arm. " Frank-k-l-lin ! " she exclaimed. " Look what this boy has done to himself ! " Father looked, then burst out laughing. " It is no laughing matter, Franklin ! " Granny said indignantly. " No *gentleman* would submit to such a—such a *mutilation* ! " " Oh, yeah ! " said Pa, using a bit of slang he had picked up from Johnny. " Well, one of your favourite nephews over in England, Charlie Gordon [Charles Fellowes-Gordon], is a gentleman—at least, he's an officer in the Royal Navy—and *he* has tattoos on both arms." We never heard Granny express herself again on the subject of " mutilations."

Father used to rib his Press secretary, the late Steve Early, unmercifully about playing the horses, but he himself was a ringleader in organizing White House betting " pools " on baseball games and other sporting events. I find in his handwriting a memo on a pool he got up for a St Louis-Detroit World Series game in 1934, showing the following profits and losses : " H. the Hop " (Hopkins), $37 (won) ; " Marv the Mac " (Marvin McIntyre), $6 (lost) ; " Pa the Wat " (" Pa " Watson), $4.50 (won) ; " Steven the Earl " (Early), $25.50 (lost) ; " Hal the Ick " (Secretary Ickes), $8.75 (lost) ; " Father " (himself), $12.25 (won) ; and " J. the Rose " (me), $6 (lost). I hope economists will not read too much significance into the fact that Father added up the " win " column for a total of $51, instead of $53.75, and that the two columns do not balance. I'm sure he could explain it somehow if he were here.

Father's personality also shone in his relationship with the Press. He liked newspapermen individually, and he enjoyed his

Press conferences, of which he held approximately a thousand. However, he was a master at baiting the Press in general, and, on rare occasions, even dressing down an individual editor or correspondent. When world events were not too pressing he delighted in conjuring up tricks to call out the reporters on some fool's errand. For instance, at Warm Springs he would summon an " important " conference at his farm. The newsmen, though they came to grow suspicious, could not very well ignore it. When they assembled he would have " Od " Moore, his tenant farmer, trot out some livestock, and Father would lecture the reporters at great length on the importance of having " good mules " or sound " stud bulls " on a farm.

One of the intriguing bits of memorabilia dealing with Father's Press-needling propensities is a memo, dated June 19, 1935, now in the Hyde Park files. It is scribbled in pencil on plain white paper in the handwriting of Father's friend, Felix Frankfurter, later to become a Supreme Court Associate Justice.

> I, Franklin D. Roosevelt . . . do hereby solemnly agree [it reads] to submit in ample time for full discussion to Marguerite LeHand and Felix Frankfurter . . . any and all proposed attacks, direct or indirect, upon the press or parts thereof, under any form or pretexts. So help me good [sic].

The document is witnessed by Grace Tully, and is signed, quite irreverently, " Nerts—Franklin D. Roosevelt."

I had never heard of this memo and what provoked it, and Grace Tully couldn't remember. So a special query was addressed to Mr Justice Frankfurter, who responded with the following explanation :

> I was staying at the White House. . . . One night at dinner with the President, at which besides myself there were present Misses Marguerite LeHand and Grace Tully, the President went on a gay rampage about some journalistic irresponsibility for which he was going to call the press to account at one of his press conferences. Both Miss LeHand and I expressed the hope that he would not get into a needless scrimmage with the press. Our attitude evidently intensified the President's shadow-boxing against the press. He simulated such seriousness that he took us in and we exacted a promise from him that he wouldn't waste his time on his planned attack on the press. The talk gradually gained hilarity and it took the form of a spurious formal agreement.

The most devastating verbal surgery I ever witnessed Father perform on a Press critic was at the 1934 dinner of the famous Gridiron Club, the association of Washington correspondents which annually puts public officials on the frying-pan and listens to off-the-record speeches from certain of the " victims." Father's target that night was the late, formidable Henry L. Mencken of Baltimore, who, preceding Father as a speaker, had hit the New Deal with just about everything but an old linotype machine.

Father began his remarks with a blandly innocent reference to " my old friend Henry Mencken." Then, abruptly, Father launched into an unbridled, really vicious attack on the Press. It was couched in language not at all like Father's usual style— for example, an assertion that the American Press was steeped in " stupidity, cowardice, and Philistinism."

At this point the stunned guests were beginning to wonder if Pa had gone off his rocker. Then a number of the more erudite and well-read correspondents began laughing, and it became noticeable that Mr Mencken, who had the wonderfully expressive countenance of a slightly bawdy cherub, was taking on an alarming, boiled-lobster colour. I was closer to Father than I was to Mencken and could not hear the latter's remark, but, according to Edgar Kemler's *The Irreverent Mr Mencken*, the Sage of Baltimore whispered furiously to his tablemate, Maryland's Governor Ritchie : " I'll get the --- -- - ----- ! I'll dig the skeletons out of his closet ! " Then, gradually, it dawned on the assembled newspapermen that what Father was doing was reading from something Mencken himself had written—in this case Mencken's essay " Journalism in America " from his *Prejudices : Sixth Series.*

The real crusher came when the dinner was over. Every one waited, according to protocol, until the President left the room. As he was leaving Pa stopped where Mencken was standing and, beaming at him, pumped his hand vigorously.

I don't think I need belabour the fact that Father was a consummate showman, even down to knowing the value of the " props " that became his trademarks—the pince-nez eyeglasses, the floppy white hats for the fishing-trips and cruises, and the quill cigarette-holder, gripped in the corner of his mouth at a cocky angle. The glasses actually date back to his last year at

Groton ; on April 12, 1900, he wrote his parents : " I'm writing in ' specks ' ! . . . I got them this morning, a pair of spectacles & a pair of ' *pince-nez.*' Next time you see me you won't know me." I once asked Father why he continued wearing these seemingly uncomfortable, rather prissy-looking glasses, which clip to the bridge of the nose. " Well," he said, " in the first place I'm accustomed to them and find them comfortable. In the second place, soon after I began wearing *pince-nez* various persons began chivvying me about them, saying they made me look ' snobbish.' This made me angry—I knew I wasn't snobbish —so I just kept on wearing them." (He could have added : ". . . out of Dutch stubbornness.")

The floppy white hat also was an early fixture. In the same Groton letter cited above he told his parents that some tennis equipment he had ordered had arrived from a New York shop. " They sent me a *lady's* white hat, so I shall send it back & get a real one," he said.

To the best of my knowledge Father's quill cigarette-holder was discovered for him by Louis Howe. It was sold by a Washington tobacco-shop. I doubt that filters were in general use when Father became addicted to his quill holder ; in any event, his had no filter. He simply liked the way he could clench it between his teeth and the way he could gesture with it. Being economical by nature, Pa let the quill mouthpieces get pretty dirty before he'd change them.

In thoughtfulness and loyalty to his family, his co-workers, and his friends Father had no peer. To me it has always been astounding how Pa, in the midst of banking crises, political campaigns, and wars, could find time to dig up some little keep sake for a child or a grandchild, and send it to him or her with a warm little note. The family correspondence files are crammed with such memos : he sent every one of us everything from books, naval prints, photograph-albums, silver, and woollen socks to family heirlooms—anything he thought we might treasure, enjoy, or just plain use. In those critical days less than six months after the United States entered World War II, Pa found time to send Anna a silver bottle—a souvenir from a submarine christening at which she had officiated—which he found at Hyde Park. In the same parcel he had Grace Tully pack a lemon-squeezer which " Sistie might like to have to make her own lemonade." Anna wrote Miss Tully : " It is continually amazing to me how Father finds the time to go through these things and send them along to his long list of children and grandchildren ! " During World War II my wife got an old copy of *The Grotonian* which Father had found, because he thought she " would be interested in the story about Jimmy when he . . . broke his leg on the first play." Each son received a gold watch which at one time or other had been used by Father, and, since he had no watch that would have been appropriate for Anna, he sent one to her son, Curtis (Buzzie), with a note explaining that " one of my watches would have gone to your Mother if she had been a boy ! "

His consideration for his staff was remarkable. He was such a good boss, in fact, that when I was in the White House as a member of his secretariat all of us felt guilty as dogs when he found it necessary one day to address a handwritten memo to Marvin McIntyre, Steve Early, Missy LeHand, and myself, saying : " From now on till the close of the session *please* don't take any afternoons off—& *please* don't be gone more than 1 hour for lunch. I've been put in hole a number of times ! FDR." What had happened was that Pa usually lunched at his desk, and had been unable to find any of us on several occasions when he needed us.

I recall an example of Pa's genuine consideration for others. One of his friends from the Warm Springs area was Cason Callaway, the now retired president of Callaway Mills and director of a number of corporations which did not and do not regard Father as their hero. Although their political and economic views differed, Father and Callaway liked each other personally, and shared an enthusiasm for developing Georgia's land resources.

Father had invited Mr and Mrs Callaway to come to Washington, spend a night at the White House, and attend the President's dinner for the Supreme Court. It was a white-tie affair, and somehow the multi-millionaire Georgia industrialist failed to bring the proper studs for his white vest. He discovered this just before he was due downstairs, and sent a valet to inquire if Father had an extra pair. Father sent back word that he was lucky to have one pair of white studs. At this hour the shops were closed, and it would have been too late to send out for studs.

Deeply chagrined, Callaway inserted his black studs into his white vest and slunk down to the reception room, " reproaching myself all the while that these important Justices would think that this Georgia boy just didn't know how to dress ! " When he came to Father in the reception line he noticed that Pa sort of winked at him and made a gesture with his head indicating his own vest. Callaway looked at Father's vest : to put his friend at ease Pa was wearing black studs, too.

Fun at the Treasury (Secretary's) Expense

Yet Father missed few opportunities to play practical jokes on certain of his associates—particularly the literal-minded Secretary of the Treasury, Henry Morgenthau.[1] Pa loved to tell of the time when Morgenthau was due to make a war-bond-drive speech on the Treasury Department steps, almost within earshot of the White House. Feeling pixyish that morning, Pa sent a Treasury official to the platform with a note he had written, instructing him to hand it to Morgenthau while Henry was speaking, and to whisper instructions to him that " the President wants you to work this into your speech." The note and instructions were delivered ; Morgenthau dutifully looked at the slip of paper, and started automatically to carry out orders and read it. Then he choked, spluttered, and tumbled while striving to regain his aplomb. On the note Pa had written something quite bawdy.

Father genuinely liked Henry, but was amused by some of his crotchets—particularly his periodic " resignations " when his feelings were hurt. I've forgotten how many times I, or some other emissary, would be sent to mollify Henry after Father had provoked him into " resigning." Sometimes Pa himself would pour on the soothing-syrup.

I was present when Morgenthau was the victim of another of Father's classic jokes. Pa's inner circle, the " Cuff Links Gang," composed of veterans of the 1920 Vice-Presidential campaign

[1] See letter from Eleanor Roosevelt to James Roosevelt on p. 341.

and a few more recent cronies, was having its traditional poker-game in Father's office on the night Congress was due to adjourn. The custom was for the group to play until Father received a personal telephone-call from the Speaker of the House—then Representative Bankhead, of Alabama—that all business had been transacted, and, unless the President had some special matter, the session would come to an end.

That night Morgenthau was far ahead. He obviously was anxious to cash in his chips, but could not do so in good faith until Congress—and the poker-game—had been declared adjourned.

Pa was determined Henry was not going to walk out with all the money. He instructed me privately to telephone Speaker Bankhead and warn him, if he heard a lot of double-talk when he made his call, not to think that the President had gone out of his mind.

The Speaker's call came around 9 P.M., and Morgenthau still was ahead. Father's end of the conversation went something like this : " Why, Mr Speaker—you mean to have to stay in session *at least* another hour ? Well, all right, I'll be right here."

Then he turned back to the table and said imperturbably, " Deal the cards."

By the time Father finally " adjourned " Congress by means of a fake telephone-call I had arranged with one of the White House ushers, we had cleaned Henry of all his winnings.

Next morning, when he read in the papers that Congress had adjourned per schedule at 9 P.M., he realized he had been " had." Over to the White House came his " resignation." He was talked out of it, of course, but for a long time he kept muttering about what a really reprehensible trick this was that Pa had played on him.

In 1941 I visited Chungking for Father

Father and Grandmother with Queen Elizabeth, Hyde Park, June 1939
Associated Press

Lieutenant-Colonel Evans F. Carlson, First Lieutenant A. C. Plumley, and myself on training manœuvres, August 1942
Harris and Ewing

Father and Mother with their thirteen grandchildren in the White House study, January 1945
Franklin D. Roosevelt Library

16

Into the White House; the Hundred Days

On March 3, 1933, the day before he was to take office as President of the United States, Father asked me to accompany Mother and him to the White House for their pre-inaugural protocol call on President and Mrs Hoover. He did this for two reasons. First, he had a strong sense of history, which he liked to share, when possible, with his children, and, second, he needed help in walking, and preferred on this particular occasion to be assisted by a member of his family.

It would be putting it mildly to state that Mr Hoover was not happy with Father. It seemed that he had taken his defeat as even more of a personal humiliation than it should have been.

In any event, in the lame-duck months between Mr Hoover's defeat and Father's inauguration the country's economic plight grew worse, and the outgoing President made repeated attempts, which have been documented by numerous political biographers, to involve Father in sharing the responsibilities on Mr Hoover's terms. Father, while going full speed ahead in formulating his own plans for the recovery programme he intended to initiate, would have co-operated with any acceptable measures for the good of the country. He had no intention, however, of letting Mr Hoover manoeuvre him into a position in which he would share the blame for the retiring Chief Executive's repudiated policies. So, politely but skilfully, Father dodged every time the gloomy Mr Hoover sought to lasso him.

All this did not tend to create a congenial atmosphere on the afternoon Father, Mother, my wife, and I paid our courtesy call to the Pennsylvania Avenue mansion which was to be Father's

and Mother's home for more years than they anticipated. The
call was made at tea-time, and we were to be received in the
Green Room on the first floor of the White House. For Father's
convenience we entered by the ground-level south entrance
(under what now is Mr Truman's famous balcony), took the
elevator to the first floor, and walked to the Green Room. In a
short while Mrs Hoover appeared. She was extremely gracious,
a thoroughgoing lady.

Then we sat. To the best of my recollection fully thirty
minutes went by. It seemed even longer. Father was imperturbable and betrayed no irritation. I kept looking at him, and could
see, however, that he did not like it.

At last President Hoover entered. To Father's astonishment,
for no hint had been given that this would be anything but a
social call, he was accompanied by the outgoing Secretary of the
Treasury, the late Ogden Mills, Father's conservative Dutchess
County neighbour and one of the principal architects of the fiscal
policies to which Father did not intend to be pinned.

Father told me later that Mr Hoover's ringing in of Ogden
Mills at this meeting was one of the damndest bits of presumption
he had ever witnessed in politics. It was plain that Mills was not
along just to have a cup of tea. It was an obvious eleventh-hour
attempt, on Mr Hoover's last full day in the White House, to
involve Father in some sort of footless contact with a subject
which he was determined to avoid.

I sat there fascinated as Father gave me one of my earliest
lessons in how to avoid political booby-traps. As soon as Mr
Hoover made reference to the fact that Secretary Mills had been
invited because his presence might be helpful Father cut in,
courteously but firmly, and observed that he certainly would not
presume to bring up any serious discussions on this purely social
occasion. Before he would undertake to discuss any fiscal
matters, he said, he would want his own advisers with him.

That pretty much broke up the party. We downed our tea,
Mother and Mrs Hoover made desultory conversation, and then
it was time to go.

At this point Father attempted to make a graceful gesture.
" Mr President," he remarked, " as you know, it is rather difficult
for me to move in a hurry. It takes me a little while to get up,

and I know how busy you must be, sir, so please don't wait for me."

Mr Hoover just stood up, looked at Father bleakly, and said in his low monotone, " Mr Roosevelt, after you have been President for a while you will learn that the President of the United States waits for no one." With that, and with no amenities, he strode from the room, Ogden Mills behind him. Mrs Hoover looked embarrassed ; she shook hands all around, and then she left, too, leaving the prospective " new tenants " on their own to make their departure.

Father was not so much angry as appalled. As for my feelings —well, I was young at the time, and my good friend Grace Tully, Father's private secretary, has recorded that Father told her " Jimmy wanted to punch him in the nose." I certainly would not claim that my own father had misquoted me.

On Inauguration Day I was again at Father's side to lend him an arm as he made his slow progress to the rostrum on the Capitol steps to take his oath of office. I had ridden on the front seat of the limousine that carried the outgoing President Hoover and Father to the ceremony. Again, so far as Mr Hoover was concerned, it was a most lugubrious occasion. As we rolled along Pennsylvania Avenue the crowds were cheering and calling out to Father, and he was raising his silk hat, confidently smiling and bowing. Already it was like a tonic after the four years of increasing gloom that had emanated from the White House.

Suddenly Father stole a look at Mr Hoover, and realized he was sitting there grim as death, looking stonily forward and not glancing at the crowd at all. It was downright embarrassing, so Father put his hat back on his head and tried to restrain his enthusiasm.

Father also tried to make some conversation with Mr Hoover, but for once in his life Pa, an acknowledged master of the art of small talk, was unable to keep a colloquy going. As we passed a Government building in process of construction I heard Pa remark rather desperately, " My, Mr President, aren't those the nicest steel girders you ever saw ! " Mr Hoover had no comment on that observation either, and shortly after that Pa just gave up.

When Father went into the White House he asked me to come to Washington to help him as a sort of unofficial aide. I was established in the insurance business by this time, and had a wife and baby to support, but I accepted immediately. Frankly, I was eager to do it. Not only did I want to be near Father, but I was intoxicated by the excitement of the campaign I had just been through with him, and I was keen to learn more about politics and government. I knew that stirring events were ahead, and nothing could have kept me from taking advantage of the ringside seat he offered me.

It was an ambiguous sort of arrangement : I had no official status, no salary, and, despite the wild stories that were written during this period about how I allegedly was coining money because of my connexion with Father, I was not capitalizing on our relationship. I was not raking in the dollars, as the scandal-mongers alleged ; in fact, because of my lack of realistic preparation for facing the fiscal facts of life, I was, as usual, pretty much behind the financial eight ball. Father thought to solve my dilemma by putting me on an allowance, as if I were back at college again, but I demurred that I was a grown man and that this would not be dignified. I stayed at the White House as his guest, did what I could to be helpful, but took no salary and no allowance.

Even before Father was inaugurated he was using me to represent him in certain quasi-official capacities. When former President Calvin Coolidge died at Northampton, Massachusetts, in January 1933 Father thought it would be a courteous gesture for the President-elect to be represented by members of his family at the funeral, so he asked me to accompany Mother to the last rites. I was travelling in the Midwest, and received word by telegram that I was to meet Mother back at Northampton, and that proper clothing would be shipped to me. When I opened the suitcase I found that a horrible mistake had been made. Instead of striped pants, cutaway, and silk hat, I had been sent a full-dress evening suit and a collapsible opera hat. By borrowing the proper kind of shirt and collar I thought I could get by if I kept on my dark overcoat throughout the ceremony. Unfortunately the church was heated almost to the temperature of a steam bath. Between mopping away the perspiration and trying to conceal my folding opera hat I presented such a ludicrous sight that Mother got the giggles. This, in turn, threw me into somewhat uncontrolled laughter. The news services thereupon got a photograph of Mrs Franklin D. Roosevelt and son apparently having a hilarious time at the Republican ex-President's funeral. When we got home both of us asked Father please not to send us to any more funerals.

One of Father's first orders when he moved into the White House was symbolic of the New Deal's humanity. He circulated word to his staff, from the top secretaries to the telephone operators, that if persons in distress telephoned to appeal for help of any sort they were not to be shut off, but that some one was to talk with them. If a farmer in Iowa was about to have his mortgage foreclosed, if a home-owner in one of the big cities was about to lose his home, and they felt desperate enough about it to phone the White House, Father wanted help given them if a way possibly could be found ; he was keenly cognizant of the suffering he had seen on his campaign trips. Many such calls were taken—sometimes by me, when I was in the White House, and occasionally by Mother. Often ways were found to cut red tape with some Federal agency. After Father's death Mother received letters from strangers who told her how, in the dark depression days, they telephoned their President and received aid. This, in short, was what the New Deal was about : it was government by humanity, not by slide-rule or advertising agency.

I remember the informal atmosphere of some of the all-night and early-morning sessions of the " hundred days," when Father would work overtime with his principal lieutenants. One night he knew a late session was in store, and he told his Secretary of the Treasury, Will Woodin, an accomplished amateur musician, who played guitar, violin, piano, and even the zither, to bring his violin with him to the White House. About two o'clock in the morning every one was getting a little punchy with fatigue, but there was still much work to be finished. Father called for a breather, sent for refreshments, and said to the Secretary, " Will, get out that violin of yours and play it for us." So the Secretary, a delightful fellow, uncased his fiddle, tuned it, and, with no accompaniment, ran through some pieces by Debussy and, if my memory is correct, a number or two that he himself had composed.

" *At Home* " *in the White House*

As the Roosevelts settled into the White House life in that historic mansion certainly took on an informal flavour. The part of it in which Father and Mother lived—the area that the general public does not see—gradually acquired the look of any Roosevelt residence from Hyde Park to Campobello. Family pictures, snapshots of the children and grandchildren (and their pets) at various ages, Pa's inevitable naval prints, ship models, assorted bric-à-brac, and all sorts of odd gadgets and outright junk which people had given him, or which Mother had picked up somewhere, were strewn about the place. The décor may not have been any decorator's dream, but, White House or not, it looked homey.

Pa's office was even more cluttered. One could hardly see his desk-top for the gadgets he piled on it. There were figurines of donkeys galore, a sad elephant or two, porcelain pigs, and mechanical toys, such as flags that waved in an electrically created breeze. My little daughters, Sara and Kate, and the other grandchildren, who all called him " Papa," would drool when they saw " Papa's " toy collection. Much as he loved his grandchildren, he could rarely bring himself to part with any gadget once it had achieved the distinction of being selected for his desk. The kids, however, gleaned much of the " loot " screened out in the earlier stages.

Grandchildren were all over the place. Father loved to have them at the White House, and often would play with them in his bed after he had finished breakfast and the morning papers. Sistie and Buzzie, Anna's children, practically grew up in the White House, and Mother created a minor national furore when she defied the White House gardener by insisting it would not hurt one of the historic trees on the lawn to tie a rope swing to it. Once, just before a formal reception, Sistie and Buzzie added their touch to the décor of the President's mansion by festooning toilet-paper on the banister of the grand staircase to the East Room.

The various grandchildren became favourites of the White House guards and attendants, and the kids learned quickly which guard could always be touched up for a candy-bar. Some

of my brothers and I agree that the kids were probably so eager
for candy-bars because the White House food was so bad.   At
night some grandchild or other was always wandering out of
bed, roaming the historic corridors.   As the grandchildren became
more numerous—I think the count was approximately thirteen,
more or less, before Father's occupancy of the White House
ended—the guards occasionally had difficulty in recognizing
just who was who and getting the right child back to the right
room.

Once when my brother John and his wife were going away
they parked their infant, Haven, at the White House.   In setting
up the arrangements John got Father on the phone—Mother
was away at the time—and asked him if he would have some one
order six dozen diapers for the baby.   Pa was fascinated.   First
he wanted to know why the baby didn't have diapers of his own.
Then, when John explained to him that it wasn't done that way
any more, Pa inquired, " Well, why so many ? "   At this point
John said rather impatiently that he didn't know why so many,
but that six dozen was the number which the child's mother had
specified, so would Pa please order them ?

When the conversation was over Pa called in his secretaries
to rehash the conversation.   He swore he was going to place the
order personally, just to hear the " didie " company's reaction
when his voice came over the telephone, saying, " This is the
President of the United States.   Please send six dozen diapers
to the White House."

As I have already noted, I never felt particularly at home in
the White House.   Elliott was rarely there, though his children
frequently visited their grandparents.   Franklin, Jr., and Johnny
would drift in and out, when they had a week-end or holiday off
from school, and they would have lively parties for their young
friends in the East Ballroom or elsewhere.

Anna lived in the White House more than any of us, and
enjoyed it the most.   " It was an amazing and wonderful residence," Sis says.   " Despite the tremendous history behind it, I
always found it a warm rather than oppressive place."

Anna's irrepressibility, in fact, helped make the White House
a home rather than an institution.   Once a visiting friend of
Mother's was occupying the Lincoln bedroom—the one that is

supposed to be " haunted." This particular guest was not over-popular with either Father or Anna. So Anna, Sistie, and Buzz began devilling her, first by making her the victim of a trick that has been a favourite in our family for as long as I can remember : they booby-trapped her bed—the big Lincoln bed— by performing various acts of sabotage with the sheets and so forth.

Then Sis discovered that the lady wore long union suits. One night she, Sistie, and Buzz decided that, since the lady was occupying the haunted bedroom, they would provide her with a " ghost." One of them sneaked in, swiped a union suit, and the three of them stuffed it with stiff paper. Then they draped it with a sheet and set it up just outside the door of the Lincoln bedroom, and went to fetch Father so he could see it. His laughter could be heard from one end of the corridor to the other. Mother, as can be imagined, took a less than dim view of the performance.

I recall another lively evening in the White House, either on the night of Father's second inauguration or during one of the Christmas holidays when all the boys were on hand. Also present was Mother's younger brother, G. Hall Roosevelt, a mountain of a man, about whom we always said, " He's just a boy at heart." They were all congregated in the bedroom of one of my brothers. A pillow-fight started, and it developed into a general roughhouse, with every one piling on Hall. The com-motion could be heard in Father's bedroom, where I was talking with him at the time. Finally it grew so wild that Father raised his eyebrows and suggested that I had better " go and see if you can arbitrate among those battling warriors ! " I did as I was told, and promptly suffered the fate of most arbitrators, the participants all got mad at me, and soon I was at the bottom of the heap.

Living in the Limelight

All of us, from Father and Mother down through the children and, to lesser degrees, even the grandchildren, learned what it meant to live in the limelight. As the New Deal honeymoon faded no rumour about Father, Mother, and their brood was too wild, too ridiculous, too libellous, or even too obscene to circulate.

To this day Mother feels that some of the problems which we have encountered have been due to our activities having been unduly publicized. The slightest slip—a speeding ticket or an argument in public—drew banner headlines. Mother had long, earnest talks with the younger boys—particularly Franklin, Jr., who fiercely resented the publicity accorded his slightest escapade. She tried to impress on him that life was not so bad—that he'd always had a good place to live, plenty to eat, a proper education, and other advantages—and that it really was not so awful for him to have to learn to live with what he considered undue publicity. At this point Brud would blow his top about how unfair it was that he should make the headlines for things which passed unnoticed when the Joneses or Smiths did them. The discussions always ended with Mother's getting nowhere.

On the other hand, some officials, seeking to court favour with the White House, would excuse offences for which one of the boys should have been penalized, which was just as harmful. There were examples concerning driving offences.

Another hazard was that every one of us was exposed to blandishments offered by seasoned operators and promoters who thought they could win some influence with the White House by being " nice " to the young Roosevelts. Sometimes we were not so bright as we should have been, and Father suffered some unfortunate publicity because of our poor judgment.

And finally came the time of the divorces, unfortunately coinciding with Father's accession to the highest office in the land. We thought less of Father's position and more—selfishly, if humanly—of ourselves. Yet throughout the waves of sermons by certain clerics and the holier-than-thou editorials and letters-to-the editors Father's loyalty—and Mother's loyalty too—never wavered.

Father was hurt a good deal because of the divorces—and it is a personal, not political, hurt about which I am talking. Yet he held to his line of interfering as little as possible in our private lives. In her autobiographical *This I Remember* Mother, commenting on Father's reaction to the first two divorces in the family (Elliott'o and Anna's), both after he was in the White House, writes :

> In each case Franklin had done what he could to prevent the divorce, but when he was convinced that the children had made up their minds after careful reflection, it never occurred to him to suggest that they should subordinate their lives to his interest. He said that he thought a man in politics stood or fell by the results of his policies ; that what the children did or did not do affected their lives, and that he did not consider that their lives should be tied to his political interests. He was quite right.

The mere problem of privacy becomes a rather painful thing to the son or daughter of a President—particularly a controversial President, whom people seem either to love or hate to extremes. The haters operate on the theory that they have a right to say whatever they please—even obscene things—to your face about your father and mother, and you are supposed to stand still and take it or walk away. Over the years I developed sense enough to know it was not going to help Father for me to become involved in public brawls, regardless of what personal satisfaction it might give me.

Sometimes this was hard to do. In 1940, for example, a man seated behind me on a train began speaking vilely of Father and Mother. There was no empty seat elsewhere to which I could move, so I finally told him to shut up. He started to rise. I rose first and shoved him back into his seat—rather hard—then hastily left the car before the incident went further. I'll admit there have been times when I wished I was more like Elliott, who never thought it quite so important to restrain himself. Elliott has taken a number of quite effective pokes at persons who defamed Pa in his presence. Each time, of course, it brought detrimental publicity, which didn't help Father.

The Time We Didn't Horsewhip Mr Pegler

As a matter of fact, Elliott, who can be a very persuasive guy, once almost talked me out of my non-aggression policy, and if it had not been for Father himself talking some good

sense into us the result might have been the juiciest headlines of our respective careers.   The incident involved Westbrook
Pegler, the columnist, who, as readers of his column may suspect,
has not been a constant admirer of the Roosevelt family and the
New Deal.

A state of hostility did not always exist between Father and
the columnist.   In March 1934, believe it or not, Pegler actually
wrote :

> Never have I encountered a subject . . . who lays it on the line as
> Mr Roosevelt does. . . . I am afraid I couldn't be trusted around Mr
> Roosevelt.   For the first time in my life in this business I might
> find myself squabbling for a chance to carry the champion's water
> bucket.

Mr Pegler may deny this, and I have no written documentation
by which to prove it, but Mother and I both remember that at
one time he was so enamoured of the New Deal that he sent a
feeler to the White House letting Father know he was willing
to join the administration in some suitable position.   An offer
was not forthcoming.

In any event, things had changed since the days when he
wanted to carry the champ's water bucket, and Mr Pegler was
now writing some pretty mean things about us.   One day he
wrote something especially rough that triggered Elliott's temper.
Elliott came to my house in Washington to discuss Mr Pegler
with me.   Things, he thought, had gone too far.   I agreed that
it was pretty bad.

Then Elliott came up with his proposed remedy.   " Jimmy,"
he said, " there's only one thing to do.   You and I have got to
waylay the guy and beat the hell out of him.   Something humiliating and undignified—maybe with a horsewhip."

I don't know what was wrong with my judgment that day,
but all of a sudden the idea appealed to me.   Elliott and I discussed various techniques and strategies that might be used.
Then a modicum of sense prevailed, and I proposed that before
we did anything we should advise Father what we had in mind.
Elliott was dubious about this, but I insisted, so he had to go
along.

We went to see Father at the White House, and I, as the

senior spokesman, laid the plan before him. Pa was simply wonderful ! He listened to our ludicrous proposal with a perfectly straight face, though I suspect he wanted to double up, start howling, and then send us both back to kindergarten. Then, with a judicial calm that would have done credit to any of the " Nine Old Men " of the Supreme Court which he was then being accused of attempting to pack, he started in gravely to demolish our arguments. He pointed out all the cons—no pros !—and made us see the unwisdom of our plan to horsewhip Mr Pegler, however soul-satisfying it might be. Finally, when he had our promise—Elliott's given grudgingly—that we would forget the whole thing, he burst our laughing and exclaimed, " Not that it isn't a grand idea—in principle ! "

Mother is Made to Carry a Pistol

At some time or other most of us had to put up with having our children guarded against crackpots by the Secret Service. When Franklin, Jr., was married to Ethel du Pont and they were living in New York City the Secret Service decided they should be protected too. Brud found this a nuisance, and wrote Father to " *please* have the detail discontinued " ; there was no need for it, and " the boredom of the job nearly drives the SS man insane."

Mother was driving around the country a good deal, and the Secret Service insisted that, since she would not let an agent accompany her, she must carry a pistol. All of us had great fun kidding her about this : " Dead-Eye Nell " and " Annie Oakley Roosevelt " were some of the names we called her. What struck us as particularly incongruous was the fact that Mother has never fired a shot in anger in her life, and would suffer a thousand deaths if she so much as nicked the little finger of a malefactor. The news that Mother was carrying a pistol got in the newspapers, and a Roosevelt-baiting mayor of a Midwestern town, where Mother was going to speak, threatened to have her nabbed as a gun-toter if she set foot in his bailiwick carrying the thing. The Secret Service, of course, had anticipated this by issuing her an agent's commission and badge, making everything quite legal.

One of the big difficulties of having the President of the United States for a father was the matter of getting in to see him and capturing his full attention when one of us had a problem on which we felt we needed his advice. I, personally, think Pa handled it very well, and it was amazing how patient and generous he was with his time when we wanted to talk with him. However, there were occasions when some of my brothers felt they were getting rather short treatment. Mother tells of the time when one of my brothers had made an appointment to see Father in his office— it *was* necessary to make an appointment with the President during office hours—and, on getting in, had poured out his heart to Father on some personal problem that seemed terribly important. Though Father usually was attentive, this day his mind was occupied by an important document he had been reading. At the end of my brother's recital Pa turned: him absently and said, " This is a most important document; I'd like your opinion on it." My brother, his feelings hurt, went to Mother and swore he'd never seek Father's advice again.

I always found it was possible to get Father's attention and to elicit good advice from him. It simply was a matter of picking the right time, and, if he seemed preoccupied, either postponing the conference or, if the matter would not wait, getting through to him by stressing that you had a real problem. Pa liked every one around him—including us—to lay things on the line when they talked to him ; where business was concerned he had no patience for rambling discourses or an over-abundance of details. He had an extraordinary knack for rapidly sizing up a situation. As a matter of fact, there were occasions when he wounded Mother's feelings by cutting her off when she would return from some trip full of enthusiasm and bursting to tell him *everything* she had learned.

Father certainly knew what we were missing in parental direction because of the job he had taken on. Though he never discussed it with any of us—at least, not with me—it obviously was on his mind a good deal. He was not a man who discussed his personal feelings with others, but one day—I learned this only recently from James H. Rowe, Jr., who had been my assistant when I was in the White House—Father, in a rare outburst, exclaimed to Jim Rowe, " One of the worst things in the world is being the child of a President ! It's a terrible life they lead ! "

What Makes Johnny Republican ?

I think it was our youngest brother, John, who was nine days short of his seventeenth birthday when Father went into the White House, who missed the most in the way of fatherly guidance. John, who has his own ideas, insists that there was nothing " abnormal " about growing up as the son of a man in the limelight. " To me it was normal, because I did not know anything else," he says.

It is no secret, however, that Mother, Anna, Elliott, Franklin, Jr., and I all are staunch Democrats, and that we regard it as a damned peculiar oddity that John has turned Republican. Occasionally we try to explain it by saying that he must have been traumatized by his rude experience at the White House on the morning after Pa was inaugurated.

Some time after midnight John, who had been out celebrating, drove up to the White House gates in a disreputable roadster. The guards wouldn't let him in. " I'm John Roosevelt ! " he protested. " Go on ! " they told him. " No son of the President would be driving such a junk-heap ! " So poor Johnny spent the rest of the night in a hotel lobby.

Shortly after that Johnny complained to Mother with great indignation that he had come in hungry one night, tried to raid the icebox, and found it locked. " What kind of a joint is this ? " he demanded. " You not only can't get past the gates, you can't even get into the icebox ! "

John's Republicanism, which he did not embrace until after Father's death, does create certain problems. In New York a few years ago, when Johnny was off somewhere—probably making a speech for the G.O.P.—Franklin, Jr., and I decided to take his wife, the former Anne Clark, who comes from a rock-ribbed Republican family, to dinner. We went to a certain plush eatery, and there encountered the well-known restaurateur Mr Toots Shor, who was taking a night off from his own place of business. Toots, an all-round character and a good Democrat, spotted me and gave me a bear-hug. He gave Franklin, whom

he knew better, two bear-hugs. Then he leaned over and asked,
" Who's the dame ? "

" Meet Mrs John Roosevelt—my brother's wife," I said, with
some misgivings.

Toots focused his gaze on her and, in full voice, bellowed,
" What ! You married to that Republican S.O.B. ? "

The Presidency Brings More Family Problems

The fact that Father had become President did not automatically shut off the propensity of the members of our family
to create problems. Family problems—jobs, debts, school crises,
automobile accidents, and so forth—went on.

Elliott continued to give Mother a good deal of concern.
Though she kept it a private matter between herself and Father,
she was considerably upset by Elliott's restlessness of that time
which led to his first divorce. In July 1933 she wrote Father
that she found it impossible to believe that Elliott was considering
remarriage, for he had no job. " It is better to let him fend for
himself," she said, " but I don't want him to borrow from others
or to give the impression to others that we won't give him anything."

Mother's concern for Elliott continued over the years, and on
occasions she allowed her maternal feelings to affect her better
judgment. In July 1937, for instance, when Elliott was attempting to get himself set up in a Texas radio-network operation,
Mother wrote Father from Texas that Elliott was " dreadfully
upset " because there had been no action by the Federal Communications Commission on the licensing of the stations which
were being sought in the name of his second wife. He had
become convinced—perhaps with good reason—that he was
being discriminated against because of his name, and Mother
asked, " Couldn't you or James say a word which wld. hurry them
—You know Elliott's disposition, he is beginning to think you
are both against him."

To the best of my recollection Father and I stayed out of this
situation completely, although in due course Elliott got his
licences.

Father remained as warm and generous towards Elliott as

any parent possibly could be. At one point he made a sizeable personal loan to Elliott, and wrote him : " I wish I could feel that all my loans are as good as yours." Elliott repaid every cent of it.

As a matter of fact, Father's generosity to all of us never ceased. Allowances for Elliott and me were ended soon after we left school, as it was Father's feeling at that time that a man should be on his own from then on. However, he was helpful to both of us from time to time with loans, and he carried a large insurance premium for me up to the time of his death. Anna also was assisted in various ways after her first marriage. In the case of the two younger boys Father came to modify his views, because of special circumstances, and he continued their allowances for some time after their marriages. In Franklin's case the two factors Father considered were (1) the fact that he went on from Harvard to the University of Virginia law school and (2) his marriage to the wealthy Ethel du Pont. Pa just couldn't see letting a Franklin Delano Roosevelt, Jr., live on du Pont money.

John followed Franklin at Harvard in 1935. He soon made the Boston papers with a cartoon about his alleged reckless driving—a drawing of Pa peering from the White House front door at a set of bashed-in colonnades, and a footman informing him, " It's Master John, Mr President ! "

Not every one, however, was prone to lambast the President's sons. One old Harvard graduate, who said he had seen a lot of both boys at college, wrote Father : " I have never observed finer, better behaved, quieter or more unobtrusive lads." In a reply which revealed his own resentment over what he felt was unfair criticism of his sons Father wrote back :

Your letter has touched me very deeply. It is just the kind of letter any father would rejoice to receive concerning his boys. And I thank you from the bottom of my heart for writing as you did— and from personal observation—your resentment of what I know to be a cruel, unjust and unwarranted cartoon. Yet I am powerless to voice the protest which you have expressed in such a fine spirit and with such an exact sense of justice and fair play.

Some of my activities also brought Father harsh letters. During the 1934 Massachusetts gubernatorial campaign my political friendship with Jim Curley provoked one critic to write : " Tell your son James to take that New Deal coat and false face away from Curley and bring them back to Washington." Father sent the letter to Press Secretary Steve Early with the comment : " My first impression is not to answer this at all. My second is to send a stereotype reply saying the President is taking no part in any campaign. My third is to file it. F.D.R." (It was filed.)

By this time I had ended my business connexion with Victor de Gerard and had formed an insurance partnership with the late John Sargent. Hardly a month went by without the airing of some lurid but undocumented accusation, alleging that I was using my " influence " to obtain lucrative contracts. Many of these letters were sent to the White House. In 1934, after Father forwarded to me a particularly virulent letter based entirely on innuendo, I wrote him : " Some day maybe someone will have guts enough to really make an accusation, so that we can have an out-and-out investigation. Gosh, how I would love it ! ! "

One friendly correspondent wrote Father of absurd rumours that I had extracted a huge amount of business from a Boston bank president by threatening to have the city of Boston cancel " a million-dollar " deposit. How I was to accomplish this was not explained. Father, loyal as ever, replied :

> I sent your letter to my boy James. He has, of course, heard the same story . . . and every time he tries to find out the name of the bank or the [bank] President mentioned in the story, he runs up against a blank wall. There is, of course, not a word of truth in it or the other stories which are being circulated but I suppose it is one of those things which people in public life have to put up with at the hands, not of the ignorant, but of well educated people who are perfectly willing to stoop to false propaganda.

Finally, in 1938, the *Saturday Evening Post* ran an article entitled " Jimmy's Got It," written by Alva Johnston. In it I read a lot of things that astonished me, one of which was the ambiguously worded estimate that my income ranged from about $250,000 to $2,000,000 a year, which was quite a spread ! If the article was true I was not only an unprincipled opportunist, but an outright crook, for my Federal tax returns for the period under discussion showed incomes ranging from $21,714.31 (1933) to $49,167.37 (1934), and down again to $23,834.38 in 1937.

As I did not wish to go to jail for tax evasion—that *would* have embarrassed Father—my course of action was to make my tax returns public, and to answer every question that Walter Davenport, a shrewd reporter, could throw at me in a series of articles published by *Collier's*. By this time my always ailing stomach had gone out completely, and I was in a hospital at Rochester, Minnesota, undergoing major surgery. I have kept most of the stacks of mail I received in the wake of these conflicting articles, and the letters which reached me were predominantly in my favour : the public indicated that it thought my explanation rang true.

There are some interesting behind-the-scenes family sidelights on how Mother and Father reacted to the " Jimmy's Got It " article. Mother, ordinarily calm and collected about such things, hit the ceiling. She wanted to rush into print with an article under her own name, defending me. Father took the wiser viewpoint and calmed her down. When the question of my answering the articles in the rival magazine came up he thought that was a good idea, and he took the trouble of writing me a lengthy memorandum giving me his detailed views of how the reply should be couched. It made me feel pretty good to have the President of the United States even though he was a prejudiced party, acting as my public-relations adviser. I quote from Father's memo :

[The] article, if one is finally decided on, should be alternately serious and humorous.

For instance . . . it should pour it on heavy about the gross misstatement of an income of from $200,000 to $2,000,000—asking what manner of reporter is a man who invents absurdities and what manner of magazine would solemnly print them—then going on to raise the question as to whether it is a libel or a compliment to spread a lie that a man makes ten or a hundred times more money or is worth ten or a hundred times as much money as is the actual case.

It would be well to suggest that the insurance salesman who is [not] successful generally dislikes the other salesman who is more on his toes or has a better line of goods to sell. . . . And . . . emphasize that . . . [the author] could have cooked up the same line of innuendo and misrepresentation about any other salesman, and that . . . [the magazine] by using that line of attack in one of their articles, laid themselves open to the charge of departing from ethical magazine standards for purely political reasons, i.e., to try to hit the President through his son.

Father went on to suggest that I make it plain that I had stayed clear of Government business, and that I would be delighted to make my tax returns public if some of the Republican Congressional critics who had jumped into the act would do likewise. Then he continued :

> Suggest that no son of any President can engage in business with the objective of becoming self-supporting without becoming liable to attack by innuendo from those who try to hit his Father through him. . . . The point is to keep the article on a high note of outraged decency and, at the same time, of ridicule for and disapprobation of writers . . . and magazines who would stoop to carry such vile innuendo.
>
> F.D.R.

I am not so simple as to think that it was no indirect advantage to me in the insurance business to have been the son of the President. To contend otherwise would be to argue that there is no such thing as human nature. Certainly there must have been prospective customers who favoured me because my Father was in the White House. Occasionally I even asked Father to show one of my clients a personal courtesy—but there was a definite cleavage between personal and political favours. I did not request the latter. There may have been a few occasions, particularly when I was trying to get started in business, when Father recommended me to his personal friends—not political favour-seekers, but mostly men he had known at Harvard. The best way to show where Father stood is to quote what he himself said in a letter he wrote in 1934 to a Boston newspaper executive :

> I am asking Jimmy to run in and see you about his insurance business. Being " free, white and twenty-one " and absolutely on his own he is, of course, entitled to go out and try to get business. I think he leans over backward in making it clear that he has no influence and exerts none with the Administration.

" Mother of the President "

Before closing this chapter I must make some mention of how Granny, the matriarch of the family, took to her new rôle as " Mother of the President." Granny, naturally, was immensely proud, and, on the day of Father's first inauguration, she even wrote out, in her own hand, the following statement :

> March 4th [1933]
> I shall leave my son in Washington, confident that he will give all the strength that is in him, to help his Country, & I shall be glad if every Mother will pray God to help & preserve him.
> Mrs. James Roosevelt

Granny, getting on in years, was spending most of her time in Hyde Park, though she still travelled a good deal and visited Europe several times during the time Father was in the White House. She enjoyed Father's new prominence to the utmost, though she professed to take it as a completely natural and thoroughly inevitable thing that her Franklin should have become President. Who else was more fitted ? She could not bear it, however, when " crude " persons said or wrote unpleasant things about her son.

Some of the things Granny had to read about the family troubles distressed her deeply. During the period of the first two divorces she wrote a letter to her " Darling Son " which touchingly reflected her unhappiness. " Perhaps I have lived a little *too* long ! " she wrote, " but when I think of you & hear *your* voice I do not want *ever* to leave you ! "

Some biographers have sought to portray Sara Delano Roosevelt as a parsimonious old woman with a phobia against touching the principal of her estate. While Granny was no spendthrift, the falsity of this picture is indicated by a revealing personal letter she wrote Father in 1935, telling him of physical improvements she was planning for the Hyde Park estate. She wrote :

> You need *not* chip in on my expenses here, you have enough & I can manage. I have to put in *all* new brass pipe, I can't put it off any longer & *I* can pay it out of my principal—Why not ? I *do* want to have this place perfect while I have it & leave it so for you dearest.

As long as she lived Father had no more faithful cheer-leader than Granny. She constantly fed him little bulletins on how much friends with whom she talked—even Republicans—thought of him. She organized listening parties when he was to deliver a " fireside chat." Before one such radio address she wrote him : " I have ordered early lunch & . . . Betty . . . I & Una will listen in. . . . I am sure the ' servants hall ' will be also listening, & I told Plog [the grounds superintendent] so he will be in his house listening."

Age did not dim Granny's ability to drive home the bland, subtle barb so far as Mother's highly publicized activities were concerned. The above letter was written about the time of the famous *New Yorker* magazine cartoon, depicting Mother, whose travels really were becoming ubiquitous, at the bottom of a coal-mine. Shortly after Mother *did* visit a coalmine. Granny could not resist the impulse to add the following delicious line :

" I hope Eleanor is with you this morning. . . . I see she has emerged from the mine . . . that is something to be thankful for."

17

Father and the Sea

THE sea was Father's great love, the source to which he could turn when the burdens of office became oppressive and his body and spirits needed recharging and restoring. I was with him on a number of his Presidential cruises, both official and unofficial. In retrospect I still marvel at how one could almost see his weariness disappear when Father got the smell of salt water in his nostrils and the feel of a rolling deck under him.

The sea did something for Pa that was more than merely physical. It brought out in him, in addition to a spirit of daring, a certain type of playfulness, and he would do things most foreign to Presidential dignity. It was the same sort of spirit that possessed him at Hyde Park and Warm Springs—he became Franklin Roosevelt, the good companion, rather than F.D.R., the President.

It is unfortunate that Mother, after her early attempts at keeping up with Father in Campobello sailing days, never really enjoyed the sea. He loved sharing his cruises with the family. A ship to him was a grand place for family fun, and nothing pleased him more than to take us with him on his voyages. It was as if he used the cruises as a means of making up to us for the fact that he could give us so comparatively little of his time. From one of our sea trips together he wrote Grace Tully : " The boys are having a good time and we have one continuous kidding match at which The Old Man manages to hold his own."

When he was off on these informal cruises, particularly if fishing was involved, Pa never believed in being the dude. He would get into old clothes ; out would come the floppy white hat, and if he didn't feel like shaving he would skip the razor for a day.

In June 1933, when Congress adjourned after the epochal session in which the early New Deal legislation was enacted, Father set out with me in a schooner, *Amberjack II*, which I had chartered ; unlike the *Myth II*, in which we had sailed just before the 1932 campaign, the *Amberjack* at least didn't leak. Father himself was the pilot. Midway in our cruise we were joined by Franklin, Jr., and Johnny and wound up at Campobello. There Father boarded the cruiser *Indianapolis* for his return to Washington.

The " Nourmahal Gang "

Even before this cruise Father sailed with Vincent Astor on the *Nourmahal*. He was to cruise on this luxurious yacht a number of times, and I was with him on several of the voyages. Just a few months before his death in February 1959 Captain Astor made available to me his log of the *Nourmahal*, in which Father's signature, as a cruise guest, appears repeatedly. He also refreshed my memory on some of the incidents of these cruises, including the attempt to assassinate Father, then the President-elect, at Miami in February 1933.

Father's participation in the *Nourmahal* cruises was one of the curious paradoxes of his personality. He had been elected to the Presidency as the self-avowed champion of the " forgotten man," and he lived up to that pledge during his tenure of office, even though it earned for him the contemptuous epithet, emanating from the Wall Street-Union League clique, of being a " traitor to his class." Father was a traitor to nobody—the fact is, the " class " in question might not have survived at all had not the New Deal preserved the entire economy. Be that as it may, here was Father, one month before embarking on a term of office in which he was to do so much for the " forgotten man," sailing on a pleasure cruise aboard the most splendid private yacht in the United States, if not in the world, in company with a group of blue bloods whose combined fortunes ran into astronomical multimillions.

There was a regular, self-styled " *Nourmahal* Gang " which

turned out almost to the man whenever Father sailed aboard her. To begin with, there was Vincent Astor himself, grandson of *the* Mrs Astor, founder of New York society's Four Hundred ; at the time of his death his personal fortune was estimated at from $100 to $200 million.

Then there were the following :

William Rhinelander Stewart, now deceased ; wealthy scion of a Four Hundred family. Will was associated in the insurance business with one of Father's bitterest critics, Republican Congressman " Ham " Fish, but was principally known as an amiable playboy.

George B. St George, of Tuxedo Park, New York, deceased. He was a dyed-in-the-wool Republican, married to Katharine (Kassie) Collier St George, a niece of Granny's, who became Republican Congresswoman in 1947. George was another pleasant but purposeless chap, with lots of inherited wealth.

Justice Frederic (Freddy) Kernochan, also of Tuxedo Park, deceased ; often referred to as " a patrician Democrat "—but at least a Democrat !

The late Kermit Roosevelt, son of President Theodore Roosevelt, one of the more solid members of the " *Nourmahal* Gang." He was one of the few of Uncle Teddy's brood who didn't rip Father up and down the back.

Lytle Hull, who died in 1958. Hull married the first Mrs Vincent Astor, while Vincent wed my onetime sister-in-law, Mary Cushing, who later divorced him.

These, then, were Father's shipmates—not a man in the crowd with whom he had any deep intellectual or political affinity. He did not choose the list—he too was a guest aboard the *Nourmahal* —but he joined the company voluntarily and accepted its society. Certainly he could have altered the guest list in any way he chose. From the several trips on which I accompanied him I can testify that he more than accepted his shipmates—when he was with them he was one of them, and he enjoyed himself thoroughly. It was as if the company were an escape for him— an escape back to the world of Groton, Harvard, Fly Club, Hyde Park, and other things far removed from the pragmatic, vital arena in which Father was now operating.

Over the years I have continued to be fascinated by the mystery of how Father accepted and enjoyed the companionship of this group during the period in which he was doing so much to change the sort of world of which the *Nourmahal* was a symbol. Recently I rashly suggested to Mother that perhaps he used these cruises as a means of learning what the " other side " was thinking. Mother promptly squelched me by observing that he did not have to go off on the *Nourmahal* for that—" he could get that every day of his life from Ma-*ma* ! " [1]

When the *Nourmahal* first arrived in the United States in 1928 after having been built for Astor in Germany, the *New York Times* described the sleek, white yacht as " an ocean liner in miniature . . . the biggest and fastest ocean-going motor yacht ever built." Its appointments were unostentatiously sumptuous —handsome furnishings and walnut, mahogany, and teakwood panelling and fittings. She was the flagship of the New York Yacht Club, and Father watched the 1934 *America*'s Cup Race from her decks.

Father's first cruise on the *Nourmahal* was an eleven-day sail in February 1933, when he was President-elect. It took him to the Bahamas, Nassau, and other points—ending at Miami. Taking note of the " economic royalist " flavour of his shipmates, the *New York Sun*, a now defunct newspaper of uncompromising Republican convictions, commemorated the event in its " Sun Dial " column with a bit of doggerel called " At Sea with Franklin D." I quote an excerpt :

> They were just good friends with no selfish ends
> To serve as they paced the decks ;
> There were George and Fred and the son of Ted
> and Vincent (he signed the checks) ;
> On the splendid yacht in a climate hot
> To tropical seas they ran
> Among those behind they dismissed from mind
> Was the well-known Forgotten Man !

---

[1] James A. Farley, in his unhappy chronicle, *Jim Farley's Story, the Roosevelt Years*, writes : " Mrs Eleanor Roosevelt once said, ' Franklin finds it hard to relax with people who aren't his social equals. . . .' " This sounds so unlike Mother that I asked her about it, and she flatly and unequivocally denied ever making such a statement. " I couldn't even have thought such a thing because it was not true," Mother told me. " If I were going to say anything at all on the subject, it would have been that I never understood how Franklin could have gone on those cruises and relaxed with those people."—J.R.

It was the *Nourmahal* which carried Father to Miami, where, on February 15, 1933, he addressed an American Legion gathering in a bay-front park. Ray Moley had come down from Washington the night before to bring the President-elect confidential information on how the prospective Cabinet was shaping up. Astor, Moley, Kermit Roosevelt, and one of the others rode in the first limousine behind the Secret Service car that followed Father's automobile to the park ; the rest of " *Nourmahal* Gang " was close behind in other cars. *En route* Moley and Astor talked on how " frightening " it was when a President-elect or a President appeared at such mass events because of the " impossibility " of preventing some one in the crowd from taking a shot at him.

As Father finished his brief remarks five shots were heard. Astor and his companions saw the Secret Service men go into action, punching and shoving some of the spectators nearest Father. Soon they saw a wounded man—it was Mayor Anton Cermak of Chicago, who later died—being taken into Father's car, which then drove off. Each of the five shots fired by the would-be assassin, Giuseppe Zangara, hit spectators. Father escaped completely, and no one but Cermak was badly hurt.

Without fully knowing what had happened, Astor, Moley, and the others followed. Astor pulled one of the wounded spectators into his car. They noticed meanwhile that two policemen had jumped on the large trunk rack in the rear of their limousine, and another officer was on the running-board, with Moley holding on to his belt. At one point one of the policemen began beating on the rear window with the butt of his revolver, ordering them to " drive to the jail ! " An argument ensued, and the Astor car was allowed to proceed to the hospital to which Father had taken Mayor Cermak.

" Then we discovered why the police wanted us to go to the jail," Astor related. " They had Zangara handcuffed to the trunk rack, and they were kneeling on him to hide him from the view of the crowd, which might have lynched him ! "

While the police took Zangara off to jail in another vehicle Astor went in and found Father, who had held Mayor Cermak in his arms on the ride to the hospital. " I said to him, ' Don't you think you had better telephone Cousin Eleanor and let her know you are all right ? ' " Astor related. " He looked at me and answered, ' Your mind, Vincent, works rather slowly—I did that five minutes ago.' "

On August 31, 1933, after Father had concluded a stay at Hyde Park, the *Nourmahal* picked him up at near-by Poughkeepsie and made a leisurely voyage to Washington, escorted by Navy destroyers. The newspapers reported that Father, " with his keen news instinct," asked before sailing, " Is my flag flying ? " Assured that it was, he announced that it was " probably the first time a private yacht had hoisted the Presidential flag."

It was on this cruise that Pa pulled one of his famous pranks. Each day a daily summary of the news, as it came in over the wireless, was published in a mimeographed bulletin. One day Father decided that the real news was just too dull and undertook to juice it up a bit. In his own handwriting he dashed off a series of fake dispatches. One reported that the New York State Supreme Court had just reversed all decisions handed down by Justice Freddie Kernochan, who was again sailing with the " Gang," and that the state bar association was demanding a probe of this " discredited jurist." Another told how the United States Supreme Court had invalidated all " quickie " divorces granted in Western states, thus casting doubt on the legality of remarriages made in the wake of such decress. The latter item was a real blockbuster, for it would place several members of the party in the position of being bigamists or living " in sin."

The *Nourmahal's* " newspaper " came out with Father's alarming fantasies duly recorded. After all hands had suffered sufficiently Pa and Vincent finally broke the news that it was all in fun. Just before he died Astor told the authors regretfully that he had saved the originals of Pa's handwritten dispatches for years, but that some one had finally swiped them from a desk aboard the yacht. He did not even have copies of the bulletin in which they were reproduced.

I sailed for the first time with Father as a junior member of the " *Nourmahal* Gang " over Easter of 1934. It was a rollicking fishing cruise into Southern waters. The trip was memorable because it was one of the few times I recall that Pa lost his temper completely with one of his children—in this case, Elliott—and the only time I ever knew him to display anger over a family matter in front of an outsider.

The *Nourmahal* was anchored off Guncay Island in the Bahamas when word came by wireless that a Navy seaplane was on its way out with White House mail and that Elliott would be aboard her. Elliott at this moment had two known strikes against him : (1) He had not been invited to join the party, and (2) it was one of the few periods when Pa was notably peeved with him over some of his exploits which had been in the newspapers. Father told Vincent, " Do not let him come aboard ! " and went off fishing in a small boat so he would not be there to receive him.

When the plane arrived it became apparent Elliott had a third strike against him—he had been celebrating the night before and was nursing a monumental hangover. Vincent was in a dilemma : he was loath to disobey the President, but he just couldn't leave Elliott to swelter in the bouncing seaplane anchored off the yacht. He took Elliott aboard, and hustled him into a shower.

When Pa returned he was exceedingly annoyed that his instructions had been disobeyed. " He is to go back with the plane, and he is *not* to have lunch with us ! " Father told Vincent. He sent for Elliott and read him a lecture in a voice that carried through the thick doors and walls of his cabin. Then Elliott was sent back on the amphibian.

If the irrepressible Elliott felt disgraced he certainly did not show it. On landing he hunted up the newspaper correspondents, who were unhappily sequestered in a temporary White House headquarters at Miami, and told them a fantastic yarn about the results of a fishing contest in which " Pa's luck was not so good." The correspondents " demanded " that they be allowed to visit the *Nourmahal* as an " investigating committee " to probe these rumours. Pa's anger, as usual, had blown over as quickly as it had flared ; furthermore, he was rather amused by the manner in which Elliott had carried off the situation. He sent word that the correspondents might come aboard—I was their escort— but that Elliott was to remain ashore. A mock trial was held, with Pa as the " plaintiff " and Elliott as the " absent defendant," accused of " gross libel." Pa spun a series of diverting stories, including one about how he had taken a sperm whale with a three-ounce hook. The trial was " inconclusive," but every one went back to Miami in good-humour.

Cruises, Collections, and the President's Dilemma

In addition to sailing on the *Nourmahal* Father went to sea many times on other vessels—among them the Presidential yachts, *Sequoia* and *Potomac* ; the *Sewanna*, a two-masted schooner which I chartered for a couple of summers ; and the Navy cruisers *Houston* and *Indianapolis*. Always these trips were carried out with great gusto, and anything might happen. Pa's letters to Mother and Granny reveal all sorts of details about his fishing prowess : on one jaunt he " caught a 230 lb. shark . . . 1 hr and 35 minutes—so I win the pool for Biggest Fish ! "

In 1934 Father took Franklin, Jr., and John on his fourteen-thousand-mile cruise aboard the *Houston*, which carried him to Haiti, Colombia, Panama, Hawaii, and other places. From Cartagena Pa wrote Mother how " F. and J." had gone driving with the President's daughter, " Senorita Olaya, and her girl chum, and had lots of fun." He added another parental note : " The boys are grand and really love it I think. They are thrilled by the ' loot ' we are given and when we get back we are going to have a ' dividing up ' party ! "

On his 1938 cruise aboard the *Houston* Father took along a scientist, Dr Waldo L. Schmitt, and turned collector for the Smithsonian Institution. He provided the Smithsonian with a rare specimen of *Seriola dumerili*, alias the Great Amberjack, and many new species of fish and plant life. A number of items were named after Pa, which tickled him as much as if he had carried a hitherto Republican county in an election. Among these were *Pycnomma roosevelti* (a fish) ; *Merriamium roosevelti* (a sponge) ; *Thalamita roosevelti* (a crab) ; *Neanthes roosevelti* (a worm) ; *Octopus roosevelti* (a mollusc) ; and even a new species of royal palm, which became *Rooseveltia frankliniana*.

Father was sensitive to the public-relations aspects of these long cruises. Indeed, back in 1934, when Vincent Astor proposed a particularly attractive trip to the Galapagos, Father replied regretfully :

Several jealous females, who would like to go to the Galapagos too . . . suggested that the Presidency calls for the presence of the President in the National Capitol for at least a couple of weeks during the year ! However, there are two contingencies : either the country may be so prosperous by November first that they will be thinking about profits and not Presidents ; or that the country will be so busted that they will beg me to go away for a month !

Official files show that Father carried on a tremendous amount of White House business while at sea. Radio messages on urgent matters went back and forth. In my own personal papers I have come across some historic documents given me by Father, including copies of messages in his handwriting sent from the *Potomac* (in code) to Secretaries Hull and Morgenthau in 1937 concerning policies to be followed in the event of a declaration of war by Japan against China.

For family participation, Pa's prize cruise was the one aboard my chartered schooner, the *Sewanna*, in July 1936. Johnny, Franklin, Jr., and I were his crew, and Pa was the pilot. Mother's brother, Hall, joined us for part of the voyage. We put into Campobello, where Granny and some of her dowager friends came aboard to greet Pa. Later we had a big family picnic ashore. The log of the cruise notes :

> The guests [meaning Granny and her friends] were carried ashore from small boats by the boats' crews and there was a great deal of fun. Later the officers . . . came ashore in a comparatively dignified manner—using their ship's punt.

While we were sailing a radio message announced the birth of Elliott Roosevelt, Jr. Grandpa Roosevelt and the three new uncles duly celebrated his arrival.

Father's naval aide at that time was the Commander (later Rear-Admiral) Paul Bastedo, U.S.N.—definitely a worrying type—and Pa did everything he could to give the commander a difficult time.

One evening, when we were completely fogbound, Father became impatient and decided *he* would take the *Sewanna* through the narrows, fog or no fog. " But, Mr President ! " Commander Bastedo expostulated. " You can't do that—it's dangerous ! "

" But nothing ! " Father retorted. " I'm going in to-morrow morning—and that's an order from your commander-in-chief ! "

Early that morning we took off in the fog. One of the escorting destroyers attempted to trail us, hoping to pick up the survivors if we hit anything. Thanks to Pa's elegant navigating, we soon lost her, much to his glee.

After we had been under way a while the fog began to lift, and in the distance we could see the " lost " destroyer bearing down on us at twenty knots. Just at this particular moment Pa was in an embarrassing position at the stern of our schooner. I'll never forget how Pa—the commander-in-chief—shook his fist in the direction of the destroyer and shouted into the breeze, " Stay two miles astern, damn you, or I'll have you court-martialled ! "

The " Good Neighbor " Voyage

In November 1936, after his smashing second-term victory over Governor Landon, Father sailed aboard the crüiser *Indianapolis* to Argentina to attend the Pan-American Peace Conference at which the Good Neighbor policy was further advanced. He wanted me to go along as his aide, so he " drafted " me from my Boston insurance business and, to give me appropriate rank, commissioned me as a lieutenant-colonel in the Marine Corps. Frankly, I felt like an impostor in that starched white uniform with the silver leaves on the shoulders. It didn't help any when, along the route, Pa received a letter from Mother, inquiring in that disingenuous way of hers, " Is . . . [James] a 2nd Lieut. or a Lieut. Col. ? " Father kidded me for days about that one.

Sailing down to Rio de Janeiro, where we stopped *en route* to Buenos Aires, we passed the equator, and Father, who, strangely enough, had never crossed the line, was initiated by the sailors into the Ancient and Honorable Order of Shellbacks. Gus Gennerich, I, and other members of our party were also " pollywogs," so we got the works—much rougher, needless to say, than Pa's initiation. Father enjoyed the horseplay hugely and wrote Mother a long letter about it, reflecting his good spirits with an intimate ending to his letter : " Loads and loads of love and try to get lots of sleep preparatory to that—Social Season. Another year let's cut it out and take a trip to Samoa and Hawaii instead ! Devotedly, F."

After having our Thanksgiving dinner aboard the *Indianapolis*

We docked at Rio on November 27 to call on the then President, Getulio Vargas. That night there was a dinner in Father's honour, given by the Foreign Ministry. The Palacio Carlos Guinle, private residence of one of Brazil's richest men, was turned over to Father as a place in which to rest and dress. Pa, not exactly an innocent abroad when it came to knowledge of luxurious mansions, was bowled over by this one. What particularly intrigued him was the parlour-sized bathroom, carpeted with what appeared to be white bearskin rugs. When he saw the huge, partially sunken bath-tub, almost big enough to swim in, Pa exclaimed, " Say, I'm going to take a bath in that thing ! Run the water for me."

Dutifully I went in to turn on the water, but could find no fixtures. I reported this to Father, and he took it philosophically. He'd just have to do without the bath, he said. Then, acting on impulse, he told me, " Why don't you just get in it, even without water, and tell me how it feels ? "

It didn't make much sense to me, but Pa was giving the orders, so in I got. The moment I sat down, water began to bubble up from the bottom—delightfully warm. Luckily I was in my shorts. " Pa ! " I yelled. " It goes on when you sit in it ! "

" Well, keep sitting—then come get me and I'll take a bath ! " he yelled back from the bedroom.

As the water rose past the half-way mark I became momentarily panicky when I wondered how I would turn it off. Then I realized that whatever mysterious force made it turn on when the tub was occupied would turn off the water automatically when the tub was vacated. Pa had a grand bath, not minding in the least using my water. After that he always talked about obtaining a similar tub for the White House, but never did anything about it.

Our next stop was Buenos Aires. There all of us—Father more than any of us—suffered a tragic loss when Gus Gennerich died shortly after our arrival in the Argentine capital. Father described the tragedy in a letter to Mother, written immediately after the event, as follows :

Dearest Babs :
    The tragedy of poor Gus hangs over all of us. On Monday he was happy & well all day, though it was a jumpy sort of day—a

vast surging throng all the way, 4 miles, from the ship to the Embassy
—then another equally long trip to the Presidential Palace & back
again—crowds, tossed flowers, cheers, people running out, balconies
filled.

When we got in finally at 7 P.M. Gus lay down while I had a
bath & dressed for a 9 P.M. Delegation Dinner and immediately
after the dinner Gus & Fox & Claunch [George Fox and Charles
Claunch] went in to cafe. He had nothing to eat, & only a bottle
of beer. He danced once or twice, & Capt. Bastedo & Pa Watson
saw him looking apparently cheerful & well. At about 1:30 he
came back to the table after a short dance, made a joking remark
to Claunch & suddenly fell forward. Fox got his pulse, but inside
of a minute & a half it had stopped. They did everything to revive
him but he had died without ever knowing he was ill. At 2:15
Jimmy & Ross [then Captain Ross T. McIntire, U.S.N., Father's
physician] were waked up & dressed & went right down, got the
authorities, & had the body taken to a funeral parlor. There was of
course no question that it was a straight heart attack—I knew
nothing of it till I woke at 8 & Ross & Jimmy came in after an hour's
sleep to tell me—and of course it has been a real shock & a real loss
for as you know good old Gus was the kind of a loyal friend who
simply cannot be replaced. . . .

It was a hard decision Ross McIntire and I had to make as
to whether to awaken Father or postpone telling him until later.
Never have I seen anything upset him more, though, as usual,
he kept his emotions under control. There had been some
difficulty in persuading the Argentine authorities to let us have
Gus's body, as some one had come up with a silly cloak-and-
dagger notion that " maybe he was poisoned " and they wanted
to conduct an investigation. Father told me I had done well in
insisting that the body must be delivered to the United States
Embassy, where, later, a simple service, which Father attended,
was conducted. When we finally returned to Washington
another service was held for Gus in the East Room of the White
House. That was Father's idea of a fitting farewell to his old
friend.

I later had a hand in selecting a replacement for Gus Gennerich
—a Massachusetts state policeman named Thomas J. Qualters,
who, until he joined the Army in World War II, served Father
faithfully and well. But there never was any real replacement, in
the sense of a good companion, for Gus.

On the day he addressed the peace conference in Buenos Aires Father learned he was not the only President whose sons sometimes caused him embarrassment. While Father was talking a wild-looking young man in the front row jumped up and shouted, " Down with imperialism ! " Father was startled, but went right on speaking as two Army officers hustled the heckler out of the hall. Later Father learned the demonstrator was the son of the then President, Agustin P. Justo of Argentina.

En route home we stopped for an official visit in Montevideo, and the Uruguayan President, Gabriel Terra, came aboard the *Indianapolis* to greet Father. Father noticed that President Terra seemed uncommonly nervous, and he inquired diplomatically if anything was amiss. He was told that this was the first time the President had been out in public since the President of Chile had visited Montevideo some months ago ; they rode together in a parade—just as he and Father were about to do— and a gunman took a shot at President Terra and wounded him.

Father, who should have been concerned, just chuckled and, through an interpreter, made what I thought was a pretty poor joke. " I'll tell you what we'll do," he told the Uruguayan President. " We'll put my boy, Jimmy, in the little seat directly in front of you. He's nice and tall, and if anyone takes a shot at you the bullet probably will hit him ! " All during that parade, in my gleaming white uniform, I felt exactly like a clay pigeon !

No one fired any shots that day, but I did save Pa from committing what would have been an unintentional insult to the Uruguayan Republic. He addressed a huge throng in Montevideo, and midway in his speech he drew from his breast pocket a blue-and-white handkerchief with which to mop his brow. The crowd began cheering the instant he produced the handkerchief, and, acting on some impulse, he waved it at them instead of using it for the intended purpose. Suddenly I realized the significance of what was going on ; leaning over to Father, I whispered ferociously, " For God's sake, don't blow your nose on that handkerchief—blue and white are the Uruguayan national colours ! "

As we neared Trinidad, where we were to be received by the British Governor-General, our wireless was crackling with news of the crisis over whether King Edward VIII—now the Duke of

Windsor—would renounce his throne for the American-born Wallis Warfield Simpson. Father even dashed off a note to Mother : " Do I or do I not propose the ' health of the King ? ' Awful dilemma. It is however to be solved by good manners and not by State Department diplomatic protocol."

Meanwhile Father, an incorrigible promoter of betting " pools," had tapped each of us in his party for a dollar on an Edward-Wallis sweepstakes. We wrote our guesses on paper slips, and the one who came closest to predicting what His Majesty would do would win the pot. Father's military aide, Lieutenant-Colonel (later Major-General) Edwin M. (" Pa ") Watson, was to lock the slips in a safe until the King's decision became known.

Father was unusually gleeful—but secretive—as he wrote out his prediction. He gave no one the slightest hint as to what he wrote.

Next day, after King Edward announced he would abdicate to marry " the woman I love," " Pa " Watson opened the safe. All the slips were there except Father's.

Rarely have I seen Father so disturbed—and he wasn't putting on an act. " Listen ! " he told " Pa " Watson. " You've *got* to find that slip and destroy it ! If what I have written ever gets out it may mean war ! "

" Pa " Watson searched high and low, but Father's slip was never found. I begged Father repeatedly to tell me what he had written, but he flatly refused. I suspect it was something quite ribald.

The missing slip never has turned up anywhere. My hunch is that the late " Pa " Watson—though he never would admit it to me—took a peek at Father's prediction, realized its potential danger, and destroyed it. In any event, if the slip was anywhere aboard the *Indianapolis*, it presumably went down with the ship when the Japanese torpedoed her in 1945, so the mystery of the President's provocative prediction must remain unsolved for all time.

18

I become White House Secretary—
Alias the "Crown Prince"

EARLY in 1937, following his runaway re-election the previous
November, Father asked me to relinquish active participation
in my Boston insurance business and come to Washington as
one of his administrative assistants.   Since the death of Louis
Howe in April 1936 there had been a serious gap on Father's
staff which never had been—and never would be—adequately
filled.   I came willingly, accepting the financial sacrifice
involved, for I was eager to work with Father.   Later, as a
Presidential secretary, working on a level with Stephen
Early and Marvin McIntyre, I took over the duties of
liaison with the so-called "Little Cabinet," the second strata
of the President's official family, and also of co-ordinating
activities of some twenty-odd independent and emergency
agencies.

As an administrative assistant I was supposed to function with
a "passion for anonymity," as did the other Presidential aides,
but this proved impossible.   The Press kept playing me up as
the "Crown Prince" and "Assistant President"—particularly
after Father sent me out to make speeches for him on various
issues, including the Supreme Court reform proposal.   I was
even boomed as a possible candidate, though I never ran, for
Lieutenant-Governor of Massachusetts.

It was typical of Father that he overrode vehement objections
from Mother in appointing me to his staff.   His favourite uncle,
Frederic Delano, and others close to Father also advised against
it.   Mother and Uncle Fred argued that the appointment would
expose both Father and me to unfair political criticism, and that

I, in particular, would be on the spot regardless of whether I functioned well or poorly.

Father merely told Uncle Fred that he needed some one he could trust to act as his " legs," and to Mother he replied, " Why should I be deprived of my eldest son's help and of the pleasure of having him with me just because I am President ? "

Mother's fears, however, were partially borne out, for the anti-New Deal segment of the Press seized on almost anything I did—even my *pre*-White House efforts to earn a living by selling insurance—as an excuse to attack Father.

What really got my goat was that the criticism kept up even after I was forced by ill-health to leave the White House staff in 1938. A minister, appearing before the House Un-American Activities Committee, then headed by Representative Martin Dies, testified that I was undermining true Americanism because my income-tax returns, which I had made public in rebuttal to grossly exaggerated stories of my earnings, did not indicate any church contributions. (My answer to this was that I made church contributions but did not claim them as tax deductions.) The late Raymond Clapper, noted Washington correspondent, called this attack a " new low," commenting, " In twenty years of Washington reporting I have seen a vast quantity of smearing done before congressional investigating committees, but none that outdoes this job."

I dealt regularly with an impressive list of agencies and person-alities. The Little Cabinet group embraced representatives of State, Treasury, War, Justice, Post Office, Navy, Interior, Agriculture, Commerce, and Labor Departments, including such officials as Sumner Welles, Under Secretary of State ; Louis A. Johnson, Assistant Secretary of War (later Secretary of Defense under President Truman) ; Solicitor-General Stanley Reed and Assistant Attorney General Robert H. Jackson (later Associate Justices of the Supreme Court) ; and Oscar L. Chapman, Assistant Secretary (later Secretary) of the Interior. Among the agencies with which I worked, and some of the better remembered personalities who headed these agencies at the time, were : Securities Exchange Commission (William O. Douglas, now on the Supreme Court bench) ; W.P.A. (Harry Hopkins) ; United States Housing Authority (Nathan Straus) ; Social Security

Board (Arthur J. Altmeyer), Federal Reserve Board (Marriner S. Eccles); United States Maritime Commission (Joseph P. Kennedy); and National Youth Administration (Aubrey Williams). There were also the Civil Service Commission, Civilian Conservation Corps, Interstate Commerce Commission, Federal Housing Administration, Agricultural Adjustment Administration, Federal Power Commission, Federal Trade Commission, National Labor Relations Board, Veterans Administrations, and others.

All the brickbats notwithstanding, working for Father was far more educational than Groton and Harvard combined. I learned from him by osmosis, for it was not his nature to set himself up as a teacher. On the art of speech-making, for instance, Father's yardstick was that the language must be clear and simple enough " to go over with Moses Smith "—Moses being the colourful and forthright character who ran Father's Hyde Park farm. Father, of course, had assistance in the drafting of his talks, but the final touches, which gave them the " F.D.R. trademark," were his. If, in the preliminary drafts, there was any highfalutin language Father reduced it to simple English.

I also learned from Father how to fend off importunate job-hunters and favour-seekers gracefully, and how to write a letter that said no without irretrievably alienating the recipient. Once, when I was in the hospital, struggling to catch up with a mountainous pile of correspondence, Pa wrote me that " two short sentences will generally answer any known letter." While Father himself frequently violated this rule, as he loved to write lengthy letters on subjects that intrigued him, occasionally he even streamlined his two-sentence formula down to two words. For instance, on a sizzling letter which I forwarded to him from New York's peppery Mayor Fiorello LaGuardia, assailing " cheap gutter politics " and " political cooties " in the Post Office Department, Father merely noted, " Ho-hum ! "

Father's own inter-office memos were often too flippant to serve as models of tact and diplomacy. " Tell Senator Walsh that Papa has not yet made up his mind but that you think Papa already has a man picked if B—— decides to resign " was his way of indicating to me that I should give a polite brush-off to the influential Massachusetts senator, who had his eye on a possible vacancy for a constituent. Or a note signed " F.D.R." would cross my desk, suggesting that it might be " pious idea "— one of his favourite expressions—to invite the troublesome Senator Borah of Idaho to lunch with the President. Concerning a proposed court appointment in Chicago, much favoured by local politicians and labour leaders, Father noted sardonically, "Typical New Deal Judge."

Another of Father's memos which I shall always remember concerned our temperamental Republican cousin, Alice Roosevelt Longworth—the " Princess Alice " of Uncle Teddy's Presidential days, who never became quite reconciled to the fact that the Hyde Park rather than the Oyster Bay Roosevelts were now in the White House. When I was Father's assistant I once sent Pa a note suggesting that we might appease Cousin Alice by appointing her to a vacancy on a certain harmless commission. His reply, which I shall censor somewhat, was, " I don't want anything to do with that woman ! "

Still another side of Father's nature was revealed in the thoughtful memos he sent when he felt that some one had been working too hard. Once, for example, when he decided that Daniel W. Bell, then Budget Director, needed a vacation, he instructed me, " Will you please phone Dan Bell every few hours to ask if he has gone away for that holiday and if he does not go in a day or two, get angry and put him on a train." He had the same consideration for faithful party workers in need of employment. " Take up with Harry Hopkins," he instructed me, " the case of ——, who ran for Congress last Fall. Did a good job. Was beaten and is bust. We owe him a job quick.

He had to borrow $50 the other day to live. How about WPA ?
F.D.R."

My education as a White House assistant was expedited by
the fact that I was fortunate enough to inherit as my private
secretary Miss Margaret Durand, a pixyish, freckle-faced,
knowledgeable young woman who had been trained by Louis
Howe. Louis had bestowed the nickname " Rabbit " on the late
Miss Durand—she always seemed to be scurrying somewhere—
and everybody, including Father, addressed her as Rabbit. Not
only was Rabbit a wonder at juggling appointments, soothing
the feelings of ruffled bureaucrats and congressmen, and writing
diplomatic letters, but her pert private memos to me always
brightened up the day's routine. Of a particularly fidgety congressman she would write, " ' Nervous Nellie ' was in to-day
with his delegation." Advising me that the Naval Academy was
getting ready to brace the White House for approval of a one-
and-a-half-million dollars officers' quarters, she would observe,
" They are not taking care of themselves, are they ? " Or,
" George A. Nelson saw you and was kind enough not to say
' Hello.' You have a friend in this world."

My other able assistant at the White House was James H.
Rowe, Jr., now a well-known Washington attorney. Jim, a
Montanan, had come to Washington to serve as law clerk to
Justice Oliver Wendell Holmes, and had then worked in several
of the Governmental agencies whose activities I was co-ordinating.
Thomas Corcoran, of the White House staff—better known as
" Tommy the Cork " in those exuberant early New Deal days
when every one had a nickname—had brought us together because
of circumstances directly attributable to my administrative
naïveté. I was attempting to cope with all my duties, see all the
people who wanted to see me, and at the same time handle the
speech-making assignments routed to me by Father. Corcoran
stopped by to see me one morning and discovered that I had
barricaded myself against all callers for two days in order to
write a speech. He persuaded the Rabbit to let him past my
barricade, and proceeded to educate me on some of the facts of
life pertaining to my job. One of the things he told me, which
I was already beginning to suspect, was that I simply couldn't
shut off all other operations every time I had to make a speech.

Corcoran suggested that I take on Jim Rowe as an assistant, and the arrangement worked happily.

White House routine began each morning in Father's bedroom. The three secretaries, Steve Early, Marvin McIntyre, and I—and sometimes " Pa " Watson, his military aide, who later joined his secretariat—would troop up to discuss the day's order of business. By this time Father would have had breakfast and read the newspapers in bed. Sometimes he would be still in bed when we came in, but usually he was dressed and ready for us. Occasionally he would be in his adjoining bathroom, shaving himself, so we would crowd in the doorway and commence the conference.

In my capacity as White House secretary—and even earlier—I occasionally made unguarded statements on public issues that sent the reporters running to Father's Press conferences with probing questions. Father took these skirmishes with equanimity and never reprimanded me in public, even if I had gone out on a limb. Early in the New Deal, when the banking activities of the House of Morgan were being investigated, I made a speech which was interpreted as a defence of the Morgans and an indictment of the existing banking laws. Asked about it at his next Press conference, Pa replied, " I will have to make it perfectly clear that Jim is more than twenty-one and that I have not seen him for ten days." Later, asked to comment on a newspaper story quoting me as allegedly making some injudicious prediction concerning the future of the National Recovery Administration, Father shot back, " He was also quoted as *not* having said it. You pays your money and you takes your choice ! Being his father, I prefer to believe him."

If any long memoried listeners recall one of Father's " fireside chats " when it sounded as if some one had dropped a tray of crockery, that was me. While Father was on the air I managed to trip over a chair, making considerable clatter. Pa looked at me sharply, but he never missed a syllable.

The hottest issue into which I was precipitated was Father's unsuccessful fight on Capitol Hill to liberalize the then ultra-conservative Supreme Court, partly by increasing its membership from nine to fifteen justices. This was the measure which Father's opponents sought to damn by labelling it the

" court-packing bill." Though he lost the fight in Congress, the attrition of time made it possible for Father to mould a Supreme Court more in tune with contemporary problems.

In some histories of the New Deal I have been depicted as one of the chief bunglers in carrying out the court reform fight on Capitol Hill. The fact of the matter is that I operated on the Hill hardly at all. My station in the court fight was my White House desk, except when I ventured into the speech-making arena.

While the battle was still smoking Father sent me to Athens, Georgia, to make a speech for him. I asked the local congressman, Paul Brown, what I should talk about, and he replied, " Anything but that damn court-packing plan ! " I reported this conversation to Father, who instructed me firmly, " That's the only thing I *do* want you to talk about." To this day Paul Brown, who still represents the same district, tells anyone who will listen, " If you ever invite that fellow to make a speech, for heaven's sake don't tell him what *not* to talk about ! "

Even though we lost the legislative fight, we retained our sense of humour. At a lull during the court battle Father went off on a fishing cruise, and reports came back that the Presidential party, which included Father's military aide, " Pa " Watson, had caught nine tarpon. I sent Father a radio message :

PRESS REPORTS CONCERNING CATCH OF TARPON NUMBERING NINE GREATLY DISTURBING AS ALL FEAR PA [WATSON] HOOKED THE FOUR CONSERVATIVES. URGE IMMEDIATE REVISION TO FIFTEEN. Father promptly radioed back : WE GOT EIGHT KING FISH TODAY ALL OVER SEVENTY YEARS OLD.

Gifts, Autographs, " Touches," and Swindles

Gifts to the White House, as some Presidents—and Presidential assistants—since Father's time have discovered, also become a troublesome problem. The President, the First Lady, and sometimes members of their family are inundated with gifts, or offers, from every conceivable source. The gift problem is a booby-trap of the worst order.

Big, excessively valuable gifts were automatically turned down. In Warm Springs, Father's former tenant farmer, " Od " Moore, recalls how a Texas breeder offered to stock Father's farm with a carload of prize heifers. Moore describes how Father, sitting at the wheel of his open car, puffing on his cigarette-holder, firmly told him : " No, ' Od,' we can't do that." Later Father permitted Moore to accept one or two bulls with the understanding that they would be available without fee as stud bulls for any farmer in the area ; thus the gift took on a public nature by serving as a non-profit means of improving the livestock of the entire community.

Some smaller gifts of purely sentimental interest, with no ostensible strings attached, were accepted, just as they have been accepted by all Presidents, largely because it would have been a pointless breach of good manners to send back such items. Mother, after she had lived in the White House for a while, learned there was sometimes danger in accepting the most trifling gifts, or even in sending along such items to hospitals or charitable organizations ; frequently, after such gifts had been accepted, the " donor " sent in a request for payment. Mother solved this problem by setting up a bin in the White House basement where such odds and ends were stored. If a bill for the " gift " arrived later, Mother simply had it brought up from the basement and returned to the sender.

As White House secretary, I had to cope with the delicate task of being diplomatic about unsolicited gifts. On Father's behalf I had to discourage a movement to start a fund to provide him with a " floating White House." A Philadelphia manufacturer wanted to supply the President with special shoes ; Father instructed me to tell him that " I have worn the same pairs of shoes for so many years that I don't need any others." Among items that came in or were proffered were dogs, brandy inhalers, hideous portraits (some four times lifesize) of Father, recordings of Father's speeches (which he never wanted to hear), bottles of home-made wine, food specialties from various regions (which had to be tested by the Secret Service if the President were going to sample them), *ad infinitum*.

In addition to the incoming gifts there was the ceaseless stream of requests for gifts, services, and contributions. Bushels of requests came in from persons who wanted signed pictures or articles of clothing worn by Father.

Many of the thousands of requests for Father's autographed picture came across my desk. In the beginning Father tried to oblige as many of these as possible. By 1937 the volume was so great that he could no longer cope with it.

One thing Father would not sanction was to allow anyone to imitate his signature for him on a presentation photograph. During the 1928 and 1932 campaigns some thousands of letters went out over his name ; some of these necessarily were signed by an aide, who developed a real facility for imitating Father's signature, but Father didn't like it. He once showed me how to detect the difference between his genuine signature and these imitations—there was a certain little twist he gave the final " t " that the imitator did not quite have.

Living in the spotlight as the President's son and secretary, I received hundreds of " odd-ball " letters. A gentleman residing in the Bronx, New York, propositioned me : " I resemble you in looks. . . . In case some one offers me a worth-while opportunity to impersonate you, would you have any objections ? " (I would, indeed, and told him so !)

More serious were the efforts by crooks and confidence men to involve me in fantastic swindles and promotions. Some crackpots actually invited me to come in on their schemes. Others—utterly unknown to me—would go around the country, representing themselves as my " agent " in multi-million-dollar promotions of everything from non-existent oil-wells to implausible business ventures. I still have one pathetic letter from an old man who turned over part of his life's savings to such a swindler. Another incredible letter came from a man who said he was vice-president of a New York business firm, asking me to confirm an offer made to him by my " agent," who told him that Father and I were ready to invest ten million dollars in his candy business ! All such letters I promptly turned over to the Attorney-General.

The invitations that poured in—mailbags full of them !—were still another part of my education. There were bids to the Mullins (South Carolina) Tobacco Festival, the Malta (Montana) Rodeo, the Fiesta de San Jacinto, and the Daniel C. Roper Annual Watermelon Party. Any day of the week there was an embassy cocktail party to which I could go, and I could take my choice of a dozen barbecues or picnics in any part of the country. A single morning's mail might bring bids to movie *premières*, American Legion shindigs, a dinner for the Fourteen Young Turks of the United States Senate, the Annual Caraboa Wallow, the Redwine (Georgia) Methodist Reunion, and the Citizens of Muscle Shoals Association Dirt-Breaking Jubilee. (I am not making this up ; the names are all taken from a file of souvenirs which I have saved since 1938.) Now, I enjoy a party as well as any man, but, after all, I had but one stomach to give to my country—and not too good a one at that. Thus, Rabbit Durand had to develop a special genius for writing letters explaining why, on a certain evening, I could not attend the Slash Pine Forest Festival or the Progressive Democrats Get-Together Clambake.

Pa's Family Kibitzers

I still marvel at Father's remarkable patience with all of us during his years in the White House. I have in mind not only our scrapes, but also the efforts of every one of us to " advise " him on public issues, job applicants, political strategy, and how to run the White House in general. Even Johnny, a Harvard undergraduate, in May 1936 was writing him, " Why don't you tell Congress to go home and the Supreme Court to go to hell the Republicans would love it . . . and it would simplify your problems—just an idea." Father would let all of us talk, but, except when he specifically elicited our opinions—as he frequently did with Mother and occasionally did with me when I was his assistant—I doubt that we influenced him much.

One typical telegram from Mother during the Spanish Civil War, sent to him in Warm Springs from Seattle, where she was visiting Anna and her family, read :

> JUST RECEIVED WIRE SIGNED EINSTEIN, DOROTHY THOMPSON, ETC., ABOUT IMPORTANT LEADERS TRAPPED IN MADRID. ARE YOU OR STATE DEPARTMENT DOING ANYTHING ?

Father's answer, an example of adroit fielding, was :

> STATE DEPARTMENT DOING EVERYTHING POSSIBLE IN SPAIN. HAD SUCCESSFUL DEDICATION OF MEDICAL AND EDUCATION BUILDINGS. LOVELY WEATHER. MUCH LOVE TO ALL SIX OF YOU—F.D.R.

As World War II drew closer Mother became even more forthright in expressing her opinions to Father. On October 1940 she wrote him :

> I've just read the State Department report to me on their attitude on trade with Japan & the figures on that trade. What you told me on scrap iron being only a small amount was incorrect & their whole attitude seems to me weak. We help China with one hand & we appease & help Japan with the other. Why can't we decide what is right & do it ?

In May 1941 there was considerable furore over Father's comments and actions concerning two of his outspoken critics. He had categorized Colonel Charles A. Lindbergh with defeatists and appeasers, likening such persons to the " Copperheads " of the American Civil War. Lindbergh subsequently resigned his Air Corps Reserve commission. Mother wrote Father :

> I wish I knew more of what really led to your refusal to renew Johnson's appointment, when the War Department asked you to do so. I suppose there is some valid reason, but . . . to a great many people it looks as though you had simply indulged in annoyance because Hugh Johnson has been attacking the Administration on its foreign policy. Some people feel that you have done that with Lindbergh, and just at this moment the Johnson incident feeds fuel to that fire. A lot of people think Lindbergh has a right to say what he chooses and you should guard yourself most carefully in every statement you make on him, or on any similar person because you must never be annoyed !

Even Granny bombarded Father with urgent, underlined messages that he do something about so-and-so. Her letters with the telltale legend in the upper left-hand corner, " To the President—*Personal*—S.D.R.," were received regularly at the White House.

When Granny went abroad she was received by heads of Government and other prominent persons. She doted on sending Father what he and I called her " Assistant Secretary of State bulletins "—not always to Father's taste. For example, in July 1937 she wrote from Italy, where " the Duce sent me a grand bunch of flowers," that " all seems very flourishing & peaceful & the devotion to the ' Head of the Government '

[Mussolini] is general in all classes. . . ." In the same letter she relayed the information, which she had picked up from a Spanish-born countess, that " there is great hope that the ' rebels ' under Franco will win, as they are the only hope for poor Spain." Sometimes Father was irked by these observations, but usually he would read me an excerpt from one of these letters and wryly say, " Well, Ma-*ma* is having a grand time ! "

While Father didn't seem to mind too much when we addressed our kibitzing solely to him, he didn't want any of us interfering in Government matters that were none of our business. He wanted no member of the family involved, however innocently or naïvely, in anything that smacked of influence-peddling. Once he batted my ears down in a fatherly but firm fashion. After I had left the White House I undertook in the best of faith to put in a good word for a Hollywood friend of mine whom I felt was being unfairly persecuted—and I use that word advisedly—by the Treasury Department on an income-tax matter. " I am a good deal upset," Father wrote me, " because the Treasury Department is much concerned over some effort on your part to telephone to the Secretary or the Undersecretary . . . about the income tax case of one of the movie magnates."

Pointing out that some lawyers operated on the theory that " a word to the top people in Washington . . . may be helpful," Father went on :

As a matter of fact, such theoretical " helpful " words generally make the Department suspicious and cause them [*sic*], rightly, to lean over backwards because, stripped down to the naked reality, this is an effort to get " political influence ". When any member of the President's family or any person close to him communicates in any way with the Treasury Department or the Department of Justice in an income tax case, it is a simple fact that people charge attempted political influence.

There, I think you should realize two things :

1. That any action on your part will, rightly or wrongly, be charged to attempted political influence, putting you and the Government in a difficult position.

2. This second consideration relates to the taxpayer who is under investigation. The tendency on the part of the Government is to lean over backwards and give him the third degree—just because

somebody close to the Administration has spoken a word in his behalf. It is right that this should be so. . . .

Washington being what it is, it is possible and even probable that any time you telephone or write or interview any Government official in behalf of a friend or a client, the papers or the Congress will get hold of it and play it up for its political effect. That the telegram or letter may have been entirely innocent makes absolutely no difference. It is not your fault that you happen to be the son of the President, but it is the fact and it cannot be altered.

I hope that this particular episode will not be made public because I am sure you telephoned without any thought of monetary gain and merely to do a friend a good turn. I know you will understand the difficulties.

Perhaps Pa's greatest tolerance and loyalty in those days was demonstrated towards Elliott, who had become a Texas radio network executive and commentator and had aligned himself with a crowd that started in early to head off a third term for Father. Being an independent sort of fellow, Elliott went on the air and said some things about the New Deal that provoked many of Father's supporters to violent anger, which they expressed in letters to the White House. Yet, in replying to one of the most bitter of the anti-Elliott letters, Steve Early expressed Father's sentiments as follows :

Mr Elliott Roosevelt is an American citizen—free and of adult age. He, therefore, enjoys, among other things, the right of free speech and is entitled to the exercise of that right. There is no censorship in this democracy of ours. Those who hear him are entitled to their opinions—to speak or to write them. I do not believe that you would change these fundamental principles of democracy in government.

The Du Pont Wedding and That Cannes Affair

Even though Father was in the White House, those old, familiar family budget problems continued, particularly for Franklin, Jr., and Johnny at Harvard. Franklin, following in Father's footsteps at the university, lived pretty expensively. In a letter to Pa he apologetically discussed his money problems, as follows :

This is my third attempt . . . to explain both my car and financial situation. . . . I have sold my La Salle for $935, actually a new Ford

($700) plus a $235 check. I agree with you that such a big car is too expensive and a little bit of an eye-sore, so that situation is settled.

But when it comes to finances I run into difficulties in my explanations. Part of this is very simple, namely that you told me you would pay my initiation dues for the Iroquois and the Fly and its [sic] $950. . . . Now we get into the question of allowance . . . and that's the part I want to postpone until I see you.

Rarely have I seen Father appear to have a better time at a social function than he did at Franklin, Jr.'s wedding in June 1937. It richly appealed to his sense of humour to be the centre of attraction at the lavish affair, given by his new in-laws, to whom, as Father well knew, his name was a dirty word. He also relished infiltrating the du Pont nest, flanked by such staunch New Deal aides as Harry Hopkins, Labour Secretary Frances Perkins, and Henry Morgenthau. Also, it was a good party ; Pa enjoyed the rich food and champagne, and, as I remember it, kissed all the bridesmaids.

Franklin, Jr., enrolled in the University of Virginia Law School at Charlottesville. During his stay there Father had to take note of one embarrassing incident, although Brud was entirely blameless. In the spring of 1938 some fraternity house jokers, inspired by Franklin, Jr.'s presence on the campus, decided it would be amusing to place a transatlantic telephone call to Prime Minister Daladier of France in the name of Franklin D. Roosevelt. (Brud, who had no knowledge of the prank, tells me it was not even his fraternity) By the time the call got to Paris the operators were assuming it was *President* Roosevelt, and it is Brud's recollection—or so he was told—that Daladier himself came on the line. After the State Department and French Foreign Office finished exchanging notes about the incident Father sent Franklin, Jr., the following memorandum :

> As you know, there was a somewhat serious international flurry over the call that was put in from the Fraternity House on May 21st to Prime Minister Daladier. The French Government asked for a check-up and the State Department got the enclosed which you can read and return to me.
>
> It was, of course, purely a prank but I think it would do no harm for you to let them know at the Fraternity House that that kind of prank can have serious results !

In June 1938 Father attended another family wedding—John's marriage to Anne Clark at Nahant, Massachusetts. The previous summer had been Johnny's season in the limelight. He took a trip through Europe, culminating in his highly publicized visit to Cannes. There was a festival in progress, and John and his travelling companions set out in a carriage to view its climax—a " battle of flowers." Even to-day it is not entirely clear what happened, but Johnny was accused of having joined the " battle " by crowning the Mayor of Cannes with a bouquet of flowers, and then of " watering " the bouquet by emptying a bottle of champagne on the head of the mayor. I was at the White House at the time, and I recall how calmly Father took it, particularly after receiving a detailed telegram from Ambassador Bill Bullitt, stating that " the story . . . is completely untrue." But let John speak for himself through excerpts from the letter he wrote Father about the day's happenings :

Dear Pa :

 . . . I know you want to hear the facts in the recent case which caused so much stink. We had been in Cannes for eight days prior to the Sunday night battle of flowers and had never heard or seen any officials of the city and expected to see none. On Sunday night . . . I went out in a flower bedecked carriage to participate in the festival. There have been three different allegations. . . . One that the mayor approached me while I was on foot in the street, another while I was sitting on the terrace of the Carlton Hotel, and the last while I was in the carriage. I am supposed to have been pouring champagne out of a bottle into a glass at the time he approached and to have soused him in champagne both the glass and the bottle. I am also supposed to have, at the same time, taken the flowers beaten him over the head with them and then thrown them into the gutter. How I ask can I have been holding a glass in one hand a bottle in another and taken the flowers in a third [?] . . . It's ridiculous. . . . What is more how could we have been as plastered as he [the mayor] says as this episode was supposed to have taken place at eleven o'clock and we stayed up until three [?] Before eleven we had had two bottles of champagne between the four of us and afterwards three more.

 . . . All I can say is that it is a cheap attempt at publicity . . . but what in hell can you expect from a bunch of people of their calibre [?] . . . it's all a bloody lie.

This earnest disclaimer by John, backed up by the clean bill of health from Ambassador Bullitt, satisfied Father and Mother. When John returned to the United States Mother met him at the dock. She told reporters that John had denied the story and that she believed him completely, for he always had been a most truthful young man and " one of the most dignified of my children."

My Illness, Resignation, and Impending Divorce

In addition to my keen interest in my White House job, my personal relations with Father during this period were delightful. We were closer than at any period of my adult life. My wife and I lived in the White House for a while. Father and Mother made it as homy as possible. We were encouraged to have our own friends in for cocktails or dinner, and Father was always delighted to greet them. Still, it wasn't the most relaxing place in the world, and one of the hazards of being around there in the evening was that you might get roped in on one of the musicales or Virginia Reels which Mother was always arranging.

When we moved into our own place in the old Georgetown section of Washington I had a ramp built from our garage to the first floor so that Father could visit us with the least possible inconvenience. He enjoyed coming over to spend an evening with us, and we would have a dinner of the type of food he liked— steak, roast beef, or game—quite different from the uninspired White House fare against which he lodged so many futile protests. Sometimes he would come with some of the White House staff, and occasionally we would invite a friend who would be good company and eschew weighty conversation, for we knew that Pa did not want to remake the world every evening.

There were occasions when Father and I would have serious talks and he would reveal to me the deeper side of his nature and the essence of what he was trying to accomplish. Then there were the times when he would take off with his irreverent observations on personages and happenings, and it was just sheer fun to be around him. He opened a window for me on the most fascinating spectacle I ever hope to see—the inside workings of government and politics.

He also found time for us to do father-and-son things together. For example, he had never made an effort to transmit his lifelong

interest in collecting stamps and other items to any of his children
—although Johnny, while at school, developed the stamp-
collecting bug on his own, and all of us picked up stamps for
Father wherever we went. However, when I was in the White
House I became a keen collector of papers, books, and letters
relating to past Presidents, and Pa was as delighted as if he had
discovered a new hobby himself. He helped me with my
collection and presented me with some choice items which he
had acquired over the years.

How emotionally I felt my responsibilities to Father was
indicated in the letter I sent him on Christmas Day 1937. I
wrote :

> Dearest Pa :
> It's almost exactly a year since we came to be with you and so
> I want to tell you a little about it. In the first place Bets and I
> have been happier than ever before and enjoyed every minute of
> it. Secondly only you can know what it's meant to me to be able
> to try to help you out in the grandest job of getting things done
> and fighting for things that really count that any of us will ever
> see or know about. I know it's an experience and confidence few
> sons have ever been privileged to have. But much more than that,
> Pa, just to be able to be near you and hope to make you feel how
> fully you can depend on us who love you is what we want so much.
> I often fear so greatly of doing something big or small which will
> bring some hurt to you, and I pray so hard that somehow it may
> never happen. Anyway you have given us so much that we hope
> you know what a happy Christmas it is for us and hope it is for you.
> Take care of yourself please and this takes heaps of love to you.
> Jimmy

I was not able, however, to adhere to my desire to remain
near Father and to do nothing to cause him hurt. By the middle
of the following year my marriage to Betsey Cushing, which had
seemed so secure the previous Christmas, was drifting on the
rocks. I also became critically ill with a serious ulcer condition
that required major surgery.

While I was in St Mary's Hospital at Rochester, Minnesota,
being built up for the operation, I had plenty of time for intro-
spection. I knew how silently wounded Father had been by
Anna's and Elliott's divorces, and I wanted to try to hold my
marriage together if I could. In July 1938 I wrote him :

The hospital has been a grand place to get many things straight in my own mind. And one thing I want *you* to feel sure about. Whatever personal troubles I have are on ice as long as they even might be used to attack you. I believe so much with all my heart in what you stand for and love you . . . so don't let any worry on that score linger.

When I was operated on in September Father came to Rochester to see me before I went under the knife, and remained there several days until I was out of danger. He was in my room, squeezing my hand, soon after I came out of the anæsthetic, and suggesting jokingly that, if the doctors really "knew us Roosevelts," they'd be giving me baking soda instead of carbon dioxide for my post-operative hiccups.

When the doctors pronounced me out of danger and Father left he made these informal remarks to citizens of Rochester gathered to see him off :

I am going away not only with a full realization that every care will be taken with my oldest boy. . . . I want to thank all of you for what I can best describe as an understanding heart on the part of the people of Rochester. You have understood that I have come here not as President but as a father ; and you have treated me accordingly. I am going away knowing that you are still going to pull for that boy of mine, and that his wife and my wife are going to be in very good hands during the period of recovery.

After some weeks of convalescence the doctors told me it would be some time before I recovered my full strength. I did not think it fair to Father to give him anything less than all out effort at the White House. Also, I was disturbed because I had come to realize it was going to be impossible to preserve my marriage.

While I was resting on a California ranch Father, for the only time in my adult life, made an indirect attempt to influence me in a major, purely personal decision. He was fond of my first wife—more so, in fact, than Mother was—and he did not want to see us divorced. Instead of talking with me directly or writing me about it he sent out his closest White House lieutenant, Harry Hopkins, as his emissary to attempt to dissuade me. Not even Mother knew that Father was sending Harry to talk with me on this matter.

Hopkins was embarrassed and uncomfortable over what he had been asked to do. Though I was devoted to Harry, I made it plain to him that I resented his intrusion into what I considered my private affair. I was hurt that Father had sent him instead of taking it up with me himself. In retrospect, however, I have come to realize that Father felt he could not broach it to me—all his life he had told us that he would advise us, if asked, but that our personal decisions were our own to make.

If I had any pique I swallowed it, and shortly after Hopkins's visit in October 1938 I wrote Father about my future plans. Addressing him as " Dear Mr. Bean "—a sentimental nickname by which I sometimes addressed him in my Harvard days (I have long since forgotten the significance, if any, of that nickname)—I said I would have to absent myself from the White House until I recovered, but that I hoped to come back. I also stated that my wife and I would be together that winter.

> To be with you, work with you and see the way you make things work is a privilege and a joy I've always felt and always will feel in a dream come true [I wrote]. To give it up is like a blow in the teeth but I know it's right and fair and after all it is the job for our Country that counts. So Mr. Bean I enclose my resignation with a busted heart but a world of love, admiration and respect for my old man first and for Mr. President next.

I was utterly unable in this letter to express my resentment over his having sent Hopkins to talk with me on a matter which I felt should have been handled between Father and me. All I said was that " Harry the Hop spent a couple of days here and we had some grand talks which he will tell you all about."

Father's first reaction was to temporize about my resignation and treat matters as if I were coming back. The following month, however, it became obvious I could not return to the White House any time soon, so, full of emotions, I wrote Father a more formal note of resignation, as follows :

Dear Mr. President :
Simply for the record, for you already know how difficult this is for me to do, I submit to you my resignation as Secretary to the President of the United States. I would appreciate it if it might be effective the 15th of November, 1938. To you as my

Father the blow of not being able to give you the fullest physical strength which the proper administration of my position demands is hard to take. I can only hope that you will always have comfort in what is in my heart. In the ever increasing stress of the days to come, to you as the President of my Country in whose plans and efforts I have such a full faith, goes my never swerving loyalty.

All my love and affection to you from your son.

James Roosevelt

November 3d, 1938.

Father's handwritten, very warm reply to me—redemonstrating and reaffirming the loyalty he always had shown to each of his children—was a wonderful document. It has been lost or misplaced somewhere—I hope some day I can find it—but I remember how he wrote me that I had his full confidence and his love, and that he intended to have me back with him soon. His letter gave me much courage to face the difficult period of my personal life that was ahead.

19

The Lonely F.D.R.;
Third-term Decision

THE President of the United States is rarely alone ; yet his can be the loneliest job in the world. Father's great loneliness became intensified during his precedent-breaking third term and the coming of the War. Mother's travels and activities had become global ; the rest of the family was widely scattered, and Father himself had to live with the terrible decisions on which so many human lives—and freedom for the world—depended.

But Father's loneliness really began a long time earlier, after polio had cut him down in his physical prime. He never talked much about it, but occasionally, through something he wrote or something he did, he would let slip a hint of how he felt. There is a bare but revealing sentence in a rather poignant letter he wrote his mother in the mid-twenties, when he was floating around without his family on the houseboat off the Florida keys. " I wish I might be with you all—somehow down here I feel just as far away as if it were Europe . . ." he said.

In 1934, when Father was on a fourteen-thousand-mile good-will cruise, he wrote Mother that " the Lord only knows when this will catch up with my Will o' the Wisp wife." Later Father teased Mother unmercifully when, to cover her movements during her extensive World War II travels, the British gave her a code name—" Rover." In fact, Father was almost as bad as the cartoonists when it came to twitting Mother about her boundless energy. At lunch one day the former Empress Zita of Austria-Hungary remarked that Mother would probably be exhausted by a fearsomely strenuous war-time Pacific tour which she was undertaking. According to Bill Hassett, Father replied, " No, but she will tire everybody else ! "

Because of the way they were brought up Father and Mother were reserved in their display—in public—of affection towards each other. I know of only one picture which shows Father kissing Mother—one taken on her return from Puerto Rico. Nor can I recall or find—though there may be some around that I do not know about—any of the traditional, corny politicians' poses showing Pa bussing Apple Blossom Festival queens or beauty-contest winners ; he just didn't go for that type of exhibitionism. Mother once said that she and Father believed there are certain things that should be done privately, and that kissing is one of them.

This reserve may have stimulated the malicious gossip that Father and Mother did not get along. The truth of the matter is that a deep, unshakeable affection and tenderness existed between them. This is evidenced by his numerous " Dearest Babs " letters, and by the letter which Mother wrote him in May 1931, just after he had sailed for Europe, in which she said :

> I hate so to see you go. . . . We are really very dependent on each other though we do see so little of each other ! I feel as lost as I did when I went abroad . . . !
> . . . Dear love to you. . . . I miss you & hate to feel you so far away. . . .
>
> > Ever devotedly,
> > E.R.

When I was living at the White House I made it a practice to drop in to see Father before retiring. Often I would find him sitting up late at night, working at his beloved stamps, a hobby he had pursued since boyhood when Granny turned over to him a Delano family collection. Occasionally he would be playing solitaire—he knew many varieties of this lone game. Once I asked him if his mind ever really was at rest when he engaged in these diversions ; he just laughed.

Sometimes in bed he would peruse a paperback mystery before turning out the lights ; more often he was doing his " homework "—reading official reports—or going through a pile of selected letters which Mother would cull for him from her own vast correspondence and leave on his night table. It was her theory that the persons who wrote to her were less inhibited than

correspondents who addressed themselves to the President, and
that Father could get a better insight into what people were
thinking by reading her mail. Father evidently agreed, for he
read the letters.

In unexpected little ways he kept track of even the most
minute details of our activities, and he let us know he was thinking
of us. For instance, when some eager beaver in the department
store where John was working sent Father at the White House a
complimentary report on John's progress, Father passed it on to
Johnny with a note of his own : " It makes me very happy—
Pa." How much he missed the family as the War came on and
scattered us is indicated in his March 1944 note to an old friend,
Leighton McCarthy, then Canadian Ambassador to the United
States. McCarthy had sent Father and Mother congratulations
on their thirty-ninth—and next-to-last—anniversary, and Father
replied : " That a war is on is shown by the fact that my Missus
is in Recife, Brazil ; Anna is in Boston ; Jimmy is in Hawaii,
Elliott is in a camp near London, Franklin, Jr., is at the Miami
camp and Johnny is on an aircraft carrier headed out. . . ."

On all his travels—even from the tremendously busy and
important war-time conferences at Casablanca, Teheran, Yalta,
and elsewhere—Father would find time somehow to compose
fascinating letters to various members of the family. Usually
he wrote them himself in a hasty, pencilled scribble on plain
tablet paper.

I always felt that these letters were his substitute for conversation. Yet, except when he did so unwittingly, Father revealed
little of his inner feelings in these latter-day communications.
His great lack in life—particularly towards the end—was that,
while he had lots of persons to whom he could talk, he had no
real confidants. It was part of his rigid Hyde Park upbringing
that private, personal matters were a man's own business, not
something to be discussed with a second party. Even his minister,
the Rev. Frank R. Wilson, to whom Father was close, told me
that their conversations never probed into Father's personal
sorrows or disappointments or hurts.

Mother herself recently told me : " I don't think I was his
confidante, either. He never would discuss an intimate family
problem unless it was something that had reached the stage at

which it just would have to be discussed. Then we would talk it over, he would tell me what he wanted done, and I would do it."

Mother added emphatically that Father, while he might sound off occasionally against the " grind " of his job, was not given to expressing regrets or frustrations about the kind of personal life he was required to lead in his later years. He never said he would have liked to have done things differently, or that he wished he could have spent more time with us, Mother said. " He lived his own life exactly as he wanted it."

As the end of the road came closer Father keenly felt the loss of many of his trusted friends and co-workers of the early days. Louis Howe was gone. So was Gus Gennerich, who also had filled a very special personal rôle. Marvin McIntyre, of the White House secretariat, was dead. Missy LeHand, Father's personal secretary since the 1920 campaign against Harding and Coolidge, died in 1944. The same year saw the passing of old Dr Peabody, the Groton headmaster who had taught Father, officiated at his wedding ceremony, and prayed with him and for him at Presidential inaugurations ; as Father sombrely wired Mrs Peabody, " the whole tone of things is going to be a bit different from now on . . . I have leaned on the rector in all these many years far more than most people know."

Finally, General " Pa " Watson, a lovable, loyal, uncomplex man, in whose company Father could relax, died on the way home from Yalta. Of the " old crowd "—men with whom he really felt at home—there were but a few left : his uncle, Frederic Delano, who was old and ill ; Basil O'Connor, his former law partner and his tireless associate in the Warm Springs Foundation ; and a handful of others.

The death of Sara Delano Roosevelt in September 1941 had been a grievous blow to Father. Grandmother lived to be almost eighty-seven, and there was a timeless permanence about her that made it even more of a shock when she died. Though Father often chafed and bridled under her efforts to treat him as if he were still the little boy she had raised with such fierce, almost consuming adoration, Father loved her dearly and sincerely. He took a keen delight in " Ma-*ma*'s " truly magnificent performance as a grand matriarch—one of the last of her kind.

And Granny was magnificent—right up to the end. I was

travelling abroad on a military mission for Father when she died, so I missed saying good-bye to her, but the Rev. Mr Wilson, who was visiting at Campobello when Granny began failing, has described for me a scene which is fixed in my mind for all time as Granny's last farewell.

The doctors had decided Granny should return to New York, and they suggested—they knew better than to order—that she allow herself to be carried down the rather steep flight of stairs for the journey home. The rector was standing at the foot of the stairs, waiting to say good-bye, when he heard a commotion from above. Granny was objecting strenuously to being carried ; she always had walked down those stairs, and she would walk them once more. Half-way down, gripping the stair rail but still holding herself proudly erect, she paused to rest. She saw the rector, smiled wryly at him, and said, " You've never seen the ' old lady ' in this condition before, have you ? " She made it to the car on her own feet and left Campobello for the last time.

With so many of his old friends dead, Father turned almost desperately to reviving old acquaintances and to seeking out new companions. Almost as he did on the houseboat *Larooco* when he was recovering from polio, he wanted light-hearted, attractive persons around him—particularly in the few off hours he could squeeze out for himself during the War years ; he did not want to be burdened with heavy, intellectual talk and discussions of serious problems. He needed—as a tonic—a little touch of frivolity and sparkling, occasionally aimless conversation. Obviously I do not write this in any derogatory or critical sense, but one of the few things that Mother never could give him—and Mother, who gave him so many things, would be the first to point it out—was that touch of triviality he needed to lighten his burdens.

In those increasingly lonely years Pa turned to various sources for companionship. A cousin, Laura Delano, became a frequent visitor. Father enjoyed her company ; while vivacious and witty, she had—and still has—a touch of the same patrician approach towards life as his mother did. For instance, once, during a total eclipse of the sun, when Pa mischievously convinced her that the sudden darkness might portend some approaching natural disaster, Cousin Laura went to her room and returned shortly with the one possession with which she proposed to meet the possible end of the world—her jewel-box. " I love it ! " Pa exclaimed as he told me this story. He also enjoyed the company of another distant cousin, the quiet and gentle Margaret Suckley ; it was she who gave Father his favourite and best-known Scottie, Murray the Outlaw of Falahill—Pa called him " Fala " for short.

Father also made new acquaintances, ranging from actresses to royalty. At a Hyde Park picnic which he and Mother gave for actors and writers who were supporting the third term, he was perfectly delighted when Katharine Hepburn waded ashore from an amphibious plane that landed her on the Hudson. Pa thought it showed great élan when Miss Hepburn showed up at the Summer White House, barefooted and slightly damp, and he personally drove her to the picnic at Mother's cottage.

He had sympathetic bonds with the war-time procession of exiled royal visitors whom he received at the White House : Crown Princess Märtha of Norway ; the Grand Duchess Charlotte of Luxemburg ; the then Princess—now Queen— Juliana of the Netherlands ; and others. He even became attached to Juliana's mother—formidable old Queen Wilhelmina, though she was one of the few living persons of whom he was slightly in awe.

In this period Hyde Park—anything connected with the scenes of his childhood—came to mean more and more to him. He took intense pleasure in his Hilltop Cottage, which he designed him self ; he particularly seethed when feature writers referred to it as the President's " Dream House." My brother Elliott and his third wife, Faye Emerson, the actress, lived there for a time after Father's death. Mother authorized Elliott to dispose of certain land at Hyde Park (the family real-estate holdings were the only assets, outside of personal property, which Father did not tie up in trust in his will in order to guarantee a lifetime income for Mother). Elliott, who never felt about Hyde Park as the rest of us did, sold off the property, including Hilltop Cottage. I am deeply attached to this individualistic, loyal brother of mine, but I—and some of the rest of us—have never quite forgiven him for selling Pa's cottage.

At Hyde Park Father would visit with Moses Smith, who ran his farm, and listen to his salty observations, punctuated with eloquent expectorations of tobacco juice, about the Republican Party. Or he would drive to the field of a neighbouring farmer to discuss the purchase of some additional acres which Father wanted to acquire.

Yet, at best, Hyde Park could be only a palliative, not a cure, for the loneliness that was eating inside Father, and all the new acquaintances—the sparkling conversationalists from the entertainment and literary worlds, the displaced European royalty— were merely names and faces with whom Father might talk and relax for a few fleeting moments. Nowhere in the world really was there anyone for him with whom he could unlock his mind and his thoughts. Politics, domestic economy, war strategy, post-war planning he could talk over with dozens of persons. Of what was inside him, of what really drove him, Father talked with no one.

Hollywood Interlude

After I resigned as Father's secretary in 1938 because of ill-health and personal reasons, it was several months before I was able physically to resume working. Although I had not been active in my Boston insurance business during the time I was in the White House I had retained an interest in the business. However, I decided to sever my ties with the East in so far as residence was concerned. I went to work in Hollywood as a twenty-five-thousand-dollar-a-year assistant to Samuel Goldwyn, one of the motion-picture industry's pioneers. My duties for Goldwyn were mostly administrative. After I left him I formed a small company and even produced one opus called *Pot o' Gold*, which, if not the worst movie ever made, was certainly a close contender.

Granny was still alive when I went to work in the fleshpots of movieland, and her reaction was even more electric than it had been when she discovered Johnny was working at the ladies' panties counter in Filene's basement. A letter from her to Father came coursing to the White House, demanding, " What is all this about Jimmy and Hollywood ! ! ! "

The hate-Roosevelt clique, which didn't like it when I sold insurance for a living, liked it no better then I tried to support myself in the picture business. At one point my little independent company made a tie-in with a legitimate venture to produce short films that were to be viewed via a slot machine into which the customers would drop a coin. Up popped a rabid Republican paper and accused me of making " indecent " movies, featuring nude females, for distribution to what it called " speak-easy night clubs " ! Father got indignant letters—pro and con—at the White House about that one, too. At this point I began to wonder if I hadn't better drop all attempts at working for a living and ask Father to put me on the W.P.A.—but the critics wouldn't have liked that either.

That Visit from British Royalty

Father had told me when I left the White House that he did not intend for us to drift apart. He kept his word. While I was on the West Coast memos went back and forth between us on matters in which he thought my opinion might be of some use.

Then, in 1939, when I went to England in connexion with the overseas promotion of the motion picture *Wuthering Heights*, Father gave me a mission to perform for him. He made me his emissary to arrange details of the forthcoming visit of the late King George VI and Queen Elizabeth, the now Queen Mother, to the United States. The present Queen Elizabeth and her sister, Princess Margaret Rose, whom I met on that visit, were little girls—and awfully cute ones—at the time.

Ambassador Kennedy arranged for me to be a week-end guest at Windsor Castle. I was unable to resist doing exactly what so many overnight guests at the White House do. I snitched a piece of stationery bearing the royal crest, and wrote a letter home, saying, " Dear Pa : It's a little larger than the White House but the beds are no longer ! "

I'm afraid I was a real hick at Windsor Castle, but the King and Queen were very kind to me. I had been carefully coached that I was to bow when presented, and that I was not to extend my hand unless they offered to shake hands with me. I completely forgot my instructions, neglected to bow, and stuck out my hand, just like any good American politician. Luckily, the King and Queen overlooked my breach of protocol and smilingly accepted my handshake.

I had also been told it was the custom at dinner to finish everything put before you, and that the next course would not be served until the preceding one was consumed. I was seated at Queen Elizabeth's left, and I started talking so much that I forgot the protocol again and ate only a few spoonfuls of soup. Suddenly I realized everybody else had their fish, while the cold soup was still before me. Again the Queen rescued me with a signal to the butlers, and by eating fast I almost got co-ordinated by the time the meat course arrived.

When the party broke up I went with Ambassador Kennedy to his suite, which was in a different part of Windsor Castle from mine. We talked until about 2.30 A.M. I finally left him, started down the hall of the castle, and suddenly realized I hadn't the faintest idea where *my* suite was located ! I almost panicked—what if I should open the wrong door and walk in on the sleeping King or Queen ? Fortunately, I found a guard, decked out in a uniform that made him resemble a fugitive from a Gilbert and Sullivan operetta, and he helped me locate my quarters, thus avoiding any international incidents.

When I got home I related all these misadventures to Father. I don't know how long it had been since I had heard him laugh so uproariously.

When the King and Queen arrived they were entertained both in Washington and Hyde Park by Father and Mother. At Hyde Park they spent a night in Grandmother's house, which, by royal standards, was relatively modest. Next day, at Pa's Hilltop Cottage, there was the famous " hot-dog " picnic at which Father and Mother—to Granny's utter horror—entertained their majesties. (Actually, there was only one platter of hot dogs for the King and Queen to sample.)

Father took the protocol connected with the visit of the King and Queen with tongue in cheek and tried to make it as informal as possible. It was a hot afternoon at Hyde Park, so Father suggested a swim to the King, who thought it a capital idea. Father put on his usual two-piece bathing-suit, and the King appeared in a one-piece dark-blue bathing garment—a thing with at least vestigial remnants of legs and arms that appeared to me to be a genuine relic from the era of his grandfather, King Edward VII.

The two of them got into Father's car, with Pa driving, and set out for the pool in the grounds of Mother's cottage some miles away. I was riding in the back seat. They drove past a line of National Guardsmen, who saluted them snappily ; this amused Father but seemed to worry the King, who apparently did not like the idea of reviewing troops in his bathing-suit.

Then, as they approached the gate, Father spotted a drove of news-cameramen. He stopped the car hastily and sent me to call off the cameramen. I was instructed to tell them that unless they gave him their word of honour that no pictures would be taken Father and the King would head back immediately and would be cheated of their swim. Pa wouldn't have minded pictures being taken, but he thought the King would not like it. This was one time I was distinctly leery about carrying out a mission for Pa ; the wails of anguish and protest were heart-rending when the frustrated lensmen realized they were going to be cheated out of photographing the King of England and the President of the United States in their bathing-suits.

I shall never forget the more formal Hyde Park dinner for the King and Queen—preceded, of course, by a pitcher of Father's famous Martinis. Granny could scarcely conceal her disapproval when the drink tray was brought into the drawing-room.

Pa, enjoying the byplay hugely, turned to the King and artlessly observed, " My mother thinks you should have a cup of tea—she doesn't approve of cocktails."

The King—not a garrulous man—pondered this a moment, then said, " Neither does my mother."

Then the President and the King raised their glasses to each other and downed their Martinis.

As the dinner got under way Granny's anguish mounted when a serving table loaded with china—some of it borrowed— collapsed. Granny's stepdaughter-in-law, Mrs James Roosevelt Roosevelt, widow of " Uncle Rosy," piped up, " I hope, Sally, that none of *my* dishes were broken ! "

Then, after dinner, a butler fell down the library steps in front of the King, the Queen, and the President, dropping a drink tray copiously laden with decanters, glasses, and ice. At this point Granny was ready to die of humiliation. The crowning blow came later when Mother, who agreed with Pa that it was all pretty funny, wrote an account of all the disasters in her syndicated column, " My Day."

Family Opposition to the Third Term

One of the few serious arguments I ever had with Father was in 1940 when I attempted to talk him out of running for a third term. As the Democratic convention in Chicago drew nearer it became obvious—even though he had not committed himself publicly—that Father both expected and would accept the precedent-breaking nomination. I argued with him against it on two grounds. The first was tradition—I thought the two-term precedent should be respected (though I do not believe it should be enforced by constitutional amendment, as has now been done). The second was a purely selfish reason : Mother and every one of us felt that Father had done his job, had done it well, and that he deserved a rest. Frankly we did not want to lose him.

Mother was so thoroughly opposed to the third term that, as early as August 1938, she advised Father that she thought it " most unwise " and " you know I do *not* believe in it." Out in Texas, Brother Elliott was so much against it that he went to the convention as a delegate and seconded the nomination of Jesse Jones for Vice-President in opposition to Father's choice—Henry Wallace.

However, once the nomination went to Father we closed ranks and were behind him. Brother Johnny—this was in his pre-Republican phase—campaigned in Massachusetts for the Democrats. Franklin, Jr., became an extremely effective speaker for the Young Democrats. He made close to three hundred speeches, and helped organize some three thousand young voters' clubs. " Mr Willkie is probably a pretty fine man," Brud would tell his audiences, " but I am sure you will agree with me when I say I know my Old Man is an awful lot finer ! " This tickled Pa so that, one month before election, when Franklin, Jr., omitted the line from a radio speech, he wrote him, " You did a grand job only I wanted to hear you say ' my Old Man '."

One thing was certain : of the four Republican candidates defeated by Father, Wendell Willkie was the only one for whom he had any positive liking and respect. Father was completely disenchanted with Mr Hoover, whom long ago he had admired ; he regarded Governor Landon as a decent man, but secretly felt a little put upon that the Republicans did not offer a tougher candidate for him to beat ; and he genuinely disliked his 1944 adversary, Thomas E. Dewey. Willkie was a different story : he regarded him as a formidable and able opponent and felt they had a lot in common, despite their different party labels.

I had played a part in Father's first contact with Wendell Willkie. Father occasionally gave me the assignment of serving as his advance agent in making contact with some personality whom he was not quite ready to meet. One day he told me there was a utility executive he wanted me to sound out for him, a chap by the name of Willkie, who wanted to sell his company's Southern properties to the Tennessee Valley Authority. " I understand he's quite a clever fellow," Father said. " I want to know more about him before I talk with him. I wonder if you'd have him out to your house for breakfast and get a line on him for me ? " I extended the invitation to Willkie, who accepted, and we had an extremely interesting three-hour breakfast conference.

Some time after he defeated Willkie in 1940 Father invited him to the White House for a private dinner—just the two of them. Grace Tully describes how, rather than expose his recent opponent to Mrs Nesbitt's cooking, Father called in an outside chef to prepare the terrapin—one of Pa's favourite dishes. He wanted the dinner to be just right. The two former rivals sat up talking in Father's study until after midnight a late hour for Father—and at regular intervals great bursts of laughter from the two congenial men could be heard coming through the closed door. Later it was with Father's blessing that Willkie, titular head of the Republican Party, made his fact-finding " One World " trip abroad. Had Willkie lived I am convinced there would eventually have been a place for him in Father's Cabinet.

My Personal Marital Troubles

My divorce from Betsey Cushing took place in 1940. In April 1941 I was married to Romelle Schneider, who had been my nurse after my serious operation in 1938. Though Father did not approve of the marriage, he took the position, consistent with the policy he always had followed with each of his children, that it was my business. He made a special point of asking Mother to attend the wedding and he sent me—Mother brought it to me by hand—the warmest letter a son possibly could ask from a father under such circumstances. This letter is not in my possession, and there was no carbon since Father wrote it by hand and gave it to Mother personally, rather than routing it through Missy LeHand or Grace Tully, who sometimes made copies for the record of his handwritten correspondence. My reply, however, has been saved, and in it I noted : " Dear Pa : That was the swellest letter and I'm so very, very grateful for it. And I guess you know how much it meant to have it in my pocket as we were married."

However they may have felt about my second marriage, Father and Mother welcomed Romelle into the family. During the War years she was often a guest at the White House. At the time of our divorce in 1954 there was much unfavourable publicity, centring around the fact that I had signed a letter making certain admissions. As I stated then, I signed this letter under rather desperate circumstances, hoping to avert a marital break-up. I knew at the time that Father was ill, and I wanted to spare him the shock of any scandal. At least, he was not alive when the unfortunate charges were publicly aired. I am now married to the former Irene Owens, and I am serving my third consecutive term in Congress, doing my best, I hope, to work for some of the ideals in which Father believed.

20

Back Together Again; We go to War

On December 7, 1941, I was in Washington as a captain in the Marine Corps Reserve. I was assigned to liaison between Marine Headquarters and the Office of the Co-ordinator of Information, forerunner of the Office of War Information. This stateside job was not to my liking, and I had been working on Pa to get me sent overseas. He kept telling me to take it easy, that my health really was not up to a hardship assignment.

I was off duty that Sunday afternoon and was resting at my suburban home. My radio was not on. I was awakened from a nap by a telephone call from the White House, telling me that the Japanese had bombed Pearl Harbor and that Father wanted me to come down right away. I got there as fast as I could.

In moments of great crisis irrelevant thoughts sometimes flash through one's mind. The first thing that struck me when I saw Father was, *Why, Pa's wearing an old sweater of mine!* It was one I had given him a long time ago when he expressed a liking for it, and, being an old-clothes saver, he still had it.

Then I became aware of his extreme calmness—almost a sad, fatalistic, but courageous acceptance of something he had tried to avert but which he feared might be inevitable.

The first thing Father said to me was, " Hello, Jimmy. It's happened." (Later I learned that he had been planning to spend a quiet Sunday afternoon with his stamp collection when Secretary of the Navy Frank Knox got through to him with the news of what had happened to the fleet at Pearl Harbor.)

Father was too busy to talk much ; after greeting me he instructed me to stand by in case I could be of any personal help to him. That was what I did. I saw the top military figures, as well as Father's own staff, come in. I listened to the conference that led to the drafting of the message which Father delivered to the Congress next day, asking for a Declaration of War against Japan.

I watched Father as he worked on that message, and I can confirm what the late Robert E. Sherwood has written—namely, that all but one sentence in the brief, simple, but eloquent message (the exception was the next-to-last sentence, suggested by Harry Hopkins) was Father's own language. Father himself was the author of the memorable phrase " a date which will live in infamy."

I stayed with Father all that afternoon and evening until he was ready to retire ; then I helped him into bed. We talked for a while before I left, and I told him there could no longer be any question about my staying in Washington, but that I would have to have a combat assignment. Father asked me again if I thought I was up to it physically, reminding me that I had been through a major operation in which two-thirds of my stomach was removed. Other than that, he did not try to dissuade me.

In uniform I was with him next day on the platform in the House Chamber as he faced both houses of Congress and delivered his fateful message. As I stood behind him my mind went back to the first time I had helped him in a public appearance—that ·day in 1924 when he walked on crutches to the rostrum in Madison Square Garden to nominate Al Smith for President. It seemed a thousand years ago.

After Father had delivered his call to arms I was entrusted with the original copy of the Declaration of War message from which he had read. In the excitement of the occasion I laid it down somewhere on reaching the White House, and, to my everlasting mortification, it disappeared. Even the Secret Service has never been able to trace where it went. Either it was inadvertently thrown away or it was picked up by some one.

None of us had waited for Pearl Harbor to put on uniforms. In September 1940 Elliott volunteered for the Army Air Corps. I was already in the Marine Corps Reserve ; Franklin, Jr., was in the Naval Reserve ; and John was commissioned as an ensign early in 1941.

My sister Anna has described how, after Elliott volunteered, there was a family gathering at Hyde Park at which Pa toasted Bunny as " the first of the family " to join the armed forces, and how my brothers and I later held an " indignation meeting." It is quite true that the three of us were certainly riled and a little puzzled, but we have since come to understand what Pa was driving at. He was impressed and touched—rightly so—by the manner in which Elliott had scrapped and wheedled to make his flying ability available to the Air Corps. All his life Elliott had experienced more than his share of hard luck and unpleasant publicity ; Pa simply wanted to boost his morale and give him the rousing send-off that he thought Bunny deserved.

My Round-the-world Mission for Father

My own Marine Corps career began in 1936 when I was commissioned as a lieutenant-colonel to serve as Father's aide on his South American goodwill tour. I was quickly infected with the *esprit de corps* of the leathernecks and wanted to remain a Marine, but I realized I had no right to such a high rank, which I had not earned. In September 1939, after a state of national emergency had been declared, I resigned my commission, stating : " I am impelled to take this step for the simple reason that I do not feel that my age or experience would justify my holding such a rank."

It was my intention all along to go back into the reserve at a lesser rank, and I did so in December 1939, re-entering as a captain. Without my knowledge, Father and the Marine Corps commandant of that time, General Thomas Holcomb, had been discussing my status, and Father had suggested that my rank be scaled down.

I trained hard with my unit on the West Coast, went on amphibious manœuvres, and began learning something about being a Marine. In September 1940—the same month Elliott volunteered—I was called to active duty. In April 1941—less than a week after my second marriage—I was on my way around the world on a military-diplomatic mission for Father. In company with Major Gerald C. Thomas—since retired as a four-star general—I visited the Philippines, China, Burma, India, Iraq, Egypt, Crete, Palestine (now Israel), and various beleaguered African desert outposts. The trip had been planned before my marriage, and, in the letter he had sent me by Mother, Pa had cautioned me to " take care " when I went into zones where the bombs were dropping and the bullets were flying. I answered him, " Don't worry. . . . I'll keep the head down ! "

There was a little human touch quite typical of Pa in connexion with my departure. In the haste of taking off I left unpaid a bill for $2.70 owed to my newspaper delivery boy in San Diego. The lad, a good businessman, wrote Pa at the White House, calling attention to the debt. Pa not only paid the bill, but sent the young man a nice note.

Major Thomas and I had the mission of observing military requirements and how American-supplied materials were performing in various theatres of war, a task for which Thomas was far more qualified than I. However, I had an additional mission, a rather delicate one, which had been entrusted to me by Father. I was to call on heads of state or governing officials in the places we visited. In addition to presenting formal letters, expressing in broad terms the goodwill of our nation, I was to assure them verbally in Father's name that, although the United States was not in the war against Hitler and Mussolini, we were doing all that a neutral nation properly could for the Allies. Furthermore, I was to indicate that, if and when we became actively involved against our will, we would do everything possible to ease their particular problems. In effect, I was telling them, " Hang on, help may be coming."

I had numerous never-to-be-forgotten experiences on this trip. I saw things which opened my eyes both to the ugliness of war and to the vast differences between American values and standards in other parts of the world.

Leaving Hong Kong, for instance, I saw a little Chinese boy— a rather nice-looking little boy—pushed overboard in the great crush aboard the ferry. No one raised a finger to help him, and he drowned.

Somewhere in China I saw a great airfield for American planes being built by hand labour performed by ten thousand coolies.

I saw mothers with infants strapped to their backs carrying and crushing rock.

In Chungking, China's war-time capital, a city of great contrasts between wealth and utter wretchedness, I had a panoramic view of literally millions of Chinese living in abject poverty.

I dined with Generalissimo and Mme Chiang Kai-shek on excellent American food. Mme Chiang repaid the hospitality Father had shown her at the White House by providing milk and eggs for me in deference to my suffering stomach. I made small talk and exchanged hot rice-wine toasts with Chinese aristocrats who had known Father's Delano uncles and great-uncles in the China trade. In the modern, Western-style house where I was quartered I bathed in a pink-tiled bathroom equipped with some of the most modern American plumbing I'd ever seen. The only hitch was that there were no water connexions, and the tub had to be filled by coolies bearing buckets.

In Egypt I met the since deposed King Farouk, and after I had presented him with a custom-made shotgun as a gift from Father, he boasted of having once slaughtered four hundred birds in an afternoon's hunting.

In Egypt I also had the thrill one morning of listening to one of Father's " fireside talks " via short-wave radio. We received the broadcast at an early hour, and I probably made myself vastly unpopular with a number of Americans in Cairo by insisting that they " come in to hear Father and stay for breakfast."

We flew into Crete—over strong objections from the British, who were worried about our security—after the Nazis had already begun their aerial assault on that island. Coming into Suda Bay, where we were to land, our relatively slow Sunderland flying-boat actually took a few shots at a Nazi patrol vessel, and then had to dodge Luftwaffe fighters as we made our own landing on the water. I was deeply impressed by the heroic King George of Greece, who, in uniform, was with the defending troops on Crete, and by the coolness of the British, who were taking the ordeal as if it were some adventuresome picnic. The British, however, hustled us out of Crete the day after we arrived—and none too soon, for right after our departure the aerial envelopment of the island by parachutists and glider-borne troops began.

In Palestine I met the exiled King Peter of Yugoslavia—a rather pathetic young man, who had the courage to resist the Axis against overwhelming odds.

Moving on to Iraq, we learned to hit the ditch and dive for foxholes to avoid enemy strafings. At the R.A.F.'s Air House one morning Messerschmitts struck just as Major Thomas was getting out of his pyjamas, and he had to run for shelter in his birthday suit.

Our final adventure was being forced down at Gambia, Africa, when our flying-boat lost an engine. Lord Louis Mountbatten—later Earl Mountbatten of Burma—was a fellow-passenger. Our pilot, with admirable British nonchalance, prepared us for a possible night-time crack-up on the water by breaking out a bottle of Scotch and saying : " Better have a nip—may be the last, y'know."

While the plane was being repaired " Dickie " Mountbatten and I were enforced guests for more than a week at the residence of the British Governor, who was lamentably short of food. We tried to ease our embarrassment, as well as the food-shortage, by shooting pigeons in his patio. Father heard about it and, after my return, sent me a mock-stern letter, accusing me of endangering our relations with the British by shattering the Governor's windows with my bad shooting.

My last informal recollection of Lord Louis was flying out of Gambia with him after our plane was finally repaired. He kept scratching his chest. Finally I could contain my curiosity no longer and asked him point-blank, " Dickie, have you got fleas ? " Lord Louis replied, " No, dammit, it's just these things I'm bringing home for my wife ! " Whereupon he put his hand inside his shirt and brought out a couple of chameleons—he was keeping them there for warmth—that he was taking to Lady Edwina for pets.

Father Keeps an Atlantic Rendezvous

That August Father went off on one of the first of his own military-diplomatic missions—the Atlantic Charter meeting off Newfoundland with Winston Churchill. Both Elliott and Franklin Jr., were on military duty in the area, and Father took

an almost schoolboyish delight in arranging for them, without
their knowledge, to be ordered to report aboard his flagship, the
cruiser *Augusta*, for unspecified duty. The reaction of each when
they received their mysterious orders was, " What in hell have
I done now ? "

The story of the Atlantic Charter meeting, however, can
be best told by Father himself. With his keen sense of history,
Father personally dictated a memorandum, relating how the idea
for the meeting was conceived and how he carried it out. To
the best of my knowledge, this memorandum has never before
been published—I am reproducing it here, just as Father wrote
it :

THE WHITE HOUSE

Washington

August 23, 1941.

MEMORANDUM OF TRIP TO MEET WINSTON CHURCHILL, AUGUST, 1941.
(THESE NOTES ARE DICTATED FOR HISTORICAL PURPOSES AND FOR
POSSIBLE USE IN PREPARING A MAGAZINE ARTICLE)

When Harry Hopkins went to England the first time in January,
1941, I told him to express my hope to Churchill that we could
meet some day to talk over the problem of the defeat of Germany.
Before Hopkins could deliver the message, Churchill expressed
exactly the same thought to Hopkins. Thus it may be truthfully
said that the meeting was suggested by both Churchill and me.

The date mentioned at that time was March or April, and the
places mentioned were Bermuda or Newfoundland. I found it
impossible, on account of legiolation, to get away from Washington
until April, and by that time the war in Greece—and later the war
in Crete—prevented Churchill from leaving.

The trip was mentioned again in May and June and early July,
and was finally decided upon about July fifteenth. Bermuda was
decided against on account of the long and rather dangerous re-
planing hop from there to England in case Churchill had to hurry
back. The neighborhood of Newfoundland was decided on. The
date of the actual rendezvous was set for August eighth, ninth or
tenth.

About July twenty-seventh, the British Admiralty sent us a
secret recommendation that Loon Bay, on the north coast of Newfoundland, be chosen, raising certain objections to Placentia Bay,
on the south coast, and another Bay west of it on the south coast.
My Naval advisors and I told the British Admiralty we much

preferred Argentia Harbor off Placentia Bay, especially as there was the new Base recently placed in commission by the Navy and already fitted with radio and manned by a number of planes, mine sweepers, etc. The British Admiralty acceded to this choice.

We were then notified that Mr. Churchill would leave from Scotland on H.M.S. Prince of Wales, accompanied by several destroyers, on August fourth, and that he would bring with him Admiral Pound, General Dill, Air Marshal Freeman and Harry Hopkins. I notified him that I would bring Admiral Stark, Gernal [sic] Marshall and General Arnold. A day or two later I was notified that he would also bring Under Secretary of State, Sir Alexander Cadogan, and I decided to bring Under Secretary of State Welles and Mr. Averell Harriman.

It was constantly emphasized, both in London and Washington, that the utmost secrecy before and during the trip was essential. This was, of course, obvious because the Prime Minister would traverse, both going and returning from Newfoundland, long distances in dangerous waters—the danger being from bombing planes, heavy raiders and submarines. This was true, to a lesser extent, in the case of the President, whose Flagship would have to traverse waters from Nova Scotia, passed [sic] Halifax, to New-foundland, where submarines or raiders could readily operate. It is obvious that the return trip of both the Prime Minister and the President should be kept secret.

All of this being accepted, I was faced with a practical problem of extreme difficulty. I knew that the British Minister is not constantly accompanied by newspaper men nor camera men, whereas I was always accompanied—the only exception being long distance cruises on heavy cruisers, when three newspaper men, representing the Press Associations, followed me on one of the escorting destroyers.

I considered the possibility of visiting Ottawa, being met by a cruiser at Quebec, and departing without newspaper men on a trip ostensibly to survey the defenses of the lower St. Lawrence. I realized, in the first place, that it would be difficult to explain my failure to take Prime Minister Mackenzie King with me, and I knew that it would be difficult to take the head of one Dominion Government to the Churchill Conference in the absence of the Prime Minister of the other Dominions. I then remembered that I had told my Press Conference about ten days before that I hoped to get off for a cruise on the U.S.S. Potomac to the eastern coast of Maine in order to get some cool nights—the Summer of 1941 being extremely hot in June and July. This became the basis for the plan of escape.

Several days before my departure I told the Press Conference that I intended to take a cruise on the " Potomac " but that being unable to accommodate three Press Association representatives on the small escort ship " Calipso " [sic], and, feeling unwilling to use an active destroyer for this purpose, I could not take the Press Association representatives with me.   They asked me whether I was going to go ashore at any time, and to this I replied definitely in the negative.

Therefore, on the morning of Sunday, August third, I entrained, accompanied by General Watson, Captain Beardall and Admiral McIntire, going on board the U.S.S. Potomac at New London, Connecticut, that evening while it was still daylight.   Many persons saw me and we stood out of the harbor into the Sound in full view of thousands, my Presidential flag flying from the main top.

It was still imperative to establish my location beyond a doubt, so on Monday morning, August fourth, we entered the harbor of Nonquit, Massachusetts.   The launches went ashore and brought on board, again in full view of hundreds, the Crown Princess of Norway, her brother, Prince Carl, her three children and two nurses, and also Mrs. Ostgaard and Mr. Bedell [Countess Ragin Ostgaard and G. A. Wedel-Jarlsberg].   We went off-shore two or three miles and fished in full view of the beach—the entrance to New Bedford harbor, and many passing yachts.   At about 6.30 P.M. we returned to Nonquit harbor and I took the party ashore and was seen by several thousand people.   Returning to the " Potomac " we stood out into the dusk headed toward the Cape Cod Canal.

At eight o'clock we reversed course and, going around the south end of Cuddyhunk Island, we anchored in the midst of seven U.S. Warships at about 11 P.M., at Mememsha Bight on the western end of Martha's Vineyard.   All ships were darkened.   At dawn Tuesday, August fifth, the U.S.S. Potomac ran along side of the Flagship " U.S.S. Augusta " and we transferred my mess crew, provisions, etc.   We found on board Admiral Stark and General Marshall, who joined the " Augusta " via a destroyer from New York late the previous evening.   At 6:30 A.M. the U.S.S. Augusta and the U.S.S. Tuscaloosa, accompanied by five new destroyers, stood out into the open sea.   We headed east passed [sic] Nantucket Shoals Lightship until we were far outside any shallow waters where hostile mines could conceivably be laid.   That evening we were 250 miles out in the ocean.

At this point fits in the delightful story of what happened to the U.S.S. Potomac and her little escorting ship.   When we left her at Martha's Vineyard she returned to Buzzards Bay, and in the late afternoon entered the Cape Cod Canal.   Captain Leahy had dressed four or five of his crew in civilian clothes and had them sit on the after deck pretending to be the President and his party. Colonel Starling, the head of the Secret Service detail, swears that he knew all about my actual location, but I have my doubts, as the Secret Service on shore and the Massachusetts State Troopers guarded the " Potomac " on her way through the Canal, and the next day the good Colonel asked at John's house at Nahant whether he and Anne expected their father to turn up there that day or the following day !

After we had got well out into deep water, east of the Nantucket Shoals, the seven ships headed north and continued toward Cape Race, Newfoundland, at about twenty-one knots all day Wednesday. Early Thursday morning we found ourselves approaching the coast of Newfoundland. The approaches to Placentia Bay and the harbor of Argentia were swept by mine sweepers and we anchored at the head of the latter harbor at 9:30 A.M. Soon afterwards the old battleship " Arkansas " entered the harbor accompanied by two destroyers.

I had no previous knowledge of where my boy Franklin, Jr.'s ship, the destroyer " Mayrant " was, though I had been told that the ship was doing patrol duty somewhere off the north Atlantic coast. It was, therefore, a complete surprise when one of the destroyers accompanying the " Arkansas " turned out to be the " Mayrant ". Captain Beardall, my Naval Aide, sent a message to the Commanding Officer of the " Mayrant " directing that Ensign Roosevelt report to the Commander-in-Chief on " U.S.S. Augusta ". I think they believed he was to report to the Commander-in-Chief of the Atlantic Fleet on board the " Augusta ", and Franklin was, therefore, completely surprised when he found on coming on board that he was to report to the Commander-in-Chief of the Navy himself. I detailed him as my Junior Naval Aide for the great occasion and he borrowed what I always call " the gold spinach ", i.e., the aiguillettes, which a Presidential Aide wears on his right shoulder and which all other Aides wear on their left shoulder.

That afternoon Franklin and I got into the whale boat, cruised close along shore inspecting the waterfront and the Argentia base development, and doing some bottom fishing for small cod and flounders.

In the evening I had for dinner and a conference Admiral Stark, General Marshall, Admiral King, General Arnold, Major General Burns, Admiral Taylor, Commander Sherman and Colonel Bundy, in order to discuss many matters prior to our conference with the British.

On Friday, August 8th, my boy Elliott flew down from Ganda [*sic*] [1] Lake and was also detailed to me as Presidential Aide. He did not know until the previous evening that I was in Newfoundland waters and was almost as much surprised as Franklin, Jr.

At four in the afternoon Sumner Welles, the Under Secretary of State, and Averell Harriman, recently back from London, arrived by plane from Washington. They dined with me but were quartered on the " Arkansas ". It should be noted that every night of the whole trip, either when we were at sea or in Argentia harbor, we " darkened ship " after sundown, and although there were twenty-eight warships in Argentia harbor, this was carried out so effectively that not a single light could be seen on any ship.

After the historic Atlantic Charter meeting had been accomplished and the news had been given to the world, a card, commemorating the meeting between Father and Winston Churchill, was printed and widely distributed. Father sent autographed copies to Anna, my brothers, and me, with the following personal memo attached :

Here is a memento of my meeting with Churchill. These cards are being circulated all over England. I got Winston to sign in one corner and I signed in the other.

Much love,
Affectionately,
Pa

" *I Really Hope One of Us Gets Killed. . . .*"

It was not long after Pearl Harbor that Father and Mother were experiencing the same pangs of apprehension as were millions of other American parents whose sons were on the war fronts.

My brother Elliott, a pilot, was soon flying reconnaissance missions in unarmed photographic planes over murderously defended enemy territory in war theatres ranging from Europe to North Africa. All of us are immensely proud of Bunny's war record. He didn't have to volunteer. Because of physical disabilities, plus his age and family status, he would never have been drafted, but he pulled strings all the way up to General

[1] The memo, obviously dictated by Father, contains these typist's errors. The Coast Guard tender was the *Calypso*, and Elliott flew down from Gander —not Ganda—Lake.

" Hap " Arnold, chief of the Air Force, in order to get into the fighting. He even signed waivers for his physical disabilities, which included his rotten eyesight—certainly no guarantee of longevity for a combat zone flier ! Objective war correspondents have praised my brother as among the bravest of the brave. He rose by his own merit to the rank of brigadier-general, commanded a wing of more than 5000 men and 250 planes in North Africa, and, among other decorations, won the Distinguished Flying Cross. Yet what is principally remembered of his war career is that some enlisted men were once ' bumped ' from a military air transport, travelling to the West Coast, to make room for a dog named Blaze which belonged to Elliott. My brother was overseas at the time, and the whole affair was mismanaged by some eager beaver underling in the States, who acted entirely without Elliott's knowledge. The men who served under my brother in combat will tell anyone that their commanding officer would no more have asked for or permitted such a favour than he would have deserted his post in action.

Franklin, Jr., known as " Big Moose " to his men, trained with the Navy from June 1940. He became executive officer of the destroyer *Mayrant*, which was bombed at Palermo in the Sicilian invasion. Quentin Reynolds, the war correspondent, wrote Mother a glowing letter about how bravely Brud performed in that show, in which five of his men were killed and six were wounded. Franklin won the Silver Star for exposing himself under fire to carry one of the critically wounded sailors to safety. Later, as a lieutenant-commander, he commanded his own destroyer escort.

Johnny, because of his merchandising experience, was routed into the Navy Supply Corps. Right away he began agitating with Pa and anyone else who would listen about getting him shipped out to sea. " I don't care what the ship looks like or is as long as she at least floats for a while," he wrote Pa. Finally he got himself moved out into the combat zone as a lieutenant aboard an aircraft-carrier. He came out as a lieutenant-commander, won the Bronze Star, and was commended for service under enemy fire.

As for me, I must admit that I felt a little immodest glow when a national magazine referred to me as a " hopelessly 4-F " reserve officer with gastric ulcers, who " used his father's prestige shamelessly to get into the shooting." I saw action in the Pacific with one of the proudest of all Marine outfits—Carlson's Raiders. I was second in command under that brave and controversial military genius, Lieutenant-Colonel—later Brigadier General— Evans Carlson in the bloody raid on Makin Island.[1] We went to Makin on submarines, travelling some three thousand miles from Pearl Harbor to reach our objective, and I had a walkie-talkie shot out of my hand on the beach. I was also in other operations elsewhere in the Pacific and the Aleutians.

I have reason to believe that Father tried to keep up with my activities, though he took pains not to let me know he was inquiring about me. I have seen one letter in which he commented to Carlson :

I am . . . glad that Jimmy is working with you—but don't forget that he had part of his stomach taken out and that a diet of condensed cubes would probably lay him low in forty-eight hours. For Heaven's sake don't let him know I mentioned this or he would slay me.

For my part, I kept Pa in mind when I went ashore on Makin. I captured a bloodstained Japanese flag, and, through Colonel Carlson, sent it to General Holcomb, the Marine Corps commandant, to be presented as a trophy to Father. Later I learned that Pa put on a wonderful show of recoiling from the object and

---

[1] For his part in the Makin operation Major Roosevelt—later promoted to colonel—was awarded the Navy Cross, second only to the Congressional Medal of Honor. The official citation, signed for the President by Navy Secretary Knox, states :
" The President of the United States takes pleasure in presenting the Navy Cross to Major James Roosevelt, U.S.M.C.R., for service as set forth in the following citation :
' For extraordinary heroism and distinguished service as second in command of the Second Marine Raider Battalion against enemy Japanese armed forces on Makin Island. Risking his own life over and beyond the ordinary call of duty, Major Roosevelt continually exposed himself to intense machine-gun and sniper fire to ensure effective control of operations from his command post. As a result of his successful maintenance of communications with his supporting vessels, two enemy surface ships, whose presence was reported, were destroyed by gun-fire. Later during evacuation, he displayed exemplary courage in personally rescuing three men from drowning in the heavy surf. His gallant conduct and his inspiring devotion to duty were in keeping with the highest traditions of the United States Naval Service.' "

refusing to touch the " evil banner." He directed that it be sent to the Marine Corps war museum.

Pa was deeply hurt in 1943 when, despite the fact that none of his four sons seemed to be exactly shunning combat, a Republican representative from Kansas, William P. Lambertson, took the floor of Congress to attack our war records, and implied that we were being protected. Mother recalls that Father one day was literally white and shaking with anger when he showed her a letter he had received from Elliott. " Pops," Bunny wrote, " sometimes I really hope that one of us gets killed so that maybe they'll stop picking on the rest of the family."

The Lambertson smear caused a row in the House, with numerous members arising to assail the Kansas legislator. Majority Leader McCormack asserted : " Outside of the House anyone making any such statement I would say tells a deliberate lie." This is strong language indeed for the floor of the House.

Father himself saw Elliott in North Africa and personally brought home a letter which Elliott had written to his own congressman, Representative Fritz Lanham, of Texas. In it Elliott made the eloquent plea :

> Please explain . . . to your colleague . . . that we, as soldiers, don't care whether or how much he disagrees with the President, but for God's sake let us fight without being stabbed in the back for the sake of politics. . . .
> I don't care whether a man is a Republican or a Democrat. Let's get together and get this damn war won. I'm tired and I want to go home and live in peace on my ranch with my family. The sooner the better.

Representative Lanham, amid applause, read Elliott's letter to the House. Later Father wrote him to express his thanks, and commented that " the thing that hurts most " was that the Republican minority leader had made no protest. " The Minority leadership, by its failure to do the decent thing at the right time," Father said, " seems to me to have missed a wonderful opportunity to show a regard for decent ethics in wartime." This comment was typical of Father, for, while he could take political smears directed against himself with equanimity (he had plenty of practice !), he was sensitive to what he considered unfair criticism of his children.

The only " favouritism "—if you can call it that—Pa showed us was his understandably human effort to catch a glimpse of us if he was anywhere near our stations. As commander-in-chief he travelled to certain war zones, and caught up with Elliott and Franklin, Jr., several times. At Oran, *en route* to the Casablanca conference, Father duplicated the almost conspiratorial measures he had taken at the Atlantic Charter conference to have my two brothers detailed for " special duty " aboard his ship, without letting them know that they were going to see him. Elliott also was with him at Casablanca, Cairo, and Teheran. When he was in North Africa Pa made a special point of personally reviewing Elliott's command.

Johnny's overseas assignments never coincided with the time and locale of any of Father's war-zone visits, but Pa made him the recipient of one of his most intriguing war-time letters, describing the joint efforts by Father and Winston Churchill at Casablanca to bring together the two dissident Free French generals, de Gaulle and Giraud. Father wrote Johnny :

> It really was a great success and only General de Gaulle was a thoroughly bad boy. The day he arrived, he thought he was Joan of Arc and the following day he insisted that he was Georges Clemenceau. Winston and I decided to get him and Giraud to come to Casablanca and to hold a shotgun wedding. I produced the bridegroom from Algiers but Winston had to make three trys [*sic*] before he could get the bride.

My own war-time contacts with Father were all in the States on my trips back from the Pacific. I have one priceless memento —an endorsement of my military travel orders from " The Commander in Chief," authorizing Captain James Roosevelt, Marine Corps Reserve, to proceed from Hyde Park to the San Diego Marine base. As Father started to sign the endorsement I told him, " You don't have to do that—I can get some one else to sign it." He replied, " Oh, no ! This probably will be the only document of its kind in existence." Then he wrote his signature on it in big, bold letters.

4th Endorsement

Hyde Park, N. Y. •   March 27, 1942.

FROM: The Commander-in-Chief
TO: Captain James Roosevelt, Marine Corps Reserve.

    1. Duty completed.

    2. You will stand relieved from temporary duty at
    Hyde Park, New York, and will proceed by air to
    Marine Corps Base, San Diego, California, and
    resume your regular duties.

    3. The travel here enjoined is necessary in the
    public service.

Franklin D Roosevelt

Another cherished letter from Pa, marked " HIGHLY CON-
FIDENTIAL," advised me :

I don't suppose that I should even tell you about it but . . . about
five days ago General Vandegrift [Alexander A. Vandegrift, who
had just become Marine Corps commandant] sent me word that
you had been recommended for promotion to Colonel, both by
the Navy and the Marine Corps, on the ground that you are the
best qualified man to be in charge of the amphibious training and
preparations for task force landing operations. There were a lot
of mighty nice things said about your work.
    However, the Board met and turned the promotion down, on
the ground that there are five hundred Lieutenant Colonels ahead
of you on the list and they did not want to jump so many.

Then Pa, unable to resist the opportunity to do a little needling,
went on :

It is a great mistake to belong to the Navy or the Marine Corps.
If this were the Army (of which I also happen to be Commander-
in-Chief) they would have paid no attention to seniority on the list.
The Army has its advantages.

Those critics who contended that the Roosevelt boys wanted
to be coddled should have been with Franklin, Jr., and Pa at
Oran when Father tried to argue Brud into leaving his damaged
destroyer and accompanying him to Cairo and Teheran, then
home, as his aide. I was in the Pacific and first learned of it

through Mother, who wrote me that " Pa ordered him to . . . come home with him. . . . I tried to make Pa *ask* but not *order*, but he said he needed him & that was that."

What happened, I later learned from Brud, was that the argument lasted all the way from Oran to Tunis on Pa's plane, the *Sacred Cow*. Pa kept telling him that the destroyer could do without him, and Brud kept arguing that he had no intention of running out on his men after what they had been through in the Palermo bombing. Pa said he *needed* him, which was hard for Brud to answer, but he still refused.

Then Father got a little sore and said, " You know, I *am* the Commander-in-Chief and I can *order* you to join me." Brud admitted that would make things a little difficult, but he grinned at Pa and said he hoped he wouldn't do it that way. Finally, as the plane approached Tunis, Pa threw in the sponge and said, " You're a pretty stubborn fellow—but if that's how you feel I guess you should go back to your ship."

I know Pa was proud of Brud for his decision, for he wrote Mother : " He finally decided he had best go back with the ship. . . . I think he is right to want to see her safely to Charleston."

Pa did not lose his parental touch because of the War. With the four of us overseas, more than ever he kept in touch with our wives, sending them chatty and cheery little notes when he had some information on our whereabouts. Early in the War, Franklin, Jr., having completed his law course and passed the Bar examination, was admitted to the Bar in New York City. A telegram came to him from the White House : " We have not had a judge in the family for a hundred years and he was only a distant cousin. Don't let this cramp your style. Pa."

The most incredible thing I ever saw happen at the White House occurred one night during the War when Father was watching a motion picture in the upstairs hall (there was no special projection room at the White House in those days). Mother was there, I was home on leave, and Secretary Morgenthau and other guests were present.

The movie ended, the lights were turned up, and there was a neatly dressed young man—a complete stranger to all of us— standing near Father. Before anyone had a chance to say anything the young man thrust a piece of paper and a pen towards Father and said, " May I please have your autograph, Mr President ? " Father was as surprised as anyone, but he gave him the autograph.

Then the Secret Service took over. Agents ushered the young man out of the room and began questioning him. It developed that he had just wanted to see if he could walk into the White House and get the President's signature. Although war-time security was in effect and the guard on the White House was even tighter than usual, the outside guards somehow let him pass, assuming he was a guest of the family. On reaching the front door he merely asked an usher where the President was, and the usher obligingly directed him upstairs.

The Secret Service really caught the devil, particularly as their chief, Secretary of the Treasury Morgenthau, was a horror-stricken witness of the event. Father, however, had a grand time kidding the rather humourless " Henry the Morg " about it.

21

The Fourth Term: End of the Road

THE fourth-term race in 1944 was Father's death-warrant. I saw him only twice during that period—once just before the campaign, and again on Inauguration Day. Each time I realized with awful, irrevocable certainty that we were going to lose him.

I think Father himself both knew it and, with that indomitable buoyancy—and stubbornness—of his, refused to know it.

He did little things, such as catching up on the autographing of his large collection of books and digging mementoes out of musty trunks and boxes for his children and grandchildren. His letters to old friends took on an increasing note of nostalgia for bygone days.

Yet he also talked with enthusiasm and conviction of what he planned to do when the War was over. First he was going to try to finish the job of securing a real peace. He was on fire with the United Nations vision. He was going to fulfil the dream of his early political idol, Woodrow Wilson, of creating a real international league for world peace.

He was going to England to return the pre-War visit of the King and Queen and the many war-time calls of his old friend and fellow-fighter for democracy, Winston Churchill.

Finally, when his public tasks were over and he could retire to private life, he had plans for a long trip around the world. He wanted to visit the North African desert; he even talked of buying land there and of demonstrating to the Arabs what could be accomplished through irrigation, reforestation, and electrification, the things that his New Deal had accomplished in our own arid West and in the Tennessee Valley country.

He went so far as to discuss with Mother how he would like to travel—on a slow freighter. When Mother demurred that she had never liked long sea journeys and would not enjoy travelling so far on a freighter, Father proposed that he take the boat, because he so loved the sea, and that Mother travel by air, meeting him along the route at various locations which he wanted to visit and explore.

Mother recalls that Father even had a time limit in mind, that he said, " I think it would be fun to go and live in the desert for two or three years and see what we could do." She replied to him, " My heavens, haven't we met enough crises ? Aren't you tired of crises ? I think the time has come to deal with one normal situation." Father answered, " Well, it could be interesting, you know. It really would be fun."

All these plans and dreams, of course, were to be put into execution at the conclusion of Father's fourth term in January 1949.

During the last seventeen months of Father's life my sister, Anna, whose husband, the late John Boettiger, a newspaperman, was overseas with the Army, lived at the White House. She came for what was to have been a short visit in November 1943. Sensing Father's need to have one of his children near him, Anna resigned her position on a Seattle newspaper and stayed on. She served as Father's unofficial and unsalaried secretary, and did much to help him and to ease the loneliness of his last months. She even taught herself shorthand at night, so she could be of greater assistance. As Sis herself has written :

> It was immaterial to me whether my job was helping to plan the 1944 campaign, pouring tea for General de Gaulle or filling Father's empty cigarette case. All that mattered was relieving a greatly over-burdened man of a few details of work and trying to make his life as pleasant as possible when a few moments opened up for relaxation.

Anna was with Father just before the Normandy invasion when he visited " Pa " Watson's house at Leesville, Virginia. She and her husband, who was home on leave, helped him write the preliminary draft of the prayer which he read to the nation over the radio when the landing craft began unloading American fighting men on Omaha Beach ; the final version, Anna says, is Father's own language.

Mother sent me a copy of the prayer, and I was much moved by its eloquence. Father prayed :

> Almighty God : Our sons . . . this day have set upon a mighty endeavor, a struggle to preserve our Republic, our religion, and our civilization, and to set free a suffering humanity.
>
> They will be sore tried . . . until the victory is won. . . . Men's souls will be shaken with the violence of war.
>
> For these men are lately drawn from the ways of peace. They fight not for the lust of conquest. . . . They fight to liberate . . . to let justice arise, and tolerance and good will among all Thy people. They yearn but for the end of battle, for their return to the haven of home.
>
> Some will never return. Embrace these, Father, and receive them, Thy heroic servants, into Thy kingdom.
>
> And for us at home—fathers, mothers, children, wives, sisters, and brothers of brave men overseas . . . help us, Almighty God, to rededicate ourselves in renewed faith in Thee in this hour of great sacrifice. . . .
>
> Thy will be done, Almighty God.
>
> Amen.

Perhaps I am not objective—perhaps I have a son's uncompromising bitterness for the premature and, in my opinion, unnecessary loss of a beloved father—but I never have been reconciled to the fact that Father's physicians did not flatly forbid him to run, or at least insist that he curtail his activities more than he did during those last months of his life.

I do not wish to be unfair. I realize that they tried to slow him down. I also know how impossible it was to control Father's actions when he had his mind set on doing something. I must accept that the doctors acted in good faith and in accordance with their best professional judgment. Yet none of us was warned that Father's life might be in danger.

The Strenuous Summer—First Alarm

Between the approaching political campaign and the onrushing climax of the War, the summer of 1944 was a strenuous one for Father. I, meanwhile, had frequent bulletins from Mother on

the state of his health. On New Year's Day 1944 she wrote me :
" Pa has had the flu but I hope it will not be bad. . . ." In April,
when he was resting at Bernard Baruch's plantation, Hobcaw
Barony, in South Carolina, she wrote : " Anna & I went down
to see Pa last Tuesday—He looked much better but said he still
had no ' pep '."

On May 29 Mother wrote :

> The doctors are very pleased with Pa's comeback & say he is
> really fine again—They took some last digestive tests last week that
> I haven't heard from but I'm sure they turned out well or Anna
> would have told me. . . . Pa is enjoying not doing things which bore
> him & he's getting so much pleasure out of having Anna around
> that I think he's going to shirk any but the office hour things for
> some time but it isn't necessity—just preference !

Then, early in July, I heard from Mother : " For your private
information Pa is going on a trip to Hawaii & Alaska, leaving
here the 14th. . . . I will go as far as the coast & fly back. Pa is
very well but we feed him carefully & see he gets plenty of rest."

At the time I received this letter I was temporarily stationed
at Camp Pendleton, near San Diego, California, as intelligence
officer on the staff of Rear-Admiral (later Vice-Admiral) Ralph O.
Davis, commanding officer of the amphibious base. Father paid
us a visit to review a landing exercise being staged by the Fifth
Marine Division as a dress rehearsal for its next Pacific operation.

Before the exercise began I was alone with Father in his
private railroad car. We talked of many things—the War, the
family, and politics. At that time the Democratic convention in
Chicago was wrangling over a Vice-Presidential nominee. I
was struck by Father's irritability over what was happening in
Chicago and by his apparent indifference as to whom the convention selected as his fourth-term running mate. He made it
clear that he was resigned to the dumping of Vice-President
Henry A. Wallace ; he felt that Wallace had become a political
liability. Although Father did not commit himself, I came
away with the distinct impression that he really preferred Justice
William O. Douglas as the Vice-Presidential nominee. But he
professed not to " give a damn " whether the delegates came up
with Justice Douglas, Jimmy Byrnes, or Senator Harry Truman.

His mind was on the War ; the fourth-term race was simply a job that had to be accomplished, and his attitude towards the coming political campaign was one of " let's get on with it."

Just before we were to leave for the exercise Father turned suddenly white, his face took on an agonized look, and he said to me, " Jimmy, I don't know if I can make it—I have horrible pains ! " It was a struggle for him to get the words out.

I was so scared I did not know what to think or do. I gripped his hand and felt his forehead. We considered calling the doctor, then decided against it. Both of us thought he was suffering some sort of acute digestive upset—Father himself was positive it had nothing to do with his heart. We talked some more, and I told him that, if he possibly could summon the strength, he should try not to cancel his appearance at the exercise, as it would create much alarm.

" Yes," Pa said, almost sighing, " it would be very bad. But help me out of my berth and let me stretch out flat on the deck for a while—that may help."

So for perhaps ten minutes, while I kept as quiet as possible, Father lay on the floor of the railroad car, his eyes closed, his face drawn, his powerful torso occasionally convulsed as the waves of pain stabbed him. Never in all my life had I felt so alone with him—and so helpless.

Then he opened his eyes, exhaled deeply, and said, " Help me up, Jimmy." I did so. I helped him get ready, and the Commander-in-Chief went out to review the exercises.

In the many photographs taken of him that day Pa looked tired. In most of them, however, he wore a big smile ; no one would have guessed what he had just been through. Looking at one of those pictures which hangs on the wall in my home, I am reminded of what Father's close friend Basil O'Connor told me recently : " I never saw the President in my life when he had his chin down. Always he was joyful. He was a buoyant fellow, even in his illness, even when he was physically weak."

The only reference Pa ever made to what happened in the railroad car, so far as I know, was in a letter to Mother, who had flown back East, in which he glossed over the incident. Before taking off for Pearl Harbor for his conference with Fleet Admiral Chester Nimitz and General of the Army Douglas MacArthur on Pacific war strategy, Father wrote her : " Dearest Babs : Off in a few minutes—All well. . . . Jimmy & I had a grand view of the landing operation at Camp Pendleton and then I got the collywobbles & stayed in the train in the p.m. Better today. . . ." He added : " It was grand having you come out with me—and the slow speed was a good thing for us both."

On the way back from Honolulu Father made the long, tiring detour to inspect American installations in the storm-swept Aleutians off the Alaska Peninsula. He made the last part of the trip in a destroyer and ran into much rough weather.

Soon after he travelled to Quebec for another conference with Churchill, Mackenzie King, and others.

" *The Little Man Made Me Pretty Mad.* . . ."

Father's political biographers have fully covered the 1944 campaign, in which the Republican nominee was Governor Thomas E. Dewey of New York, whom Father disliked and distrusted deeply. Once again, all of us, while recognizing that this time Father could hardly refuse to run, viewed the prospect with heavy hearts and wished he had not been called upon to sacrifice himself. At one point early in the campaign, when Father's vitality and spirits were low, Mother wrote me :

> I don't think Pa would really mind defeat. If elected he'll do his job well I feel sure & I think he can be kept well to do it but he does get tired so I think if defeated he'll be content. . . . I am only con-cerned because Dewey seems to me more & more to show no understanding of the job at home or abroad.

Here I must respectfully dissent from Mother's opinion. I think Father would have minded horribly being defeated for anything by Thomas E. Dewey.

Father had hoped to avoid partisan political speeches in his last campaign, but, shortly after the above letter was written, Dewey's methods got his Dutch up, and Father began swinging mightily and effectively. The old F.D.R—the seasoned political virtuoso—was back on the hustings.

Among their other mistakes, the G.O.P. strategists spread that silly story, which was pure bunk, about how Father's little

Scottie, Fala, had been left behind in the Aleutians and how Father ordered a destroyer to go back and retrieve him. In his speech to the Teamsters Union Pa took delight in debunking that one in a manner that set people laughing at Dewey.

Then in New York City, to combat the whispering campaign about his health, Father rode bareheaded in a cold, driving rain—in his open car—for approximately four hours. It was a magnificent performance, but the drain on his vitality was terrible.

When the ballots were counted on Election Day Father once more was the victor—the first man in history to be elected President of the United States for four terms. It was not a joyous victory, however. " The little man made me pretty mad," he confessed in a letter written me just after the election. Later he wrote an old friend who was knitting him a pair of socks for his inauguration and wanted to know what colour he would like : " I would suggest black or blue because that is a little bit the way I felt after going through THE DIRTIEST CAMPAIGN IN ALL HISTORY."

Inauguration Day—Second Alarm

The next—and the last—time I saw Father was on Inauguration Day, January 20, 1945. I was on active duty in the Philippines when I received a letter from him, asking me if I would come to the inauguration. He pointed out that I had stood with him at each of the preceding three and that he would like for me to be with him again. I replied that this was a matter for him to decide, as the only way I could leave my post in the Philippines was for him, as my commander-in-chief, to order me to Washington.

So he called me home, just to stand with him that day. Frankly I was hoping fervently that he would. I wanted to see him.

The first moment I saw Father I realized something was terribly wrong. He looked awful, and, regardless of what the doctors said, I knew in my heart that his days were numbered.

The inauguration was on the South Portico of the White House. It was a bitterly cold, raw day, and Father insisted on going through the ceremony without an overcoat. I begged Father to throw his naval cape over his shoulders, but he brushed aside my suggestion.

Later, just before he proceeded to the reception in the State Dining Room, Father and I were alone for a few minutes in the Green Room. He was thoroughly chilled, and the same type of pain, though somewhat less acute, that had bothered him in San Diego was stabbing him again. He gripped my arm hard and said, " Jimmy, I can't take this unless you get me a stiff drink." I said I would, and as I started out he called to me, " You'd better make it straight." I brought him a tumbler half full of whisky, which he drank as if it were medicine. In all my life I had never seen Father take a drink in that manner.

Then he went to the reception, and no one there—no one but me—knew how he felt.

I was deeply disturbed. Before returning to the Philippines I ran around like a chicken with its head cut off, trying to get one of his physicians or some one close to him to tell me what was wrong with Pa. The only person who would admit to me that he thought Father was a sick man was Lieutenant-Commander George A. Fox, U.S.N., Father's physical therapist.

Had I discussed the matter that day with Bill Hassett, his devoted secretary, or with Basil O'Connor, they would have told me that they shared my fears. Regardless of all the soothing talk from the doctors, they felt, as I did, that Father's days were surely numbered. It showed in the way he talked, the way he looked. There was a drawn, almost ethereal look about him. At times the old zestfulness was there, but often—particularly when he let down his guard—he seemed thousands of miles away. That was the mental picture I carried with me as I returned to the Philippines, depressed and worried over Father's condition.

Of the various things we discussed on that last time I saw Father one subject alone stirred the old fire in him. That was his prospective trip to Yalta to confer with Stalin and Churchill. Father felt deeply and intensely that the hopes for a decent and just peace depended largely on what he would be able to negotiate with Stalin at Yalta. As he talked about it one could almost see him throw off his fatigue as he became stimulated with the thought of the challenging task that faced him.

Pa was insistent on one thing for that last inauguration. He wanted every one of his grandchildren with him in the White

House—perhaps he had a prescience that this would be the last time they would all be together. There were thirteen grand-children at that time and it took a bit of doing, but Pa assembled them all ; as Mother has written, " We bulged at the corners." He made personal calls and even paid for some of the railroad tickets to make certain every one was there.

Yalta and Ibn Saud

Soon afterwards Father sailed for the Yalta conference—again a tremendous drain on his ebbing vitality. This time it was Anna who accompanied him. With all the vital international problems that were weighing upon him, the family was still very much on his mind. The Senate row over confirmation of Elliott as a brigadier-general was in progress, and the unfortunate publicity over the transportation of Elliott's dog in a military plane was providing plenty of ammunition for the Roosevelt-haters. Stopping at Malta *en route* to Russia, Father first sent Anna out to buy presents for the family, then personally dashed off a note to Mother on tablet paper, advising her of his safe arrival and remarking, " I hope for news of the Senate confirmation of Elliott."

Pa was tired at Yalta. It showed in the increasing gauntness of his face and in his general loss of weight—yet he was in-domitable as ever. He maintained a gruelling schedule at the conferences, and just before sailing from Sevastopol on February 12, 1945, he again wrote Mother : " Dearest Babs : We have wound up the conference successfully I think.   I am a bit exhausted but really all right."

Instead of heading straight for home Father insisted on stopping for conferences with King Farouk of Egypt, King Ibn Saud of Saudi Arabia, and the Emperor Haile Selassie of Ethiopia. Another " Dearest Babs " note went off :

> Headed in the right direction—homeward ! All well, but still need a little sleep. A *fantastic* week. King of Egypt, ditto of Arabia and the Emperor of Ethiopia ! Anna is fine and at the moment is ashore in Algiers. Give John and Johnnie [John Boettiger, Sr., and Jr.] my love. I hope to come to Washington when you . . . are going to be there. . . . Devotedly, F.D.R.

Father's time was running out fast. A revealing, description of how Father appeared physically is contained in the excellent little book *F.D.R. Meets Ibn Saud,* by Colonel William A. Eddy, U.S.M.C. (retired), the first United States Minister to Saudi Arabia, who set up the meeting and served as Father's interpreter. He wrote :

> Throughout this meeting, President Roosevelt was in top form as a charming host, witty conversationalist, with the spark and light in his eyes and that gracious smile which always won people over to him whenever he talked with them as a friend. However, every now and then I would catch him off guard and see his face in repose. It was ashen in color ; the lines were deep ; the eyes would fade in helpless fatigue. He was living on his nerve.

While Father was sailing home Mother was in a mood of high elation over the announced results of the Yalta conference and in anticipation of the United Nations Organization meeting in San Francisco, which Father planned to address. She wrote him the following remarkable letter :

Feb. 13th [1945]

Dearest Franklin :

We seem to be almost united as a country in approval of the results of the conference. I think you must be very well satisfied & your diplomatic abilities must have been colossal ! Jonathan [1] is happy. John [1] is happy. All the world looks smiling. I think having the first U.N. meeting in San Francisco is a stroke of genius. At last will Marshal Stalin leave his own country or won't you three have to be on hand ?

You must feel a great let up in strain & satisfaction & I hate to think that you must return to the petty partisan struggles here. I had Mr. and Mrs. Wallace [1] to lunch on Tuesday. He says Vandenberg [1] is bring[ing] up the question on purely party lines it will depend on how much you really want to bring pressure.

[1] Some of the personalities referred to may need identification at this date. "Jonathan" was Jonathan Daniels, Father's Press secretary. "John" apparently was Anna's husband, the late John Boettiger. "Wallace" was the former Vice-President, then awaiting confirmation by the Senate as Secretary of Commerce, and "Jones" was Jesse Jones, the displaced Commerce Secretary, who was kicking up as much trouble as possible for his successor. "Vandenberg" was the Republican Senator from Michigan. "Aubrey" was Aubrey Williams, whose nomination to head the Rural Electrification Administration was being fought fang and nail by old Senator McKellar of Tennessee. Mary Norton was a New Jersey congresswoman.

They tell me Jones [1] still goes to his office, but he's not a sensitive person, is he ? Aubrey [1] was accused of all the crimes by McKellar [1], so you will have to fight for him too. His seems to be a miniature fight but similar to the one of Wallace, they are afraid he might build liberal farmers thro R.E.A. Oh ! well, I guess we are as prejudiced in our way as they are their way—I wish I knew what you really thought & really wanted. I've explained your letter to Jones & wondered if I was doing some wishful thinking & Mary Norton [1] asked me the other day if you really wanted Wallace—

I have a sense of relief that Elliott is confirmed & now the attacks on him will die down but Anna will be the next victim until I do something awful !

Much love dear, congratulations & I hope you enjoy the return trip & that it is placid & uneventful so you get a rest. . . . I hope you arrive when I am home.

Devotedly
ER [1]

He Just Didn't Bounce Back

There was much comment on Father's extreme weariness when, on March 1, 1945, he reported to the joint session of the two houses of Congress on what had been accomplished at Yalta. He was seated as he delivered his report—the first time, to the best of my recollection, that he ever had addressed Congress without standing. " I hope," he said, " that you will pardon me for this unusual posture of sitting down . . . but I know that you will realize that it makes it a lot easier for me not to have to carry about ten pounds of steel around on the bottom of my legs ; and also . . . I have just completed a fourteen-thousand-mile trip." Not since his 1928 gubernatorial campaign had he publicly mentioned his crippled legs.

Father plunged back into the duties of the Presidency, and he also resumed his rôle of the proud parent whose sons were at war. On March 3 he was writing Elliott : " Dear Bunny : It is grand to be able to address you as Brigadier General ! "

In the pile of personal mail that was waiting for him was a cryptic letter from Franklin, Jr., advising him that if he would look up a certain Navy report about the sinking of a Japanese submarine on or about the date of Pa's recent birthday he would see it was Brud's new destroyer escort, the U.S.S. *Ulvert M.*

Moore, that had done the sinking as a special " birthday present " for the Commander-in-Chief. Father wrote back delightedly that it was the nicest, most unusual, and certainly the most exciting birthday present he had ever received.

Bob Sherwood, Father's speech-writing aide, back from a thirty-five-thousand-mile Pacific war-zone swing, brought him news that he had seen me in the Philippines ; also, that he had talked with the commanding officer of Johnny's aircraft-carrier. The skipper told him Johnny was doing a good job and wouldn't " stand for any nonsense about being the President's son."

Father just didn't bounce back the way he should have. He went to Hyde Park for a week-end in March. Then, on March 29, he left for Warm Springs. Sis would have gone with him, but on her return from Yalta she found her five-year-old son, John Boettiger, Jr., seriously ill. Mother too might have made the trip to Georgia, but she had no indication from Vice-Admiral Ross T. McIntire, the White House physician, that there was anything to worry about. Admiral McIntire did not accompany Father either ; Commander Howard Bruenn, a heart specialist, went along instead.

Father's companions on that trip, therefore, were his two old friends Basil O'Connor and Leighton McCarthy and his two cousins Laura Delano and Margaret Suckley. Doc O'Connor had to return to New York. Always honest—even to the point of bluntness—with Father, O'Connor saw him just before he left and gave him some advice.

" He was having breakfast in bed," O'Connor says. " I told him good-bye, and said to him, ' We're going to need you when the War is over. But, unless you go away for ninety days and do absolutely nothing so you can get your strength back, there's a good chance you're not going to be around that long.' He just looked at me and said in a rather faraway manner, ' If I could only put on some weight. . . .' "

On the night of April 11 Father telephoned Anna in Washington to ask about little Johnny Boettiger. " He knew my spirits were low," Sis has told me, " so he tried to cheer me up. His voice was strong, and he was wonderful—full of fun and quips."

He told Anna about the barbecue that a couple of his Warm Springs friends—Ruth Stevens, who runs the local hotel, and

Frank Allcorn, the mayor—were going to cook up for him and the newspapermen next day. " Lady Ruth," as he called her, was going to cook him some Brunswick stew, which he loved, and they even had arranged to have Bun Wright, Pa's favourite country fiddler, play a few hoedowns.

Sis was the last member of the family to whom Pa talked.

While Pa was having this telephone conversation with Anna Elliott was at an air base in England ; Franklin, Jr., and John were at sea in the Pacific ; and I was at a headquarters camp near a muddy little town called Dulag on Leyte Island, in the Philippines.

My job was that of intelligence officer on the staff of Admiral Davis, commander of Amphibious Group Thirteen, Pacific Fleet, and we were making preparations for our part in the Okinawa invasion. I had just finished writing Mother a long letter, chatting with her about the forthcoming United Nations meeting in San Francisco on April 25, which Father planned to address and which she expected to attend. I also told her about how friendly the people on Leyte were, and how they did our laundry for us on a twenty-four-hour schedule. " That," I wrote, " ought to make a lot of people jealous."

Casualty of War

In the Philippines, which is on the other side of the international dateline, it was early morning, April 13 (back home it was late afternoon, April 12), when I was awakened by an orderly with the routine overnight dispatches. I checked them for the admiral, lay back on my cot for a few minutes, then started to get up when the orderly returned.

He stood in the doorway—he was a young Navy enlisted man— and said in a disturbed manner, " I have something for you, sir."

I waited. I thought he was acting strangely, and I was puzzled by it.

The orderly started weeping, dropped a piece of paper on my cot, and ran out.

It was the official communication to the fleet that Father had died a few hours before.

In a very short while a personal message, sent through Navy

communications, came to me. The same message was received in England by Brigadier-General Elliott Roosevelt, and somewhere in the Pacific by Lieutenant-Commander Franklin D. Roosevelt, Jr., and Lieutenant John Roosevelt. It read :

DARLINGS : PA SLEPT AWAY THIS AFTERNOON. HE DID HIS JOB TO THE END AS HE WOULD WANT YOU TO DO. BLESS YOU. ALL OUR LOVE.
MOTHER

I sat alone with my thoughts for a while. I was too numb to think about anything very clearly, but I do remember saying to myself : *Pa is a casualty of the War, just as much as if he had been stopped by an enemy bullet.*

Then I thought of some of the things he had told me when I saw him last on Inauguration Day—his soaring hopes for an early and lasting peace and for the rebuilding of the world when the War was over ; his determination to try, through the United Nations, to finish the job in which President Woodrow Wilson had been tragically frustrated by petty, narrow-minded men.

Then Admiral Davis came in and asked me if there was anything he could do. I said that, since our outfit was not scheduled to go into action for some time, I would like to get home for the funeral if it could be arranged, and that I would return to my post before we shoved off for the next operation. I said I did not want a special flight set up. The admiral said he would see what could be done.

Our two chaplains came in, and I prayed with them in my quarters. Four hours later I was on the first lap of the long flight home, hitching rides on planes that were going my way.

22

Lonely, Too, in Death

FLYING home across the Pacific, racing against the clock in the hope of reaching Father's funeral in time, I had opportunity for meditation. It was a hard journey ; my thoughts were painful and sombre. I had to change planes several times, and at my stop in Honolulu I learned some of the details of Father's death. One of the things I learned was that none of the family was with him.

That bothered me dreadfully. I knew Pa would not have wanted it that way. He would have wanted, had he been able to recognize us and to talk to us, to have said good-bye to his " Dearest Babs " and " the chicks." He would have given us a message of love and would have told us not to grieve too much for him—and I'm sure he would have thought up some little witticism, some last gallant jest, before he closed his eyes for ever.

My thoughts went back to the last time I saw him on In- auguration Day, and when I recalled how I had tried to get the doctors to tell me the score and how I had drawn a blank the bitterness surged up in me. I accepted his passing ; from the faith in which he had raised me I drew the strength to resign myself to God's will and to the fact that the time had come at last for the soldier of democracy to lay down his arms. Yet I still hated the fact, and I could not make myself think otherwise, that Pa—our Pa, our early playmate, our sailing partner, our cruelly stricken father, so courageous in adversity, our sunny companion, our President, our Commander-in-Chief, but always our Pa had died alone. His loneliness had to be with him to the end.

It helped none when I learned later from Mother—and she has written it in her autobiography—that even after the massive cerebral hæmorrhage hit Father that afternoon and the word was flashed to Washington, reaching Mother at a Thrift Shop benefit, the White House physician still was " not alarmed." He advised her not to cancel her afternoon engagement, but, she said later, " we planned to go to Warm Springs that evening."

Along the route another telegram from Mother caught up with me. The funeral service was going to be Saturday afternoon, and Father would be buried on Sunday at Hyde Park. Our plane was bucking head-winds. I knew in my heart I was going to be too late ; yet I kept hoping desperately for some miracle that would bring me home in time.

But there was no miracle. I arrived in New York just a few hours too late to see Father laid to rest in the rose garden where Granny used to tend her flowers. Mother and Anna were there, and Elliott had made it home from England.

Of Franklin, Jr., and Johnny there is a story which I myself heard from them only recently. Although we are a talkative lot, all of us have some of Father's innate reticence about very private things, and sometimes we do not talk about them unless there is a reason.

Both Brud and Johnny were with their ships at sea when Mother's duplicate wires reached them. The aerial softening up of Okinawa had begun, and it was out of the question for either of them to attempt to get home. In their circumstances the line in Mother's telegram, " He did his job to the end as he would want you to do," meant they must remain at their posts.

On the evening of Father's death American warships were cruising off Okinawa. On board Admiral " Jocko " Clark's flagship, the carrier *Hornet*, Lieutenant John Roosevelt, U.S.N.R., had the midnight to 4 A.M. watch. At some time during that period he got the message.

Admiral Marc Mitscher, commanding Task Force Fifty-Eight, offered to put Johnny aboard a " jeep " carrier and send him to within flying distance of Guam, where he could get a plane for the States. Johnny took a look at Mother's telegram and decided that under no circumstances would he be responsible for taking a capital ship out of the shooting. He thanked the admiral and said no.

Johnny's own commanding officer very sensibly put him hard at work. The next night John was standing watch on the flag bridge. Somewhere off in the dark other ships were cruising, and one of them was the U.S.S. *Ulvert M. Moore* (DE-442), Lieutenant-Commander Franklin D. Roosevelt, Jr., U.S.N.R., commanding. From the loudspeaker of the ship-to-ship communication system John heard a familiar voice—Brud's—calling the *Hornet's* code.

John picked up his phone, and soon one Harvard-Groton-accented voice was answering the other—using no names, of course.

" Are you making it home, Old Man ? " asked the voice from the *Ulvert M. Moore*.

" No," replied the voice from the *Hornet*. " Are you ? "

" Nope. Let's clean it up out here first. So long, Old Man— over and out."

" So long."

Father's Secret Funeral Instructions

Back in New York, too late for the funeral, I had four hours to wait before I could board the train that would bring Mother back from Hyde Park to Washington, where she would begin the job of breaking up twelve years of housekeeping at the White House.

I wanted to be alone, and I wanted to keep moving. I began walking the streets rather aimlessly and found myself on Fifth Avenue. It was Sunday and the streets were not crowded. I was just another man in uniform—no one approached me, no one spoke to me, until a taxicab pulled up alongside me. The driver leaped out, leaving his door open, and said, " My God, aren't you Jimmy Roosevelt ? "

I said I was. He grabbed my hand, and the words started pouring out of him—all the things Father had meant to him.

Then an ugly thing happened—a thing that Mother and Anna and Elliott and Franklin and Johnny and I had learned long ago to live with but which, at this particular moment, when Father had just been buried at Hyde Park, was hard to endure. The cabbie had a passenger, and he leaned out of the cab, uttered a profanity, and said, " I hired you to drive me, not to talk about that —— Roosevelt ! "

Long ago I had schooled myself—for Father's sake—to put my fists in my pockets and walk away when strangers started reviling Father. That afternoon I was able to do it once more, but I had to restrain the cab-driver from assaulting the passenger. The cabbie was so angry he couldn't talk coherently. Tears were running down his face, and he made the man leave his cab. I guess I was crying a bit too as I walked away.

When I boarded the train returning from the funeral I found Mother in control of her emotions. Mother is like that—she feels things deeply, intensely, but on the surface she freezes. We embraced each other, and I did the same with Anna and Elliott.

Then Mother took me aside and handed me an envelope that had been found in Father's safe. It was still sealed, for it was addressed to me in Father's own hand, and Mother had felt she should not open it.

I had an eerie feeling, coupled with a rush of emotion, as I opened it and saw what it was. It was a four-page document, handwritten in pencil by Father. The document was dated December 26, 1937—early in Father's second term, when he was in superb health. It gave specific instructions on every detail of how he wanted his funeral conducted in the event of his death while he was still President of the United States.

As the communication from Father was opened too late, Father's funeral instructions were not carried out to the letter as he had directed. He had never told Mother of the document in the safe. Mother, however, had a general idea of his wishes, so the major details were observed.

For example, Father directed " that a service of the utmost simplicity be held in the East Room," which was done. However, his stipulation that it be " attended only by the household, by those in the Executive Office who have been close to me, by the Cabinet and their families and by such other members of the Administrative Branch as have been close to me " was not fully observed. The list of those attending was larger than he had desired.

His second instruction—" That there be no Lying in State anywhere "—was followed.

He had wanted the funeral service at the White House to be followed by another " simple service " in the rotunda of the

Capitol, to be conducted by his old Groton Headmaster and
friend, the Rev. Endicott Peabody. " Only prayers . . . and two
hymns—no speaking," Father had written.   There was no
service at the Capitol, and Dr Peabody had preceded Father in
death.

Father's directions for the removal of his body to Hyde Park
and for the conducting of services and burial there were not
fully carried out.   He had wanted his casket taken to St James's,
where he had worshipped, for a short, simple service, and then
to the house of his parents to rest " in front of the East fireplace
in the big room for the night."   Neither was done.   The funeral
train did not arrive in Hyde Park until Sunday morning, and the
casket was taken directly to the rose garden.

He directed : " That the casket be of absolute simplicity,
dark wood, that the body be not embalmed or hermetically
sealed, and that the grave be not lined with brick, cement or
stone."   The outer box of the casket was, as he had wanted, of
dark mahogany and simple design, encasing a bronze coffin.
The body, however, was embalmed, and the casket was placed
in a cement vault.   Neither Mother nor any of the family nor
his intimates know why he requested that his body be not embalmed and that the casket be placed directly into the earth ;
so far as we can learn, he had never discussed this with anyone.
Knowing Father, we can only speculate that he regarded the
embalming procedure as a distasteful invasion of privacy, and
that perhaps he had an inner yearning to follow the traditional
funeral liturgy, " Earth to earth, ashes to ashes, dust to dust, in
sure and certain hope of the Resurrection. . . ."

Father had asked : " That . . . the interment take place where
the sun dial stands in the garden, and that the casket be carried
to the garden by men from the place including the Boreel place
and the back farms and Val Kill Cottage."   (The Boreel place
was the tract purchased by Grandfather James Roosevelt in 1868,
adjoining the land and house where Father was born.)   Eight
men from the armed services carried Father's casket, and interment took place where Father directed.   (The Sun dial was moved
thirty-two feet and four inches north to make room for the
grave.)

Father had directed that " the interment be attended only by the family, the Cabinet, the President, the Speaker and not to exceed 2 Senators and 2 Representatives." Because of the circumstances I have described, of the immediate family only Mother, Anna, and Elliott were present. None of the thirteen grandchildren was there—Mother felt Pa would have preferred for them to remember him as he was on that last Inauguration Day, when he had gone to such pains to assemble them all at the White House.

There were more senators and representatives present than he had specified, as well as a number of others who had worked with Father.

Father asked :

        plain   no carving or decoration
" That a $\wedge$ white marble monument $\wedge$ be placed over the grave." [NOTE : The interlined words were inserted by Father, as indicated—J.R.] He specified a stone eight feet long, four feet wide, and three feet high. The monument is as he requested.

He also wrote :

It is my hope that my dear wife will on her death be buried there also, and that the monument contain no device or inscription except the following on the South side :

FRANKLIN DELANO ROOSEVELT
1882–19—
ANNA ELEANOR ROOSEVELT
1884–19—

The inscription is as he directed, only with the year of his death—1945—filled in, and the final date, after Mother's name, left blank. One day my wonderful Mother will be reunited there with my wonderful Father. Though he is waiting for her in the eternal sleep in which he, as a religious man, so firmly believed, I pray to God it will be many years off.

Epilogue

How do I end this story of my memories of Franklin Delano Roosevelt, my father ? I may as well ask myself how or when I will stop remembering Pa. Or when the people whom I meet wherever I go in my own country and in other countries will stop approaching me and saying, " I never met him, but I *knew* him. . . ." Or when strangers will stop saying, " Let me tell you what your Father meant to me. . . ."

I could write more. I could relate the details of how Pa drew his remarkable will, of which he named me the family trustee, wording it rigidly to protect the principal of the estate for Mother

during her lifetime, for he knew so well her impulsive, over-generous instincts and did not want her to give everything away. I could write of how Mother, instead of lapsing into lonesome, idle widowhood, has become an even greater personality than she was at the time of Father's death. I could write of all the things that have happened to my sister, my brothers, and me. Some are good, some are bad, and many—perhaps both the good and the bad—can be traced to the way in which Pa raised us.

But all of that now would be anticlimactic, a wordy appendix to this volume, which I have intended as a document of love.

I think the ending of this story rightly should come from Father himself.

He was working on an address the day before he died. It was a speech he was supposed to broadcast two nights later for the Jefferson Day dinners throughout the country. In it he spoke not of partisan politics, but of peace and patriotism.

Father read and corrected a copy of what he had dictated. The last sentence in his typed manuscript was made to read, " The only limit to our realization of to-morrow will be our doubts of to-day." Then, in his own hand—a hand not as strong as it was in those earlier days when, despite his affliction, he could pin a husky fourteen-year-old boy to the floor—he wrote a final sentence :

" *Let us move forward with strong and active faith.*"

It was on the day after that Father, while posing for a portrait, said, almost inaudibly, " I have a terrific headache," and came to the end of his road.

Acknowledgments and Bibliography

BY SIDNEY SHALETT

During the more than eighteen months in which the preparation of this volume was under way a number of persons made invaluable contributions. Most of these sources are identified in the text, but special acknowledgment is due in a number of instances.

James Roosevelt, of course, is the primary source of information for this son's portrait of Franklin Roosevelt, not as a politician, but as a father. His images of his father are as vivid as if the incidents he is describing had happened only yesterday. Possibly we have touched upon some topics that some persons may think might best have been kept private. Mr Roosevelt and I gave these matters earnest consideration ; our feeling is that, in the process of his evolution from the personal father to the public figure, F.D.R. himself made the decision to share his life, his legend, his legacy with posterity.

Mr Roosevelt adds, " There is nothing in this book, I think, that Father would not have wanted told."

To Eleanor Roosevelt, Anna Roosevelt Halsted, Elliott Roosevelt, Franklin D. Roosevelt, Jr., and John A. Roosevelt sincere thanks are due. Each gave generously of her and his time, and granted permission to quote from previously unpublished letters.

I must acknowledge my personal debt to my wife and research associate, Anita Shalett. In this undertaking to produce a human study of a man whom both my wife and I admired—and now admire more than ever—her rôle has been a major one. Not only did she assist in going through hundreds of letters and other documents at Hyde Park, Warm Springs, and in Washington, but her editorial criticism and assessment of both the rough and finished manuscripts, her sensitive feeling for the basic human story, have been of inestimable value.

In the co-author's family circle a special sort of acknowledgment is due to my two sons, Michael and John Shalett. During the long period of preparation of this story of a father's relationship with his children they were deprived of much of the day-to-day services of their own father.

Never in my experience as a writer have I had more painstaking, intelligent, unsparing co-operation than was given by Herman Kahn, director of the Franklin D. Roosevelt Library at Hyde Park. A knowledgeable and dedicated authority, Mr Kahn has gone far beyond ordinary courtesy in assisting the authors. He has suggested sources of corroborative information, and has been a judicious, scholarly arbiter of many questions concerning F.D.R. Appreciation also is due to the Library's capable staff.

Charles Forrest Palmer, of Atlanta, chairman and guiding spirit of the Franklin D. Roosevelt Warm Springs (Georgia) Memorial Commission, has helped the authors considerably. Mr Palmer believed in F.D.R. and his works, and on several occasions put aside his private business activities to serve the President in various capacities. Not only were his own recollections of aid to the authors, but he made available a series of tape-recorded interviews, collected for the Commission by Dr Rexford G. Tugwell, which supplemented our own research at Warm Springs. These interviews, pertaining to F.D.R.'s Georgia associations, have preserved much information which otherwise might have been lost to future historians.

Of the many persons interviewed, whose recollections of special phases of F.D.R.'s life are quoted, the authors are particularly indebted to D. Basil O'Connor, who had been F.D.R.'s law partner, friend, and associate in the development of Warm Springs as a centre for medical treatment of polio victims. " Doc " O'Connor knew and understood F.D.R. with a rare sympathy and sensitivity.

In some of the personal stories related by James Roosevelt there may be divergences from versions published by other authors. Mr Roosevelt has narrated the occurrences as faithfully as memory allows —and, in most cases, he had the advantage of having been there.

The punctuation—or lack of it—and occasional lapses in grammar and spelling in some of the letters from F.D.R. and other members of the family will undoubtedly be noted by readers. The authors have deliberately refrained from changing these letters, preferring to reproduce them exactly as they were written.

Certain books have been of value, some as source material, others as background ; where a direct quotation is made, if it is not so indicated in the text, it will be credited in the ensuing chapter bibliography. Of considerable help were the two autobiographical volumes by Eleanor Roosevelt, *This Is My Story* and *This I Remember*, and the four volumes edited by Elliott Roosevelt, entitled *F.D.R., His Personal Letters*. A series of six articles, written by Anna Roosevelt and published in 1949 in the now defunct magazine *The Woman* (Farrell Publishing Corporation), was useful as background.

Books consulted—and, in some instances, quoted from—are listed below. Thereafter, in the chapter bibliography which follows the reference list, quotations will be identified in most instances by the author's name. James Roosevelt and Eleanor Roosevelt will be identified as " J.R." and " E.R."

The list of books, authors, publishers, dates, and places of publication is as follows :

BLACK, RUBY : *Eleanor Roosevelt : A Biography* (Duell, Sloan and Pearce, New York, 1940).

BURNS, JAMES MACGREGOR : *Roosevelt : The Lion and the Fox* (Harcourt, Brace and Company, New York, 1956).

CARMICHAEL, DONALD SCOTT (ed.) : *F.D.R., Columnist : The Uncollected Columns of Franklin D. Roosevelt* (Pellegrini and Cudahy, Chicago, 1947).

DANIELS, JONATHAN : *The End of Innocence* (J. B. Lippincott Company, Philadelphia and New York, 1954).

DELANO, DANIEL W. : *Franklin Roosevelt and the Delano Influence* (James S. Nudi Publications, Pittsburgh, 1946).

EDDY, WILLIAM A. : *F.D.R. Meets Ibn Saud* (American Friends of the Middle East, Inc., New York, 1954).

FARLEY, JAMES A. : *Jim Farley's Story, the Roosevelt Years* (McGraw-Hill Book Company, Inc., New York, 1948).

FREIDEL, FRANK : *Franklin D. Roosevelt* (3 vols., Little, Brown and Company, Boston and Toronto, 1952–56).

GUNTHER, JOHN : *Roosevelt in Retrospect* (Harper and Brothers, New York, 1950 ; Hamish Hamilton, London, 1950).

HASSETT, WILLIAM D. : *Off the Record with F.D.R.* (Rutgers University Press, New Brunswick (copyright by Warm Springs Foundation), 1958).

KEMLER, EDGAR : *The Irreverent Mr Mencken* (Little, Brown and Company, Boston and Toronto, 1950).

KINGDON, FRANK (ed.) : *As FDR Said* (Duell, Sloan and Pearce, New York, 1950).

MCINTIRE, ROSS T., in collaboration with GEORGE CREEL : *White House Physician* (G. P. Putnam's Sons, New York, 1946).

MACKENZIE, COMPTON : *Mr Roosevelt* (E. P. Dutton and Company New York, 1944 ; George G. Harrap and Co., London, 1943).

NESBITT, HENRIETTA : *White House Diary* (Doubleday and Company, Inc., New York, 1948).

PALMER, CHARLES F. : *Adventures of a Slum Fighter* (Tupper and Love, Atlanta, 1955).

PERKINS, FRANCES : *The Roosevelt I Knew* (Viking Press, New York, 1946).

ROOSEVELT, ELEANOR : *This Is My Story* (Harper and Brothers, New York, 1937 ; Hutchinson and Co., London, 1938, under the title *The Lady of the White House*).

ROOSEVELT, ELEANOR : *This I Remember* (Harper and Brothers, New York, 1949 ; Hutchinson and Co., London, 1950).

ROOSEVELT, ELLIOTT : *As He Saw It* (Duell, Sloan and Pearce, New York, 1946).

ROOSEVELT, ELLIOTT (ed.) : *F.D.R., His Personal Letters* (4 vols., Duell, Sloan and Pearce, New York, 1947–50 ; George G. Harrap and Co., London, 1949–52).

ROOSEVELT, MRS JAMES (SARA DELANO), as told to Isabel Leighton and Gabrielle Forbush : *My Boy Franklin* (Ray Long and Richard R. Smith, Inc., New York, 1933).

ROSENMAN, SAMUEL I. : *Working with Roosevelt* (Harper and Brothers, New York, 1952 ; Rupert Hart-Davis, London, 1952).

SCHRIFTGIESSER, KARL : *The Amazing Roosevelt Family, 1613–1942* (Wilfred Funk, Inc., New York, 1942 ; Jarrolds, London, 1943).

SHERWOOD, ROBERT E. : *Roosevelt and Hopkins ; an Intimate History* (Harper and Brothers, New York, 1948).

STILES, LELA : *The Man Behind Roosevelt : The Story of Louis McHenry Howe* (World Publishing Company, Cleveland and New York, 1954).

TULLY, GRACE : *F.D.R., My Boss* (Charles Scribner's Sons, New York, 1949).

WALKER, TURNLEY : *Roosevelt and the Warm Springs Story* (A. A. Wyn, Inc., New York, 1953).

Following are specific credits for sources of quotations, information, and corroboration, listed by chapters :

Chapter I. Various quotes from Sara Delano Roosevelt are from her book ; J.R. (James Roosevelt) heard her relate most of these stories. E.R.'s teasing remark about the " lovely ladies " is from *This Is My Story* ; likewise her comments on F.D.R.'s shortcomings as a disciplinarian and her memories of her mother and father. The quotation on how F.D.R.'s foolhardy German goose " committed suicide " is from Hassett, who also relates the story which F.D.R, once told J.R. concerning the effervescent powders, the chamber-pot, and the *Fräulein*. The incident witnessed by J.R., concerning his grandmother's indignation over F.D.R.'s use of " damn ! " at the dinner-table is also related with a slightly different conclusion by Gunther. E.R.'s recollections of early settlement house work are from her first volume.

Chapter II. E.R.'s *This Is My Story* is the source for her remarks concerning her " relief " at the birth of her first son, James ; her " curious arrangement " for " airing the chicks " ; and the close sequence in which her children were born. Daniel Delano tells of Sara Roosevelt's original thought to name F.D.R. " Warren " after her father.

Chapter III. J.R.'s story of how the touring lobstermen invaded Anna's bedchamber in the White House is one known to the family ; it is also told by Ruby Black. Likewise, his account of Sara Roosevelt's encounter with Huey Long has been related by other authors, including Farley, an eyewitness. E.R.'s comments on how her mother-in-law spoiled the children are from her second autobiographical volume. Frances Perkins's *The Roosevelt I Knew* is the source of F.D.R.'s indignant explosion on the same subject.

Chapter IV. Daniels writes of F.D.R.'s reminiscences on his personal budget troubles during World War I ; also of the disastrous effects of Walter Camp's energetic " fitness " programme on F.D.R. and other officials of that era. Freidel mentions the admiring glances given the handsome young Assistant Navy Secretary. E.R.'s first volume tells of her early Washington housekeeping experiences, and Anna Roosevelt's articles in *The Woman* correspond with J.R.'s remembrance of how the Roosevelt kids tricked the young British envoy at baseball. Gunther and Grace Tully also cite the affectionate customs existing between F.D.R. and his children. Frances Perkins's book first related F.D.R.'s remark on how he loved to sing with the " Methodys " ; other authors have adopted it.

Chapter V. Anna Roosevelt has written of her scolding by the convalescent F.D.R. Hassett quotes F.D.R. on the ribald Delano " shot gun wedding " story.

Chapter VII. Averell Harriman's remark on the formidable Christianity of Dr Endicott Peabody is quoted in George Biddle's article, " As I Remember Groton School," published in *Harper's*, August 1939. E.R.'s remark on the conformity of son James at Groton is from *This Is My Story*.

Chapter VIII. The account of F.D.R.'s chilling slip into the Bay of Fundy the day *before* he came down with polio, not ordinarily related in the sequence of events used by biographers of this period, is from Earle Looker's *This Man Roosevelt*, published by Brewer, Warren and Putnam, New York, 1932.

Chapter IX. E.R.'s account of her only breakdown after F.D.R. contracted polio is from her first book. Grace Tully—and others after her—tells of F.D.R.'s rejoinder to Mme Chiang Kai-shek. The letter from F.D.R. to Governor Cox was obtained by C. F. Palmer from James M. Cox, Jr. The account of F.D.R.'s difficulty with his hat at his first inaugural, which J.R. contradicts, is from Gunther ; the story of J.R.'s " experiments " with his father's braces, which he likewise denies, is from McIntire.

Chapter X. Donald S. Carmichael, who edited the collection of F.D.R.'s newspaper columns, uncovered the F.D.R.–John Lawrence correspondence, pertaining to the houseboat *Larooco*, in an article published in the *F.D.R. Collector*, November 1948.

Chapter XI. For the reference to F.D.R.'s widespread post-polio business ventures the authors have drawn on Freidel's concise summation in *Franklin D. Roosevelt*, Vol. 2.

Chapter XII. In the Warm Springs chapter the authors were aided immeasurably by the Tugwell–Warm Springs Commission tape-recorded interviews. Although J.R. has heard E.R. tell the story a number of times, the " chickens-on-the-hoof " incident also was related by her to Dr Tugwell. Henry Wallace's recollections of his first conference with President-elect Roosevelt at Warm Springs are also from the Tugwell interviews. Former Vice-President Wallace reviewed and amplified his recollections for the authors. L. Duncan Cannon, business administrator of the Georgia Warm Springs Foundation, is the source of several of the anecdotes about F.D.R.'s pranks at Warm Springs.

Chapter XIV. Both in personal conversations and in his book C. F. Palmer gives the background of what happened at the famous " possum dinner." The prophetic and peppery quotations from Louis Howe are from Lela Stiles's biography.

Chapter XV. *Re* the controversial topic of White House menus, Sherwood's *Roosevelt and Hopkins*, Grace Tully's *F.D.R., My Boss*, and Hassett's *Off the Record with F.D.R.* are sources for some of the tart observations which season J.R.'s own recollections. The story of F.D.R.'s dispute with Dean Acheson, while originally told to J.R. by F.D.R. himself and checked for details by the authors with Acheson, is also related by Gunther. A private memo by C. F. Palmer, who heard F.D.R. tell the story, is the source for the account of how F.D.R. disconcerted Henry Morgenthau during the Secretary's speech on the Treasury steps.

Chapter XVI. Grace Tully's reminiscences again are the source for F.D.R.'s quote on J.R. wanting to punch Mr Hoover in the nose.

Miss Tully, Mrs Nesbitt, and others have used the story—a favourite in the Roosevelt family—of F.D.R.'s initiation as a diaper-procurer. E.R.'s talk with Franklin, Jr., concerning his bitterness over undue publicity was related by her to the authors ; she also tells it in *This I Remember*. The same volume is the source for her story of a son's ire at F.D.R.'s seeming indifference to a personal problem.

Chapter XVIII. F.D.R.'s remark to E.R. on his desire to have J.R. as his secretary is related in *This I Remember*. F.D.R.'s memo on Alice Longworth—a document which J.R. says is " engraved on my memory "—is one of the items which somehow has been mislaid. J.R. comments, " I preserved this memo for years ; only recently it disappeared somehow from my files."

Chapter XIX. Hassett is authority for F.D.R.'s remark to Empress Zita about E.R.'s awesome energy. Miss Tully's book relates how F.D.R. called in an outside chef, rather than expose Wendell Willkie to the regular White House cooking. As for that famous so-called " hot dog " picnic for Their Britannic Majesties, J.R. was present on the occasion, and E.R. also establishes in her second volume that only *one* plate of hot dogs was dished up, purely as a sample for the King and Queen. Hermann Kahn, director of the F.D.R. Library, comments that the saga of the " hot dog " picnic is one of the many hardy perennials that have been exaggerated over the years. " Though we have never been able to establish that any such photograph exists, and I am practically positive that no such photograph was ever taken . . . many people will swear that they have seen pictures of the King shoving a hot dog into his mouth," Kahn says.

Chapter XX. Sherwood's volume describes the drafting of Declaration of War against Japan. The " indignation meeting " which J.R. describes after F.D.R. toasted Elliott Roosevelt as " the first of the family to join the armed forces " is also mentioned by Anna Roosevelt in one of her articles and by Elliott Roosevelt in his *As He Saw It*.

Chapter XXI. F.D.R.'s plans for a long journey on a slow freighter after finishing his fourth term were related to E.R. at a time when J.R. was off at war, but J.R. later discussed these conversations with his mother. The story was also told by E.R. to Tugwell for the Warm Springs Commission interviews. E.R.'s comment that the White House " bulged at the corners " when F.D.R. brought in their thirteen grandchildren for his last inauguration is from her second autobiographical volume.

Eleanor Roosevelt's Letter to James Roosevelt, July 30, 1959

VAL-KILL COTTAGE
HYDE PARK, DUTCHESS COUNTY
NEW YORK

July 30, 1959

Dearest Jimmy :

I am sending back from here and from the apartment the manuscript which I have completely read. I think, particularly in the last chapters, that you have made this a very moving account. It has a ring of sincerity and of real devotion and love on your part which I think would have given your father tremendous satisfaction. I am happy that you have been able to write something of this kind.

Now for the things that I would like to have you change.

I know that the popular supposition is that food was always bad in the White House. I think the people who feel that way forget that all the time we lived there we were in the depression years and felt we could not allow Mrs. Nesbitt certain extravagances or we were on rationing and that there always had to be coupons saved for Hyde Park as well as for Washington, and that when we went to Hyde Park it was always more extravagant than in Washington. Also, Father did not like too many bills.

I would like you to put a note where you begin your dissertation on Mrs. Nesbitt and say : " Mrs. Nesbitt, of course, always submitted menus to Mother. The responsibility for what she spent and for what she ordered was my mother's and my mother's alone. Mrs. Nesbitt carried out her orders and later when Dr. McIntyre controlled the President's menus, she carried out the Doctor's orders."

When you list what you gave Father at your home—steaks and some other simple food—I think I must tell you that he did have those at the White House, and other people had them too, perhaps not as often as you think he should have had them, but they were served.

The children certainly had proper food, and did not take to candy bars because of lack of food. They just liked candy bars !

Mrs. Nesbitt did not cook the food. It was cooked in the kitchen by very competent cooks or it was cooked by Granny's cook in order to give Father a slight change when his appetite was failing.

Mrs. Nesbitt made every effort to meet Father's wishes in economy as well as in providing what he wanted. The cooks were not familiar at first with the way Father liked game and never familiar with terrapin. But Father once had a man come in and the cooks learned from him and were able to do it afterwards, but this was a single occasion. I remember well his disappointment when the terrapin was not prepared the first time as he had expected, but, unfortunately, neither Mrs. Nesbitt nor the cooks had lived in houses where terrapin was a usual food.

Secondly, I wish you would put a note after your first reference to Secretary Morgenthau. I think he is sensitive and will be deeply hurt. If you wish, you can say " My mother wishes me to say that Mr. and Mrs. Henry Morgenthau, Jr. were probably the closest personal friends in the Cabinet and over a long period of years." My husband never held office from the time he went to Albany without finding a place for Mr. Morgenthau. He would often kid him but underlying the kidding was a deep affection and complete trust in his loyalty, integrity and friendship.

Father never told me he wanted to get rid of Mrs. Nesbitt and he often praised the work of her husband as well as her own.

Much love,
Mother.

Index